The State in Northern Ireland 1921–72

*Paul Bew, Peter Gibbon
and Henry Patterson*

THE STATE
IN NORTHERN IRELAND
1921–72
POLITICAL FORCES
AND SOCIAL CLASSES

St. Martin's Press   New York

St. Martin's Press, Inc., 175 Fifth Avenue, New York, N.Y. 10010
Printed in Great Britain
First published in the United States of America in 1979

ISBN 0–312–75608–9

Library of Congress Cataloging in Publication Data

Bew, Paul
    The state in Northern Ireland, 1921–72.

    Includes index.
        1. Northern Ireland – Politics and government.
    2. Ulster Unionist Party. 3. Social classes – Northern
    Ireland. I. Gibbon, Peter, joint author.
    II. Patterson, Henry, 1947– joint author.
    III. Title.
    DA990.U46B36 1979   320.9'416'082   79–13020
    ISBN 0–312–75608–9

Contents

Abbreviations

BBC	British Broadcasting Corporation
CDC	Citizens' Defence Committee
CGIA	Capital Grants to Industry Act
CID	Criminal Investigation Department (Special Branch)
CPI	Communist Party of Ireland
CPRS	Central Policy Review Staff ('Think Tank')
CSJNI	Campaign for Social Justice in Northern Ireland
DORA	Defence of the Realm Act
GOC	General Officer Commanding
IDA	Industries Development Act
ILP	Independent Labour Party
IOO	Independent Orange Order
IRA	Irish Republican Army
ITGWU	Irish Transport and General Workers' Union
LGA	Loans Guarantee Act
NICS	Northern Ireland Civil Service
NIHC	Northern Ireland House of Commons Debates (Hansard)
NIHT	Northern Ireland Housing Trust
NILP	Northern Ireland Labour Party
NUU	New University of Ulster
PRO	Public Record Office (London)
PRONI	Public Record Office of Northern Ireland (Belfast)
RIA	Re-equipment of Industry Act
RIC	Royal Irish Constabulary
RUC	Royal Ulster Constabulary
RWG	Revolutionary Workers' Groups
SDLP	Social Democratic and Labour Party
SPO	State Paper Office (Dublin)
UDA	Ulster Defence Association
UDR	Ulster Defence Regiment
UIDA	Ulster Industries Development Association
UIL	United Irish League
USC	Ulster Special Constabulary (B Specials)
UUC	Ulster Unionist Council
UULA	Ulster Unionist Labour Association
UVF	Ulster Volunteer Force
UWC	Ulster Workers' Council

Preface

From its creation in 1921 until its destruction in 1972 the Northern Ireland state was ruled by a single party, the Ulster Unionists. This party was supported for all purposes exclusively by Protestants, who comprised two-thirds of the local population. In the course of its rule it departed in a number of notable ways from the normal forms of parliamentary democracy.

These three facts—whose truth is indisputable—pose a number of questions of scientific and popular interest. How was a party able to remain in power for over half a century? Why should its overthrow have coincided with the destruction of the state itself? What was the relationship of the party to the Protestant population? How did it rule this population, and that of Northern Ireland as a whole? Which social forces did the party represent and who—if the question can be put this way—did the other state apparatuses represent? What did the modifications to parliamentary democracy really signify? On what bases, in short, were Ulster Unionism and the state in Northern Ireland organised?

These questions have been posed and answered before, though perhaps not exactly in this form. The reader will want to know why he should be expected to find the answers offered in this book any more illuminating than those given elsewhere. The reasons are twofold. The present authors are the first to have had at their disposal the archives of the Northern Ireland state itself, which were made available through the Public Record Office of Northern Ireland in January 1977 (at least for the period until 1947). Moreover, we write not principally as political historians but as social and political scientists, inserting the events we discuss in a systematic framework founded upon a strategic conception of politics. This second reason should lend the book a wider interest, as a contribution to the discussion of the Marxist conceptions of the state, the national question and imperialism.

In its preparation we have incurred debts which we wish to acknowledge, chiefly to a number of fellow researchers whose co-operation proved indispensable: Michael Farrell, J. H. Whyte, Breda Howard, Rosamund Goldie, Denis Norman and Philip McVicker. In addition, the assistance of those responsible for making available specific sources should be mentioned. The trustees of the Spender papers gave permission to quote from *Financial Diary*. John McColgan gave us permission to quote from his Ph.D., while the help of Trevor Parkhill, Peter

Smythe and Sean McMenamin of the Public Record Office of Northern Ireland was most valuable. Of course, none of these individuals shares any responsibility for the positions or interpretations of the authors.

Finally it should be noted that as a result of changes in the PRO classification scheme the source referred to as Cab. 7 is now Cab. 9.

Belfast and Sheffield   P.B.   P.G.   H.P.
November 1978

1

MARXISM AND IRELAND

Marxists have striven to understand Ireland for over a century. Today, when a work on Ireland professes to be Marxist, it stands not only in relation to an academic orthodoxy but to the outline of a Marxist orthodoxy too. Over a period of a hundred years certain familiar themes, concepts and lines of argument have coalesced into something one could call the Marxist 'position' on the Irish question. The basis of this position is a substantial one. Marx, Engels, Lenin and Kautsky all took a keen interest in Ireland and wrote about it extensively. In addition, during the period of the Second International Ireland itself produced a Marxist political leader of international stature, James Connolly.

Until very recently Marxists have contented themselves with using this position primarily as a declarative resource—a well of quotations and slogans to justify certain manifestoes or illuminate descriptive agitational histories. They have chosen not to attempt to develop or even explore it thoroughly. The other side of this remarkably unambitious disposition has been what may safely be described as a total political failure. Irish Marxism has probably fewer adherents today than at any stage since 1945. The last decade in particular has demonstrated the inability of its supporters to intervene significantly in the course of unprecedented upheaval and change.

Irish Marxism is in fact in danger of extinction, politically and intellectually. Its prospects of survival, let alone development, seem slim. Of course, there are objective reasons for this sitution, but part of the responsibility must lie with the 'position'. If we are honest we have to admit that it has been unable to generate any form of successful political struggle. The time has come for a re-examination and re-evaluation.

It may seem curious for this assertion to preface a work which claims to be a Marxist history of Northern Ireland. The theoretical ambition appears somewhat grandiose compared with the limited empirical objective. But consider two points. Firstly there are no local Marxist raw materials for an analysis of either Irish state. The state has simply never been regarded as a pertinent starting point for an appreciation of past and present political forces in Ireland. Indeed, to propose an analysis of the state has been to run into the objection that local conditions are exceptional and that other concepts must take precedence, notably 'imperialism' and the 'right of nations to self-determination'. This order of priorities is justified by commonsense arguments about 'eight hundred years of British occupation', 'three hundred years of national oppression' and so on. In other words, the existing Marxist position becomes an obstacle to legitimate Marxist investigation. Secondly, it is when dealing with the Ulster question that the Marxist position shows itself most deficient, both theoretically and politically. Theoretically it is unable to illuminate a single aspect of the problem. Politically it has proved unable to generate a single effective political tactic.

The Marxist position on Ulster does not, of course, stand alone. It is one point on a compass of more or less compatible positions. Two others have already been mentioned—'imperialism' and the 'right to self-determination'. The latter involves the political nature of Irish nationalism. To clear the ground for our own operation, this system of positions will be scrutinised historically and analytically.

The Ulster question

The Marxist position on Ulster was essentially formulated by Connolly, although Marx, Engels and Lenin all propounded views which have been regarded as anticipating his. Naturally, Ulster was not the principal aspect of the Irish question for any of these writers. Their main concern was the struggle for Home Rule, its conditions and consequences, and the attitude of the working-class movement towards it. Unionism represented an obstruction to a political force whose general objectives they endorsed. This is revealing. The Ulster question is considered only in political terms, and only in relation to another purely political issue. All well and good—but this is not the same thing as a rigorously founded analysis. The concepts available for the classical consideration of Ulster have no support within an historical and scientific evaluation of the province's social and political economy. Indeed, as will become clear, none of the leaders of the international communist movement who wrote about Ireland took even the country's overall social structure as his object.

Ulster hardly figures at all in the writings of Marx and Engels: not one of their many discussions of Ireland addresses itself primarily to this question. In particular, the uneven development of Irish capitalism—for all its importance to later varieties of radical history in the attempt to explain Loyalism—is simply not acknowledged. Marx died in 1883, before Protestant opposition to any form of united Ireland had become completely clear. There is reason to doubt whether it would have registered even had he lived. Indeed, he had earlier expressed the optimistic belief that disestablishment of the Church of Ireland would ensure a unity of Catholic and Protestant popular classes. Engels seems to have shared this view and to have been bewildered by the events of the mid-1880s. His later references to the topic, beyond remarks about the 'Protestant braggarts of Ulster',[1] are rare, unclear and markedly elliptical.[2]

Much the same limitations apply, with greater excuse, to Lenin. Even more than was the case with Marx and Engels, his interest in Ireland was a primarily theoretical rather than practical political one. For him, the Ulster question was significant largely because of its delaying effect upon Home Rule. While admittedly this was its most important aspect, to define it thus was to leave no basis for understanding Unionism's origins, support, durability, contradictions, etc. Lenin's two discussions of the issue in fact suggest that he sought to derive these aspects of Unionism from its overriding political significance (and that he slightly misread an aspect of this). The UVF is described in one of these discussions as a direct instrument of English landlords[3] (who Lenin believed were still powerful in Ireland in 1914) and in another as 'armed gangs of Black Hundreds' who would 'melt away and disappear' should 'the Liberals appeal to the people of England, to the proletariat'.[4]

A more accurate characterisation is to be found in the work of Karl Kautsky, the most important theoretician of the Second International. The national and colonial question was one of his political specialities. In 1880 he published an attack on Malthusian population theory based on an analysis of the Famine,[5] and later corresponded with Engels on Ireland. In 1922, some years after deserting the international communist movement, he published a fuller treatment of the Irish question.[6]

Making use of the work of the German agrarian historian Bonn, Kautsky noted the material basis of the uneven development of the Irish economy and related it to the development of Unionism, distinguishing between its indiguous local basis and its relatively marginal English supporters. However, as Angela Clifford has pointed out, Kautsky ascribed the persistence of uneven development to English economic policy, as did George O'Brien and most contemporary Irish nationalists. This profound idealism was reproduced in his essentially psychologistic view of the relationship between uneven development and politics. After the emancipation of the Catholics in 1829

> ... the better-educated, prosperous, hard-working Ulstermen [who] had up to then looked down disparagingly at the Irish Catholics because of their ignorance, their dirty poverty, their apathy resulting from despair, now became filled with fear and with fear-engendered hatred (which is the worst kind) of the Irish—now battling actively and successfully for their further development.[7]

In his positive stress on the multi-class character of Unionism Kautsky loses sight of both the direct material basis of bourgeois opposition to Home Rule, and to the realities of the political and ideological resistance of the Protestant masses. It is a reflection of the general quality of classical Marxist writing on Ulster that Kautsky's work is nevertheless relatively superior to Marx's, Engels's and Lenin's.

In view of the sketchy treatment provided by the 'founding fathers', the principal components of the Marxist position have been provided by James Connolly. In Marxist discussion of Ulster (and Ireland generally) references to Marx and Lenin tend to supplement quotations from his work, rather than vice versa. This accurately reflects a difference in both quantity and detail between Connolly and classical Marxists, and a partial continuity in their concerns and positions. The element of continuity extends to general intentions: Connolly was another of those uninterested in producing a Marxist analysis of Ulster as such. And while he did not make all Lenin's mistakes in evaluating Unionism, he made enough of his own to demonstrate that this was a real political error.

As a Marxist organiser, propagandist and journalist Connolly was particularly concerned in 1910–14 with evaluating the significance of the Ulster question. It was the Ulster Unionist Council's mobilisation against Home Rule that crystallised the opposition between nationalist and anti-nationalist political forces, and which should have become the touchstone of any Marxist analysis of the national question. For Connolly it did not. The outstanding feature of his work on Ulster, recurrently evident one way or another, is a disinclination to take Unionism seriously. In a revealing cameo William McMullen identified the tendency perfectly:

> [Connolly] found the Northern environment trying and uncongenial and it was only with difficulty he could be patient with the odd stolid Orangeman whom he encountered in his propaganda work up to this. One such occasion was when he was speaking at Library Street on a Sunday evening and was expatiating on Irish history when one of this type interrupted him, and drawing a copy of the Solemn League and Covenant from his pocket brandished it in the air and remarked that there would be no Home Rule for Ireland and that he and his thousands of co-signatories would see to it. Connolly, with a sardonic smile, advised him to take the document home and frame it, adding 'your children will laugh at you'.[8]

Elsewhere Connolly said in so many words, 'There is no economic class in Ireland today whose interest as a class are [sic] bound up with the Union'.[9]

The basis for this extraordinary position is to be found in his economistic view of the national question, which will be discussed later. It assumed that there was no bourgeois social basis in Ireland for 'real' national independence. The Home Rule subscribed to by the Irish Parliamentary Party was a sham. *Ergo* there was no room for a 'true' class opposition to the sham. Unionist resistance to Home Rule involved a grand illusion.

There were two sides to this illusion. Firstly, it masked the true aim of the bourgeoisie. The resistance of the Belfast bourgeoisie to Home Rule was motivated not by a distinct class interest, but only by a general desire to divert the working class from revolutionary politics:

> When election time rolls around, the smug representatives of Orangeism will beat the big drum of 'saving the Union' before the working-class voters, and with that discord in their ears they will be deaf to the cry of the helpless victims of capitalist oppression . . . The question of Home Government, the professional advocacy of it and the professional opposition to it, is the greatest asset in the hands of reaction in Ireland, the never-failing decoy to lure the workers into

the bogs of religious hatreds and social stagnation.[10]

Secondly, Unionism misrepresented the true instincts of the Protestant working class. The resistance of the Protestant masses was 'stage-managed' by ruling-class manipulation of Orange prejudices—'only the force of religious bigotry remains as an asset to Unionism'.[11] Again demonstrating an economistic tendency, Connolly evidently regarded revolutionary politics in the working class as a natural condition. The contemporary Unionist mobilisation was merely the last in a long line of manipulative interventions by the ruling class to head off the development of a united popular movement. He saw the basis of such a movement in the shared experience of exploitation among Protestant and Catholic workers alike, which would ineluctably displace the artifically induced sense of division:

> . . . despite their diverse origin, the workers of Ireland are bearers of a common spoilation and sufferers from a common bondage . . . the rallying cries of the various parties, led by the various factions of our masters, are but sound and fury, signifying nothing to us in our present needs and struggles . . .[12]

In an article written the same year he welcomed some, relatively minor strikes as signs of a spirit of rebelliousness amongst Protestant workers—'the workers of the Northeast corner will get tired of being led by the nose by a party of landlords and place-hunting lawyers'.[13]

Orangeism and trade union militancy were regarded as mutually exclusive. The former was a passive instrument (confined purely to the realm of ideas) with which the bourgeoisie could divert workers from the class struggle. The latter was an expression of basic class instinct which, when mobilised, would dissolve Orange illusions and transform itself into revolutionary socialism. According to this interpretation, therefore, the Ulster question was not a serious one. The Unionist alliance was at best brittle, since both the illusions underlying it were liable to collapse.

The participation of the Unionist bourgeoisie was susceptible to collapse should the Liberal government face up to its 'great piece of theatricals'.[14] Arguing along lines almost identical to Lenin's, Connolly hypothesised that the employers would back down as soon as they weighed the possibility of armed conflict with the British state against their fundamental desire for 'business as usual'.

'Belfast itself seems bent upon its usual lines of strict attention to the business of profitmaking and when I look around for the "grim, determined faces" so celebrated in the song and story of the Tory press, I fail to see them.'[15]

On the other hand, the participation of the Protestant proletariat was susceptible to collapse should the illusions of Orangeism be overtaken either by the class struggle or by its verbal substitute—'Marxist education'. Connolly believed that Protestant workers would revert to their true class instincts when Ulster's hidden history was revealed to them. In his eyes that history was a story of previous class conflict in the Protestant bloc. The recognition of these phenomenal forms of class struggle would awaken forgotten knowledge of its essence in the breasts of the Belfast working class. In his articles in Forward, and at a series of weekly lectures on Ulster history organised by the ILP of Ireland, Connolly began his task: '. . . in the treatment of Protestant workers by Protestant exploiters in Ulster, our coming historians will find plenty of material upon which to base his appeal to the Orange masses . . .'.[16]

In 'July 12th'[17] he dealt with Episcopalian persecution of Presbyterians in the seventeenth and eighteenth centuries. The Plantation of Ulster in the seventeenth century was carried out for the benefit of the Episcopalian landlord class, and the large numbers of Presbyterian tenants acquired neither civic and religious freedom nor security of tenure. Contemporary parallels, Connolly argued, were clear. 'The fundamental historical facts to remember are: the Irish Catholic was despoiled by force, the Irish Protestant was despoiled by fraud. The spoilation of both today continues under more insidious but more effective forms . . .'.[18]

Similarly, in 'A Forgotten Chapter of Irish History' he examined the incidents accompanying the Antrim Leases of 1722, concentrating on the degree to which tenants were mercilessly exploited by their landlords despite the ties of a common Protestantism. The possessing classes always put their economic interests first, and this supposedly had specific implications for Connolly's day. Just as in the past Protestant exploiters had simply used religious ideology to bind the masses to them, if present circumstances dictated it they would jettison those same principles.

Having 'demonstrated' the brittleness of subscription to Unionism by both its major class bases, Connolly went on to forsee the consequences of its collapse. He even foolishly conceived of radical possibilities for the UVF which would develop out of popular disillusion with bourgeois betrayal. At one Belfast meeting 'He hoped that the Ulster Volunteers would keep the arms they had got and that they would not surrender them when the leaders would cry off, for they might come in useful to them yet . . .'.[19] Lenin, Kautsky and Connolly were all mistaken about the 'lack of material basis' for bourgeois opposition to Home Rule. The basis was in fact substantial,[20] and it is inexcusable that Connolly failed to register it.

A second deficiency in his treatment of the Ulster question was a failure to note that the ideology around which the ruling class mobilised both itself and the masses was not primarily Orange at all.[21] In 1886 Ulster Presbyterians, while actually retaining strong anti-Establishment and anti-landlord traditions and a general hostility to Orangeism, moved en bloc to the Unionist anti-Home Rule alliance. Although democratic, their ideology was also intensely pro-imperialist and hostile to nationalist demands. In all three anti-Home Rule agitations this relatively secular ideology was to play a dominant role in integrating the main elements of the Protestant bloc. Its durability was a consequence of the fact that it provided a specific representation of the structural division in Irish society which Connolly failed to recognise. According to the ideology, the social and economic character of the north, and in particular its monopolisation of capitalist machine industry, was the expression of two distinct racial and religious histories (Ireland— Two Nations). It centred on the backward-agrarian/progressive-industrial antithesis, which it explained in the terms recorded by Kautsky. This ideology drew its strength not from the fact that it was supported by the ruling class (although it was) but from the specific material structures which it represented in a particular way. By ignoring it completely Connolly was able to simplify the problems facing those who were trying to reverse Unionist dominance. The lesson of history was an easy one, he argued: class ties of possession and non-possession of the means of production were determinate and the pan-class ties of Unionist and Orange ideology illusory.

The third deficiency of Connolly's approach lay in what he had to say about Orangeism. Quite apart from overestimating its influence, he misread its complexity. Rather than existing as an alternative to 'pure' class consciousness, Orangeism and proletarian class ideology had interpenetrated each other. The history of the Protestant bloc from the 1860s provides numerous examples of 'independent' forms of Orangeism with a strong, if limited, sense of class awareness.[22] In particular, independent Orangeism was a powerful force in the local trade unions.

In fact the notion of bourgeois manipulation of the Protestant masses in the service of ulterior economic motives was not introduced into the discourse of Belfast politics by Connolly at all. It was a central theme in the development of the Independent Orange Order, which was founded in 1903 and was able to win substantial Protestant working-class support.[23] The Independent Orange Order demonstrated that there was already a populist strain within Protestant ideology which articulated all the lessons Connolly wanted to teach the Protestant masses. It also demonstrated that a militant populism in no way threatened the disintegration of Unionist and Orange ideologies. In fact the Independents regularly attacked upper-class Unionists leaders for their tendency to compromise in defence of Protestant interests. If the bourgeoisie had behaved in the way Connolly predicted, the most likely result would have been the emergence of a more plebeian leadership for the anti-Home Rule movement, reflecting more organic ties with popular Protestant practices like riot and expulsion. What was extremely unlikely was a passive acceptance of a Home Rule parliament.

Underlying these deficiencies in Connolly's work is an essentially pre-Marxist notion of ideology—as a system of illusions and misrepresentations of reality, whose source is the strategy of the ruling class and whose function is to prevent the exploited masses arriving at an awareness of their real situation. As Althusser has pointed out, this theory's ancestry can be traced back to the Enlightenment notion of religion as an illusion created by an alliance of priests and despots.[24] Its presence in Connolly's work is entirely understandable, since it was a key aspect of the economistic Marxism of the Second International, which is evident in many (though not all) of his other positions.

Connolly's main contribution to the development of a Marxist analysis of the Ulster question has been the negative one of stressing the artificiality both of Unionism and of divisions within the working class. These crucial elements have endured and are to be found reproduced with little modification in much modern Irish

Marxism. The principal form of radical politics to develop from them has been trade union agitation combined with didacticism—the practical and verbal forms of belief in a 'real' unity obscured by manipulation. The hope is that in the long run circumstances will allow Protestant workers to see the truth of the message. Unfortunately it has not just been a case of unfavourable circumstances, but of the wrong message.

The right of nations to self-determination

The remaining elements of the Marxist position all have as their central concern the Irish national question as a whole. It has been approached by Irish Marxists on two different levels: in the light of what are taken to be Marxist 'principles'—the 'right of nations to self-determination' and the question of imperialism; and, more concretely, in terms of the social and political character of Irish nationalism and its relation to the country's social structure. In Marxist terms this very division is of course problematic, and has had serious implications. Most important, it has led to the first set of issues being discussed in an effectively non-political way, as questions of justice and morality.

It is well known that classical Marxism repeatedly endorsed Irish self-determination, at least between 1867 and 1920. This endorsement is presented by modern Irish Marxists as part of the same ethical discourse which they share today, and to which Marx, Engels, Lenin and Kautsky are all indiscriminately absorbed. In fact, none of these figures argued for Irish self-determination on these or any other moral grounds. All approached the question politically, though in substantially different ways. A clarification of their general attitudes to it will show how far contemporary formulations conform to past ones.

As it happened the Irish question provided the context in which Marx and Engels defined their general position on the right of nations to self-determination. Instructively, however, their first comments on Irish independence were negative. They specifically opposed O'Connell's repeal movement in the 1840s, describing it as 'obsolete rubbish', 'fermenting junk' and 'a pretext for obtaining posts ... and making profitable business transactions'.[25] It represented no more than a disguise for British Whiggism. Under

O'Connell's leadership the working class would gain more than it would lose by association with England.[26]

When they eventually came to support Irish self-determination in the 1860s they did so under very specific conditions. Marx's position was that the Irish independence and social questions had become inseparable in the intervening period, and might now conceivably be the spark for revolutionary developments in England, which had meanwhile faltered. The English aristocracy and bourgeoisie had a common interest in turning Ireland into pasture land to supply England with meat and wool at the cheapest possible prices. Even more important, anti-Irish racialism was the secret of the impotence of the English working class. Yet this whole reactionary sequence had a weak link in that the landed aristocracy were vulnerable in Ireland, where the land and national questions interacted in a mutually reinforcing way. To support Irish self-determination, therefore, was to lend weight to the revolution in Britain.[27]

Marx and Engels did not subscribe to any general moral principle either on Irish national self-determination or on national self-determination generally. As Lenin was to point out, they opposed not only O'Connell's movement but the national aspirations of the Czechs and south Slavs, whose struggles were primarily in the interest of Tsarist autocracy:

> Marx and Engels . . . drew a clear and definite distinction between 'whole reactionary nations' serving as Russian outposts in Europe, and 'revolutionary nations', namely the Germans, Poles and Magyars. This is a fact. And it was indicated at the time with incontrovertible truth: in 1848 the revolutionary nations fought for liberty, whose principal enemy was Tsarism, whereas the Czechs, etc., were in fact reactionary nations and outposts of Tsarism . . .[28]

As these examples indicate, the only 'general principle' on the national question which may be deduced from the work of Marx and Engels is that it always stands for or corresponds to *some other* political question, which requires independent evaluation. This view was shared and developed further by Lenin.

The issue of national self-determination, particularly in eastern Europe, preoccupied the Second International from its London congress of 1896 to its disintegration in 1914. Hence most leading European Marxists of the early twentieth century contributed to the debate—Kautsky, Bauer, Radek, Stalin, Trotsky, Lenin,

Luxemburg, not to speak of the Mensheviks, Bundists, Fracyists and so on. Their views significantly differed both conceptually and in their conclusions. Lenin's major assaults on Bauer, Radek and Luxemburg are well known, yet it is also clear that his position was distinct from those of Kautsky, Stalin and Trotsky, particularly if his works of 1913–16 and 1922–23 are examined. In so far as there is a classical position on the question, it is in these texts that it is developed.

The most striking difference between Lenin's writings and those of most others on this question is the virtually complete absence from his work of any attempt to develop or begin from abstract definitions of nations and nationalism. This is the style of Kautsky and Stalin.[29] Without explicitly condemning their positions (except Stalin's on Georgia),[30] Lenin nevertheless remarked of his own work:

> In my writings on the national question I have already said that an abstract presentation of the question of nationalism in general is of no use at all . . . the fundamental interest of proletarian solidarity and consequently of the proletarian class struggle requires that we never adopt a formal attitude to the national question . . .[31]

This refusal does not signify an agnosticism. On the contrary, it is expressed as a prerequisite for a scientific view. According to Lenin, constructing general definitions of nationalism and deriving a general political position from them was an offence against concrete analysis. It was associated with the evolutionist conception of history, in which nationalism was invariably linked with the rise of the bourgeoisie. Of this view he remarked, 'to see [history] as a straight line moving slowly and steadily upwards . . . one must be a virtuoso of philistinism . . .'.[32]

In his writings he distinguishes between at least three varieties of the national question. These correspond to three distinct areas: pre-First World War Europe, colonial countries after the First World War, and the Soviet Union under the dictatorship of the proletariat (Georgia, 1922–23). The first will be examined here, while the second will be discussed in the next section.

Despite the publication of Stalin's 'classic' on the subject in 1913, Lenin felt it necessary between 1913 and 1916 to write no fewer than four substantial articles on the national question in Europe.[33] In them he consistently argues the necessity of distinguishing it from a number of other, related questions before it can properly be understood.

First, it must be distinguished from the question of cultural oppression. The national question in contemporary Europe was not a species of this question, which in any case was so diffusely formulated as to be devoid of meaning. Hence it could not be resolved by 'cultural autonomy', as the Austro-Marxists held. To identify national with cultural oppression was theoretically to endorse the bourgeois or petty-bourgeois 'national' culture of the oppressed nation, and more practically to endorse the demands of those classes and the clergy for control of local ideological apparatuses such as schooling.

Second, it must be distinguished from the question of economic dependence. The national question was essentially a political issue and was economically indifferent, Lenin argued strongly against Luxemburg, who believed the inability of small nations to sustain economic independence made political independence irrelevant.

> Not only small states, but even Russia for example, is entirely dependent economically on the power of the rich bourgeois countries. Not only the miniature Balkan states, but even nineteenth-century America was economically a colony of Europe, as Marx pointed out in *Capital* . . . but this has nothing whatever to do with the quesiton of national movements and the national state. For the question of the political self-determination of nations and their independence in bourgeois society Rosa Luxembourg has substituted the quesiton of their economic independence. All this is just as intelligent as if someone, in discussing the programmatic demand for the supremacy of parliament, were to expound the perfectly correct conviction that big capital dominates in a bourgeois country whatever the regime in it . . .[34]

Third, it must, generally speaking, be distinguished from the question of imperialism. As will be demonstrated further on, the question of national integrity is not linked with that of imperialism irrevocably, but as a matter of specific conjunctures. Prior to Lenin's re-evaluation of the prospects for socialist revolution (around 1915–16) he never discussed imperialism as an aspect of the national question, even in texts (such as 'Critical Remarks on the National Question', 1913) which deal explicitly with the national question within an imperialist power.

Distinguished from these related questions, the real significance of the national question in Europe could be evaluated. It represented a variant form of the question of *democracy*. It did so in a double sense. On the one hand, the struggle within an oppressor nation to remove national oppression was a democratic one. On the other, it was a condition of democracy in the oppressed nation that the oppression be broken.

The struggle within the oppressor state was democratic in that it attacked the privileges of the dominant national group on egalitarian grounds, counterposed the 'international culture of democracy' to the reactionary cultures of dominant groups, and created the conditions for peaceful relations between national groups. But, for Lenin, the progressive effects he was convinced would follow within the oppressed nation itself from the recognition of its right to self-determination played a greater role. He equated the resolution of the national question in oppressed countries with the attainment of full political democracy:

> The national question in most western countries . . . was settled long ago . . . Rosa Luxemburg has lost sight of the *most important thing*—the difference between countries where bourgeois-democratic reforms have long been completed, and those where they have not . . .

> Engels . . . did not make the mistake some Marxists make in dealing with the . . . right of nations to self-determination, when they argue that it is impossible under capitalism and superfluous under socialism. This seemingly clever but actually incorrect statement might be made in regard of any democratic institution . . .[35]

Lenin was clearer on few things than the desirability from the proletarian viewpoint of 'democratic institutions':

> . . . in a democratic republic no less than in a monarchy, the state remains a machine for the oppression of one class by another . . . [but this] by no means signifies that the *form* of oppression makes no difference to the proletariat . . . a wider, freer more open form of class struggle and class oppression vastly assists the proletariat in its struggle . . .[36]

In a word, the European national question was for Lenin one of establishing democracy, and through it the 'best conditions for the class struggle'.[37] This interpretation is supported by the programme he believed his conclusions obliged the Bolsheviks to follow—the proclamation of the right of nations to secede from others, i.e. to constitute themselves as fields of class struggle unimpeded by national diversions. On the application of this programme Lenin was equally explicit—'it refers to bourgeois-democratic national movements . . . all instances of bourgeois-democratic movements [and] only cases where such a movement is actually in existence . . .'.[38]

The national question in the colonies after World War I represented a substantially different set of issues. Here Lenin regarded national struggles as progressive not merely on the grounds that they were a variant of the question of democracy and led to the 'simplification of class antagonisms' (Marx and Engels), but because they represented a variant of the question of imperialism. Colonial national questions took an anti-imperialist colour from the post-war international situation. The issue will be examined in the next section.

In addition to Marx's principle that no abstract or absolute judgements could be made about nationality or nationalism, Lenin had in effect added another. There are only specific national questions, requiring concrete analyses. Both questions and analyses are *political* in character, not economic or even ideological. As such, their solution lies purely at the political level.

It was on the basis of these principles (and other considerations, to be discussed) that classical Marxism endorsed Irish self-determination between 1867 and 1920. There were discrepancies, however, between these ideas and those of Connolly. As it turned out, it was Connolly's that were to prove the more influential in Ireland. While their application to the issues of 1867 to 1916 led to similar (though not identical) conclusions, their application to the issues of today would not.

A major object of Connolly's career was to establish the political and ideological independence of the workers' movement from all varieties of bourgeois influence. The difficulties were numerous. In particular the meagre resources of the tiny Irish socialist movement meant that he had to combine his theoretical and practical work with long spells of full-time employment. When it is remembered that he was *establishing* a Marxist tradition under these circumstances and was to face problems that were nowhere anticipated in the limited corpus of Marx's writings on Ireland, the shortcomings of his analysis are predictable and understandable.

In his first intervention in Irish politics, the formation of the Irish

Socialist Republican Party in 1896, Connolly identified the aim he was to pursue until his execution in 1916—the assertion of a leading role for the working class in the struggle for 'real' national independence, by which he meant an Irish socialist (or 'workers") republic. One aspect of this struggle was a critique of the bourgeois and petty-bourgeois nationalist ideologies which denied the central role of class struggle in Irish history. This part of his work was to achieve its most comprehensive expression in his *Labour in Irish History*.[40]

On the national question he identified two mistaken attitudes. One was identical to that advanced in Europe by Luxemburg and Radek, which Lenin had condemned as 'imperialist economism':

> One set, observing that those who talk loudest about 'Ireland a Nation' are often the most merciless grinders of the faces of the poor, fly off to the extremest limit of hostility to nationalism and, whilst opposed to oppression at all time, are also opposed to national revolt for national independence . . .[41]

The other represented a much more significant force, based as it was in Belfast, where there was a relatively strong local socialist movement of the British ILP type. Connolly criticised the Belfast socialists for their 'West British' orientation:

> As long as the movement in this district is content to draw its literature from England and its illustrations from British conditions, so long will it be but an echo of the fight of our British brothers and sisters. So soon as we build up a literature and spoken propaganda dealing with conditions in Ireland, as our fathers knew and as we know them, so soon will the movement here draw strength and power to itself.[42]

As it has been alleged by Conor Cruise O'Brien that Connolly's view of the Protestant working class was inadequate principally because of his commitment to an orthodox nationalist position, it should be observed that his critique of the Unionist socialism of William Walker and other leaders of the ILP was based not on nationalist prejudices but on the same Marxist principles by which, during the Second International debate on the colonial question in 1907, Lenin, Kautsky and Luxemburg opposed those who, like Bernstein and the Dutch social democrat Van Kol, argued for the progressive mission of imperialism and a 'socialist colonial policy'.[43] The Belfast socialists dissented from demands for Home Rule on the grounds of the general economic and cultural backwardness of the south, which could be remedied by only inclusion in the United Kingdom, where the strength of progressive forces was greater.[44]

Not only did Connolly parallel Lenin's thinking in rejecting these positions, but at one stage very early in his work he seems to anticipate the essence of Lenin's own view. Writing in 1897, he pointed out that the national question in contemporary Ireland was no more and no less than the question of democracy—whose significance he interpreted in the classical manner:

> An Irish Republic would . . . be the natural repository of popular power; the weapon of popular emancipation, the only power which would show in the full light of day all those class antagonisms and lines of economic demarcation now obscured by the mists of patriotism . . .[45]

Yet in another article published the same year he put forward an entirely different argument. It was this, rather than the first, which was to remain his definitive position.

> If you remove the English army tomorrow and hoist the green flag over Dublin Castle, unless you set about the organisation of a Socialist Republic your efforts will be in vain . . . Nationalism without socialism—without a reorganisation of society—is only national recreancy . . .[46]

Connolly slid from the Leninist view that the working class could play a leading role in the national revolution to the very different one that there could be no national revolution without the leadership of the working class. In a curious way the argument behind this view mirrors that shared by Luxemburg and some of Connolly's own opponents. It springs from common assumptions. Luxemburg, it will be remembered, equated nationalism with capitalism. Since the leadership of nationalist movements was generally bourgeois, and, more important, since these movements endorsed existing economic relations, Luxemburg considered it obvious that demanding national independence as such was frivolous. It would undo neither bourgeois dominance nor economic subjection to powerful external forces.

Connolly actually shared *all* these views. English rule was treated as a mere 'symbol'[47] of 'foreign' (i.e capitalist) property relations which colonialism had imposed in Ireland. The Irish nationalist bourgeoisie was equally implicated in these relations. Any political independence it achieved would be meaningless. The difference between Luxemburg and Connolly was simply that while this reasoning led Luxemburg to reject all national struggles as reactionary, it led Connolly to argue that they could only be 'properly' fought as socialist revolutions.

The similarity of Luxemburg's and Connolly's views springs from a common error. Both treated the political and ideological significance of the national question as deriving from the economic position of its leadership, and neither acknowledged that political struggles can be progressive and revolutionary without in themselves settling the quesiton of capitalism v. socialism.[48] In fact, to the extent that Connolly's conclusion is less obviously economistic than Luxemburg's, it is also less internally consistent.

The notion that the Irish working class alone had an objective interest in national independence was not a serious limitation on Connolly's politics until after the Easter Rising. It affected only his views about Ulster, already discussed. The problems of applying it to the rest of Ireland were concealed by its compatibility with the Leninist notion of the leading role of the working class in the national revolution, and the fact that the revolution was still in its early stages. As soon as it reached a more advanced phase the weaknesses became clearer. Short of socialism, Connolly's supporters could never consistently acknowledge that the national revolution had ever been fully achieved. The essentially tautological argument that the War of Independence (1919–21) left the Irish revolution 'incomplete' has now become the conventional wisdom of the Marxist left. Since national liberation can be attained only by socialism according to Connolly, this is to say neither more nor less than that Ireland is not socialist. While the point will be generally admitted, it can hardly be described as an illuminating one.

In practice it is not simply unhelpful but positively misleading. Socialism is identified with national liberation, and the struggle for socialism becomes wholly reduced to a matter of 'completion'—even, in the most obvious sense, to territorial completion. Yet it is not clear that this particular issue has anything to do with democracy, let alone socialism.

When they claim that the Irish revolution is territorially incomplete, latter-day Connolly socialists mean that the north is still part of the United Kingdom. But the connection between righting this situation and improving the conditions for class struggle is tenuous. Kautsky saw things differently from Connolly's disciples. He believed that southern independence would release a class struggle in the north irrespective of 'incompletion':

> In an oppressed country the class contradictions are only too easily. hidden and obscured by national contradictions. The Irish worker will only rightly recognise his class position and become responsive to international socialism when the government confronting him as the guardian of the property of the ruling class is no longer that of the English, but of his compatriots . . .[49]

While this argument is somewhat mechanical in that it ignores what Angela Cifford has called 'the maintenance of a profound sense of national grievance over partition',[50] it is nevertheless closer to Lenin's views than was Connolly's. The relative merits of territorial completion/incompletion are more or less calculable and may be evaluated in terms rather more concrete than those proposed by Connolly.

On the side of incompletion stands democracy for three million in the south, albeit infringed by the 'sense of national grievance', accompanied by restrictions on democracy for a million and a half, in the north, the result of the forcible inclusion of a Catholic minority within the state's borders. On the side of completion stands the probability of restrictions on democracy for *four and a half million* as a consequence of the forcible inclusion of a Protestant minority within a thirty-two-county republic. The question of 'territorial completion', though it sounds revolutionary, is really Hobson's choice.

The democratic, that is to say the *national*, stage of the Irish revolution seems probably to have been as complete as it ever could be by 1921. Perhaps, had Connolly lived, he would have recognised as much. Given the discrepancy between his position and Lenin's, it seems more likely that he would not. In any case it is his 1896–1916 position that lives on today, and which has had the effect of absorbing the question of socialist revolution to that of national irredentism.

Imperialism

The third compass point of the Marxist position is that Ireland's history is best understood through the notion of imperialism, and that imperialism v. anti-imperialism has been the fundamental conflict in Irish society for a very long time. This argument is adopted as a supplement or fall-back to the idea that Irish self-determination is still an open question. It is less well worked out and has less authority—not surprisingly, since Marx, Engels and Connolly all died before the formulation of Lenin's theory, while Kautsky rejected substantial aspects of it. Hence, evaluation in this case entails not so much a review of its historical development as a discussion of its contemporary expression.

In its typical form the argument runs thus. Ireland has for hundreds of years been dominated by imperialism, which has plundered its resources, decimated its population, engineered Protestant–Catholic divisions and divided the country. After an interlude following partition it resumed economic domination of southern Ireland through the export of industrial and financial capital. In the north this domination was never interrupted. Imperialism sponsored the remnants of colonialism and their brutal repression of the opponents of partition. According to this conception, British imperialism's involvement in Ireland (not to say its moral responsibility) is theoretically and practically inescapable. Not only is the present conflict a direct result, but British imperialism remains a critical protagonist in it, striving to crush popular resistance by military force. This conclusion has, of course, clear political implications, both in Ireland and in Britain.

Is the notion of imperialism at the heart of this view really the Marxist–Leninist concept, or is it something else? Its picture of Irish history reveals a concept of imperialism which is broad, diffuse and at the same time formalistic. *Broad:* imperialism is not associated with any definite historical period, as it was by Lenin and Bukharin. *Diffuse:* beyond general violence and repression, imperialism is not associated with any specific effects, as it is in Marxist theory. *Formalistic:* its relevance is argued not from the working out of certain tendencies within and between societies, but from foreign presence as such. The primacy of the imperialism/anti-imperialism conflict is likewise asserted by reference not to a situation in which the economic and political reproduction of imperialism is threatened, but simply to one in which there is opposition to foreign presence.

Underlying the imprecision of these aspects of the concept is a substantial error. 'Imperialism' is regarded as synonymous with the foreign policies of the British ruling class. Leave aside the question of whether it was British policies that dictated Anglo-Irish relations, and of whether the British ruling class ever had anything coherent or consistent enough to be called a policy on Ireland. Consider only the identification of imperialism with policy.

Two implications suggest themselves. First, colonialism is elevated to the status of imperialism's central characteristic. Second, as it is merely a series of foreign policies, British imperialism amounts to no more than the outcome of voluntary choices to behave in misanthropic ways towards the Irish and others. 'Imperialism' in this sense, since it is specific to nothing in any particular society, effectively stands outside it.

This conception of imperialism is in contrast to that advanced by Marxist–Leninist theory and developed in its classical form by Lenin. For Lenin, imperialism was a special stage in the evolution of the capitalist mode of production, together with the accompanying social, political and ideological conditions and effects. Its principal characteristic was the reorganisation of capitalism as an international system, a 'world economy'[51] in which colonial oppression played a major part.

This stage of development was a result of structural changes in the economic constitution of the ruling classes in the advanced countries. Most marked in Germany, the changes became significant around 1900.[52] They were, first, increased concentration of production and the formation of cartels and monopolies; second, a particular form of concentration in the banking sector which transformed its relation to other sectors from one of subordination to dominance; third, the consequent birth of a new type of capital—finance capital, 'capital controlled by the banks and employed by industrialists' (Hilferding), together with a general weakening of the position of small industrial capital; and last, a tendency for capital to be transferred from domestic to overseas investment.

These structural changes had far-reaching consequences on the world economy and its superstructure. In the industrialised countries the principal economic effect was the appearance of 'parasitism and decay'.[53] Here Lenin differed from Hilferding (who accorded finance capital a progressive role), pointing out that only under monopoly conditions did it become possible for technical progress to be held back artificially and productive investment abandoned in favour of speculative lending. At the international level the globe was divided and redivided as powerful cartels apportioned markets and sources of raw materials: older forms of capitalist competition were now writ large.

Imperialism had important ideological and political effects also. It led to an intensification of colonial policy and a fiercer scramble to acquire colonies. Industrialised countries pre-emptively annexed territories for economic exploitation by their leading monopolies. Concomitantly it set in motion a power struggle in which political control of the older colonies and annexed zones (Belgium, Lorraine, Ireland) became the subject of a war of position between the imperialist powers.[54] Bourgeois opposition to consequent restrictions on political freedom was undermined by the ubiquitous trend towards reduction of free competition.

The remaining significant political and ideological effect of imperialism was the creation of a 'labour aristocracy'—a section of the working class in the industrialised countries that was allied to its respective bourgeoisie. Lenin dealt primarily with the material foundation for this alliance,[55] but his writings show an awareness that it also had a political dimension and that in consequence the labour aristocracy could not be regarded as a fixed sociological category.

Two central features of the classical Marxist–Leninist concept of imperialism may be abstracted from this summary, features which were themselves repeatedly stressed by Lenin and Bukharin. The first is that imperialism is a *special stage* in the development of the capitalist mode of production, to which a *special form* of colonialism corresponds. Colonialism is given a new motive—'the struggle for sources of raw materials, the export of capital, for spheres of influence, i.e. spheres of profitable deals, concessions, monopoly profits and so on'.[56] This revolutionises colonial policy (and the foreign policies of the great powers generally). In the past colonies had been acquired for speculative plunder, 'reasons of state', etc, but not in a systematic fashion, nor in the context of intense competition, nor even necessarily by force. The essence of the new colonialism was its comprehensiveness, which conferred upon each colony the status of a link in a chain and generated international conflicts over whose chain it should be part of. The chains of Lenin's day were not yet those of an international division of labour, but of an international carving up of the globe. Economic changes made it possible and perhaps necessary to secure an advantageous political position, which in turn meant the seizure of new territories and a strengthening of control over older ones. Imperialism and the form of colonialism associated with it were therefore highly specific historical categories tied to the period of finance capital. Neither was in any sense anticipated by earlier strategies of conquest (Macedonian, Roman, Napoleonic, etc).

> If a certain phase of development is to be theoretically understood it must be understood with all its peculiarities, its distinguishing trends, its specific characteristics, which it shares with none. He who, like 'Colonel Torrance', sees the savages' club as the beginning of capital . . . will never be able to find his way among the tendencies of capitalist development . . . The historian or economist who places under one denomination the structure of modern capitalism, i.e. modern production relations, and the numerous types of production relations that formerly led to wars of conquest, will understand nothing . . .[57]

The second major feature of the concept follows from this. It is that imperialism cannot be reduced to a policy or a succession of policies. This view, advanced by Plekhanov (who believed that 'imperialism is a bad habit of a certain nation'[58]) and Kautsky (who felt that colonial aggression could be dropped in favour of regulated peaceful competition), was ridiculed by Lenin. Moreover in his criticism of Kautsky Lenin specifically emphasised the connection between seeing imperialism as a policy and the 'one-sided, i.e. arbitrary [singling] out of only the national question'[59] as the essence of imperialism. This, he observed, was 'a more subtle and disguised (and therefore more dangerous) advocacy of conciliation with imperialism, because a fight against the policy of the trusts and the banks that does not affect [their] economic basis . . . is bourgeois reformism'.[60]

A specific form of colonialism; irreducibility to policy. These central features of the classical Marxist-Leninist conception of imperialism contrast sharply with the interpretation customarily accepted by Irish Marxists today. Imperialism, for them, is the product of undifferentiated colonialist policies. If they have been talking not of imperialism but only of something they mistook for it, the question remains of whether the real—the classical—concept should be central issue in the analysis of Irish politics.

Writers of Irish history have always tended to stress continuities. For all its deficiencies, this tendency does in one sense reflect reality. The basic lines of economic and political development (including its modern elements) were laid down in the last century, and subsequent events have represented their unfolding. To this extent the question of the specific effects of imperialism proper upon Ireland has a short answer. They are few. Interestingly, most of them have generally been more characteristic of imperialism in the industrialised countries than in the colonies. This is not to say that there have been no effects of the latter kind, as the British and Irish Communist Organisation would argue. Such a view is merely the other side of the coin under discussion and, like it, belongs to the realm of morality rather than science.

By 1900, the date Lenin assigned to the emergence of imperialism as a predominant trend, Irish politics had already taken recognisable shape. In the south the basic structure of the bloc of classes carrying on the national struggle was decided. The relation of the cause of independence to the land question and to the conflict between bourgeoisie and proletariat was also determined. The overwhelmingly agrarian and commercial bias of the economy was established, as was its relation to the world economy: the exchange of livestock and diary products, together with displaced migrants, for processed and manufactured products. In the north the dominant Protestant class bloc had achieved independent organised expression by 1905. Both this expression—and that of the opposition to it—had been anticipated twenty years earlier. Likewise, northern industry's basic pattern of shipbuilding and textile manufacture was complete, as was its dual Protestant/Catholic labour market.

The specifically 'colonial' changes wrought by imperialism in Ireland were primarily political, and can be characterised (Following Lenin) as 'a general striving towards violence and reaction'.[61] They were brought about by the international colonial aspect of British imperialism and were consolidated in the repression of progressive forces during the First World War. Their significance should not be underestimated. They played a part in the inspiration of the nationalist and republican forces in the Anglo-Irish war.

When the south achieved formal independence in the 1920s, the effects of imperialist colonialism receded. In the 1930s, under de

Valera, southern Ireland was almost entirely freed from its influence. In the north a regime of violence and reaction was founded, but its nature was not related to any specific tendency associated with imperialism and its contemporary contradictions.

Of the 'metropolitan' changes with which imperialism was associated, the formation and consolidation of a labour aristocracy had the greatest significance. Mainly in Ulster, but to some extent in the south too, divisions developed and grew more marked between workers employed by the mainly British-oriented largest establishments (the Belfast 'big six', Guinness's, etc) and the rest of the proletariat. In Dublin they found expression in the struggle over Larkinism. In the north they interacted with and intensified existing structural and religious differences in the labour force and gave labourism its distinctive 'Walkerist' characteristics. In Ireland as a whole they were one of the bases of the split in the trade union movement between north and south.

Concentration of production and migration of capital were relatively insignificant trends in inter-war Ireland, as later chapters will show. It was not until 1955 that local effects of these aspects of imperialism emerged. The growing influence of the banks and of finance capital was a different matter, particularly in the north, where they exercised considerable power at the heart of the state. This situation was due more to the crisis in shipbuilding in the '30s than to developments of the kind envisaged by Lenin and Bukharin, though. In 1969, when large-scale British military involvement in Ireland was resumed, the effects of imperialism in the classical sense upon Irish affairs were slight.

Modern Marxist writing about imperialism in Ireland discusses conditions and effects which are not imperialist in their source or their status. Imperialism's real impact upon Irish society has not been a substantial one. To translate these conclusions into Marxist terms imperialism and anti-imperialism have not historically been the major source of antagonism in Ireland, north or south. The *exception* to this generalisation is, however, instructive.

There is little doubt that Lenin considered the Easter Rising of 1916 and the Anglo-Irish war to have been essentially anti-imperialist conflicts, during which imperialism *v.* anti-imperialism did become the principal division in Irish society. This is evident from his remarks in 'The self-determination Debate Summed Up' (1916) and his reference to Ireland in 'Preliminary Draft Theses on the National and Colonial Questions' (1920). From these documents it is also evident how he conceived the whole political question of imperialism and anti-imperialism, and the circumstances in which the contradiction between these forces becomes the overriding one in a given society.

In both these texts Lenin proceeds from an analysis of the international situation to a closer examination of particular aspects of it and their development in individual countries. The significance attributed to specific conflicts derives not from their formal characteristics (who was fighting whom over what) but from the meaning lent them by international events and the international balance of political forces. So the struggle between the Kautskyist and Leninist trends in the working-class movement from 1914 to 1916 was not, for Lenin, simply a fight for influence within the German and Russian working classes. Internationally and strategically it epitomised a struggle between the forces of imperialism and anti-imperialism. This was because in this period—which Lenin characterised as one of 'nascent social revolution'—the principal confrontation at the international level was that between the imperialist powers on the one hand and the militant proletariat (anti-imperialism) on the other. While Leninism stood for the break-up of the political and ideological conditions of imperialism's supremacy, Kautskyism stood for their preservation.

These considerations formed the context of Lenin's later reflections on contemporary national movements. On the one hand, the nascently revolutionary international situation reduced the conflicts these movements represented to secondary importance. But on the other, further considerations meant that such movements might nevertheless threaten imperialism's conditions of existence and thus fuse with and ignite the principal conflict. The 'further considerations' were that the small, oppressed European nations were becoming a source of weakness for imperialism. As the struggles between the big powers intensified they found new battlegrounds, these smaller countries among them. Consequently reaction and popular resistance to imperialism increased. In this situation, nationalist popular struggle took on not only a democratic but an anti-imperialist significance. Lenin clarified this proposition in referring to the Belgian nationalist resistance during the First World War:

... the dialectics of history are such that small nations, powerless as *independent* factors in the struggle against imperialism, play a part as one of the ferments, one of the bacilli, which help the *real* anti-imperialist force, the socialist proletariat, to make its appearance on the scene . . .[62]

Naturally, what applied to Belgium applied also to Ireland:

... we must support *every* revolt against our chief enemy, the bourgeoisie of the big states, provided that it is not the revolt of a reactionary class . . . It is precisely in the 'era of Imperialism', which is the era of *nascent revolution*, that the proletariat will today give especially vigorous support to any revolt of the annexed regions so that tomorrow, or simultaneously, it may attack the bourgeoisie of the great power that is weakened by the revolt . . .[63]

In 1920 he evidently regarded the Anglo-Irish war too as an anti-imperialist struggle. Instructively, he arrived at this assessment on the basis of a fresh analysis of the international scene. In 'Report on the International Situation and the Fundamental Tasks of the Communist International' (1920) and 'Report of the Commission on the National and Colonial Questions' (1920) he expressed his new view of the world situation. In the course of the First World War, the Treaty of Versailles and the Russian revolution a completely new balance of forces had come into being. The main characteristics of the world political system now included the 'drawing in of the dependent peoples' of the new colonies into politics, the emergence of the Soviet states and the imperialist offensive against them, and the subordination of two former imperialist powers (Germany and Austria). Not only did proletarian revolution remain 'nascent' but the power of independence movements to ignite it had been increased—provided they were under revolutionary leadership. Their potential was greater because of the quantitatively larger scale on which they could add to imperialism's cumulative tensions. Lenin now believed that revolutionary national movements had an anti-imperialist significance in every colonial country, not simply those like Ireland. In this context he predicted:

World imperialism shall fall when the revolutionary onslaught of the exploited and oppressed workers in each country, overcoming resistance from petty-bourgeois elements and the influence of the small upper crust of labour aristocrats, merges with the revolutionary onslaught of hundreds of millions of people who have hitherto stood beyond the pale of history . . .[64]

Nothing could be further from his 1916 and 1920 views than a formalistic assessment of conflicts based on the nominal standing of the parties involved. The 'imperialist' and 'anti-imperialist' content ascribed to particular forces and conflicts depends on an assessment of the relation of political forces at the international strategic level and of the circumstances under which imperialism's conditions of existence may be overturned. This is accompanied by an appreciation of the specific local and tactical means through which broader forces may unfold. For Irish Marxists to demonstrate that imperialism and anti-imperialism are a living reality in Irish politics and that the confrontation between them is the overriding one, they must show that they derive their significance from their role in the overall strategic situation of which Irish politics forms a part. The exercise would be of more than academic value, since it would mean not only the evaluation of particular movements but the discovery of the kinds of alliances Marxists must secure in order to succeed in their struggle. No more than imperialism carries its name around its neck is every movement claiming to be 'anti-imperialist' genuinely so.

Consider once more in this context, too, the claims made for the importance of completing the national revolution. Irish Marxists typically employ their concept of imperialism to argue the revolutionary implications of completion. Not only is incompletion said to be an outstanding aspect of the national question, but it also has an anti-imperialist content. In this connection territorial incompletion is often associated with economic incompletion.

Lenin, of course, completely rejected the idea of any connection between the latter and the democratic aspect of the national question. It is clear too that he saw no direct relationship between economic dependence and a struggle against imperialism. While it has to be acknowledged that the presence of multinational companies, along with the depletion of the country's physical resources, indicates the hand of imperialism at work in the Irish economy, this is far from saying that it is in conflict with anti-imperialist forces, or that if it does the conflict is significant enough to create a national question. Lenin believed that such questions were generated only where there was direct foreign control (the colonies, Germany, etc). Even when a country was being exploited by several others, local political contradictions remained pre-eminent. This view was adumbrated by Mao in his discussion of imperialism, colonialism and China in the 1930s. Prior to 1935, he wrote, 'the Chinese people's struggle against imperialism, together with conflicts among the imperialist powers' had ensured for China 'a semi-independent status enabling internal class divisions to predominate'. This state of affairs was transformed when Japan's intentions became unmistakable. 'They want to convert the whole of China from a semi-colony shared by several imperialist powers into a colony dominated by Japan.' This created a new principal contradiction of an essentially national character.[65] Such conditions are not being created in Ireland. Nor is the international situation forcing imperialist exploitation in countries like Ireland into a critical position. To this extent semi- or neo-colonial influence falls short of generating an anti-imperialist national question.

Is there, finally, another side to the question of territorial unity, distinct from the democratic aspect, that offers to set imperialism and anti-imperialism on a collision course? Certainly an imperial power, Britain, has maintained a colonial relationship to Northern Ireland and is reckoned by some to be determined it should continue. But this is far from proving that struggles over the status of Northern Ireland involve the question of imperialism, or that contradictions involving imperialism have primacy in Ulster.

Struggles over the status of the north are no more automatically anti-imperialist than crimes against property are automatically anti-capitalist. Nobody to date has shown that the IRA's fight for territorial completion offers any prospect of an end to British imperialism. Most of the evidence points to a different interpretation—that in the long run British imperialism would itself prefer a form of territorial completion. The real objections to unification come not from Britain but from local Protestants. Of course the British want to crush the IRA, and are prepared to use force to do so. Yet this is a separate question. The proof is that, even if the IRA forced the British to withdraw, territorial integrity would be as far away as ever.

The political nature of Irish nationalism

The remaining compass point of the Marxist position concerns the social and political economy of nationalist Ireland, together with its political implications. This is evidently a critical aspect of the overall position, since Protestant resistance to a united Ireland is underplayed and the struggle for national liberation remains the first item on the agenda. If Marxists are to intervene in this struggle, they clearly require systematic knowledge of whom they should ally with, and whom they should not. This in turn requires an analysis of Irish society. The extent to which such analysis has been developed may be best appreciated by examining Marxist writing on the Irish peasantry and its relation to republicanism.

Understanding this question has probably been the most important task of concrete analysis that Marxists interested in Ireland have had to face. Every sustained revolutionary movement in Irish history, with the exception of today's Provisional IRA, has been predominantly peasant in social composition (though rarely in leadership). The great truth remains, though, that no Marxist has ever undertaken such an analysis. Indeed, practical Marxist concern with the Irish peasantry has, astonishingly, declined rather than grown over the years.

This concern found its most rigorous expression in the work of Marx himself. Marx was, in fact, a representative of the widespread current of critical opinion on the Anglo-Irish nexus and, in particular, the land system in Ireland.[66] At one radical end of the spectrum stood Marx himself and Irish republicanism, in the middle could be found constitutional nationalists of the Parnellite and moderate varieties, and on the right stood agricultural technocrats like R. O. Pringle, editor of the *Irish Farmer's Gazette*, and Professor Baldwin, who ran the government model farm in Ireland. Such a broad grouping could not be a united one.[67] The political differences between socialist separatists, separatist non-socialists, Home Rulers of different shades and even Unionists in this category are obvious. Nevertheless there was unity on one point. All accepted that the basic trends in Irish agrarian economic and social relations were adverse. In this consensus the agricultural transition to pasture, with its attendant effects of high emigration rates and consolidation, constituted a national crisis. Marx for his part was familiar with the various products of this tradition. He read the radical Nationalist press as well as the works of more moderate figures like J. N. Murphy. He regularly studied the Irish agrarian statistics. He analysed Irish subordination as an objective process.

'*Clearing of the Estate of Ireland*' is now the one purpose of English rule in Ireland. The *stupid* English government in London knows nothing, of course, itself of this immense change since 1846 . . .'[68] The remedy was threefold.

What the Irish need is
(1) Self-government and independence from England.
(2) An agrarian revolution.
(3) Protective tariffs against England. Once the Irish are independent, necessity will turn them into protectionists, as it did Canada, Australia, etc.[69]

It was certainly not Ireland's destiny to be merely England's sheepwalk and cattle pasture. Relative overpopulation had increased *pari passu* with absolute depopulation. In 1867 Marx phrased an argument that was to appear in *Capital* itself. 'Rents and profits (where the farmer is no peasant farmer) may increase, although the produce of the soil decreases. The total produce may diminish, and still greater part of it may be converted into surplus produce, falling to the landlord and the (great) farmer. And the price of the surplus produce has risen.'[70]

Yet despite the brilliance of occasional insights, there is little even here that would have been of contemporary practical use to Irish socialists. Marx does not discuss the combination of modes of production in nineteenth-century Ireland, and is thus obliged to remain silent on the question of divisons within the rural population.

Consider this problem, the differentiation of the peasantry. In a work which had the Irish social structure as its primary object Marx would necessarily have taken it up together with the question of its political effects. Instead, both Marx and Engels were obviously aware of the existence of a certain degree of differentiation, but were somewhat cursory on the subject of both its extent and its significance.

In *Capital* Marx wrote: 'The smaller and medium farmers—I reckon among these all who do not cultivate more than 100 acres—still make up about eight tenths of the whole number.'[71] It is possible to make two comments on this passage. While Marx acknowledged the existence of a top one fifth of Irish farmers who did not belong to the same socio-economic category of the other four fifths, he nowhere analysed the political implications of this fact. Secondly, it is certain that the bottom four fifths cannot be lumped together for the purposes of analysis. In sum, Marx's Irish writings do not allow the reader to perceive the full significance of the divisions within the Irish peasantry. The impression is given that the overwhelming majority of the peasantry shared roughly the same conditions of life and would be likely to participate in a unified manner in any agrarian social movement. In reality, there were deep internal divisions within the very forms of class struggle adopted by Irish rural movements, and these divisions set decided limitations on the radicalism of possible solutions to the agrarian question. In particular, such divisions—or to put it another way, the political and social weight of a fairly extensive Irish rural bourgeoisie—made it probable that the land question could be settled by a British Parliament in a relatively gradualistic fashion.[72]

Consider the implicatons for Marx's position. In 1870 he wrote:

> The destruction of the English landed aristocracy in Ireland is an infinitely easier operation than in England here because in Ireland the *land question* has hitherto been the *exclusive form* of the social question, because it is a question of existence, *of life and death*, for the immense majority of the Irish people and because it is at the same time inseparable from the national question.[73]

This terse passage clearly implies that Marx saw a sense of grievance on the land question as the driving force behind Irish nationalism. However, after some hestitation in the spring of 1881, he had by the end of that year clearly come to the conclusion that the land question could be settled with the framework of the union.[75] In a letter to Edward Bernstein in June 1882 Engels explicitly stated that the aim of the Land League—'the total removal of the intruder landlords'—could be achieved by 'constitutional means.'[76]

These admissions are of some importance. Marx's position on the content of Irish nationalism was largely determined by his view of the land question. 'Previously I thought Ireland's separation from England impossible,' he wrote to Engels on 2 November 1867. 'Now, I think it inevitable, although after separation there may come *federation*. How the English carry on is evidenced by the *Agricultural Statistics* for the current year. Furthermore, the form of the eviction.' Yet in 1879–82 the power of the 'English aristocracy in Ireland' had suffered an irreversible historical defeat. Marx offers no reflection on the significance of this development; nor, most surprisingly, does Engels. In consequence the latter's comments on

Ireland became increasingly inconsequential, as his position on Ulster demonstrates.

Marx and Engels circled around a double problem without ever clearly formulating it or recognising its significance: on the one hand, the differentiation of the peasantry; on the other, the relation of the land question to nationalism/republicanism. Within Marx's lifetime the trend towards the former radically altered both the land question itself and its relation to politics. The land question was effectively solved in its own terms, yet the problem of Irish independence remained at the centre of politics and still continued to generate different responses from different strata of the peasantry.

While there is a partial awareness of this situation in the work of Marx and Engels, there is none at all in later Marxist writing on the Irish peasantry. A large share of the blame for this must be shouldered by Connolly, who as a consequence of his attitudes to the national question and the 'workers' republic' displayed no interest in the social forces that were to bear the brunt of the struggles betwen 1918 and 1923. The three-volume collection of Connolly's work sponsored by the ITGWU and published between 1948 and 1951 contains only three articles on the peasantry, two written in 1898 and one in exile in 1909.[77] Together with the sections on the contemporary land question in *The Reconquest of Ireland*[78] these do little more than state that all sections of the peasantry remained oppressed despite peasant proprietorship, and endorse a land programme for all purposes identical with that of William O'Brien's United Irish League.

An even more remarkably inadequate treatment of the question is that of Kautsky, who was actually the Second International's authority on the agrarian question.[79] Reviewing the results of the Land Acts and the effects of more favourable prices in the twentieth century, he wrote:

> the position of the farmers and clergy has been changed and is now the same as in most of the older states: that is, they form a conservative element. Their demand for self-determination has not decreased with the increase of their power, but it is no longer expressed in such desperate ways. They prefer the means of parliament to those of violence . . .[80]

As it turned out, a significant proportion of 'the farmers' were showing their preference for violence over parliament while

Kautsky was writing. In Ireland, if not in Germany, this fact was inescapable. Yet the relationship of the land question to nationalism and republicanism continued locally to be registered in a half-hearted and purely formal way.

The Communist Party of Ireland, founded in 1921 with James Connolly's son Roddy as Secretary, does not seem to have mentioned the peasantry in its manifesto, which addressed only the 'workers of Ireland' and called only for a 'Workers' Republic'.[81] It was not until 1930, after this organisation had been replaced by the 'Revolutionary Workers' Groups',[82] that Irish Marxists drafted an agrarian programme of any sort. Even then it was vague and abstract, calling for the 'socialisation' of land and 'guarantees to the working farmers [of] the use of such land as they can work without the exploitation of others'.[83] A 'Campaign Committee of Irish Working Farmers' was formed, but its existence appears to have been largely a paper one.

In 1931 the RWGs published a long pamphlet by Elinor Burns[84] which was to summarise contemporary Irish Marxist reflections on the political situation and the significance of the agrarian question in relation to it. Burns argued that Irish history since 1845 could be divided into four phases. In the first, between 1845 and 1881, Ireland's increasing oppression as a food-producing colony generated the conditions for the Land League to emerge as the major revolutionary force in Irish politics. In the period between 1881 and 1918 land reform made possible a degree of rural capital accumulation which was mirrored by a similar process in urban areas. This in turn generated a revolutionary working class. Between 1919 and 1921 sections of the peasantry became immiserated and followed this class into revolutionary politics. After 1921 the rural and urban bourgeoisies consolidated their dominance. According to Burns, however, adverse economic conditions were making worker–peasant unity again a practical possibility in the 1930s.

A number of themes emerge from this analysis. First, all sections of the peasantry are seen as being still exploited, no longer by landlords but by imperialism. The phrase 'the exchange of one set of masters for another' recurs again and again. Nevertheless, the significance of the revolutionary qualities of the poor peasantry is stressed especially. Secondly, Republicanism is treated as the political expression of this economic oppression. This functions as a

kind of surrogate for socialism, since oppression is experienced in a
'political' rather than economic form. Thirdly, the bourgeoisie are
treated as the permanent turncoats of 'genuine' land reform. Their
destiny is to always sell out the peasantry, just as it is to always sell
out the national revolution. Finally, Republican politics can still
play a role in achieving socialism, since through the flight of the
bourgeoisie from the 'anti-imperialist' struggle they will come to
recognise the leading role of the working class and its
corollary—that national revolution means socialist revolution.

This is in reality yet another variant of the 'incomplete revolution'
thesis. 'Genuine' land reform is added to national revolution as
another goal the bourgeoisie is congenitally unable to realise, and
is again equated with socialism (despite the fact that the RWG's
programme was redistributivist). Republicanism is treated as a kind
of peasant syndicalism. The bourgeoisie's relation to it is deduced
from their economic position. Divisions within the peasantry are
secondary. The correct strategy for the working class is simply to
declare its solidarity with republicanism. All that has changed from
Connolly's day is that the peasantry have been acknowledged as a
potential ally. In Burns's pamphlet the words 'and Peasants' are
added to the 'Workers' Republic' slogan.

This economistic analysis, which fell below the level of Marx's
reflections—themselves inadequate—formed the basis of the CPI's
agrarian strategy (and overall political strategy too) when the party
was reconstituted in 1933. To implement it the party strove to
secure unity with the left wing of the Republican movement. In
September 1934 a 'Republican Congress' was called by the latter, to
which the CPI were invited. They supported a resolution proposed
by Peadar O'Donnell and George Gilmore in favour of a 'united
anti-imperialist front'.

Ironically, the Congress turned into a debate between those
who, like the CPI, perceived the need to adapt Connolly's position
to include the peasantry as an ally (albeit in an inadequate way) and
those who preferred to rely on the word of the master. Almost half
the delegates, under the leadership of some of the first CPI's
founders, opposed the O'Donnell–Gilmore resolution on the
grounds that it ran counter to the concept of a 'Workers' Republic'.
The latter, they asserted, continued to be on the agenda. The
outcome was a split.

[While] O'Donnell won the battle [he] lost the war, for the

substantial minority, when they found they were beaten, left the hall
. . . and left Congress. Congress survived for several years afterwards
but finally O'Donnell and his committee disbanded it rather than see
it disintegrate . . .[85]

The ghost of Connolly had claimed its first victim (through the
intervention of two of his children, Roddy and Nora). The CPI
continued to espouse its albeit defective programme, but without
an audience.[86] It was left to a German non-Marxist writing twenty
years later to indicate even the *empirical* relationship between the
land question and republicanism.[87]

The reader should require no reminder of the other side of the
coin to the peasantry's (lack of) analysis—the Marxist position on
urban social classes. This requires no lengthy restatement, since it is
implicit in each of the formulations already discussed. The Catholic
urban bourgeoisie's 'historical role' has been to (at least) divert or
(at most) betray the leadership of the national struggle, the true
bearers of which are the revolutionary working class. The
significance of the national struggle for this class is obviously a
problem. Calling it a surrogate obviously begs further questions,
and most Marxists have 'solved' this in the manner of Connolly, by
regarding national liberation and socialism as the same thing.
Moreover, struggles for these objectives are typically seen as the
logical extension of the militancy of the volatile Dublin trade union
movement. (Connolly, rather than analysising this syndicalism,
simply endorsed it.) The urban petty-bourgeoisie receive attention
only from Kautsky, who predictably explained its republicanism in
terms of its desire to displace English cadres in the Irish Civil
Service.

Quite apart from failing to detect the theoretical errors in all
these formulations, modern Irish Marxism has largely failed to
register even their empirical refutation. The Anglo-Irish war or War
of Independence (1918–21) clearly demonstrated that important
sectors of the rural and urban bourgeoisie could play a leading role
in the national struggle and that this struggle could enlist the
support of rural and urban working classes without putting forward
any socially radical aims. Connolly for one believed this impossible,
notwithstanding the work of other Marxists.

Yet 1978 still finds these same lessons mainly ignored. Most of
Connolly's formulations continue to be uncritically repeated, only
without the same excuses. Connolly reflected the generality of the

militant section of the Second International's reception of Marxism and was executed before Lenin's critique of it became available. The impulse behind his work is uniformly progressive, yet his actual theoretical construct prevented it from finding expression in any but his most fundamental position: his support for national liberation. The Marxist 'position' on Ireland today amounts to no more than a reprise of Connolly's position as a whole, combined with a selective reading of Marx and Lenin in its light.[88] Conspiring with these figures' own inadequate formulations when Ireland was their direct subject, the outcome is a melange of non-Marxist postures, whose few implementable implications have no forseeable progressive effect.

The state

Two conclusions may be drawn from this historical and analytical review of the Marxist position on Ireland. Firstly, the great unfulfilled need of Irish Marxist politics is a scientific analysis of Irish society. This objective, however, is a long-term one. It is not possible to wish such an analysis into being, as its construction requires a substantial period being devoted not only to the assembly of raw materials but to the clarification of concepts.

Indeed, it is only exceptionally, as in the case of Lenin's *Development of Capitalism in Russia*, that such a work appears ready-made and complete in a single initiative. The authors of this work have set themselves a more modest goal—a partial survey of the economy and politics of Northern Ireland—in the hope that it may provide a kind of signpost for this larger objective.

A second conclusion of this review is that much of the Marxist position described here has a very close association with dominant bourgeois ideologies. One precise reason why Irish Marxism is backward and why there is no significant Marxist–Leninist political grouping in Ireland is that Marxism has invariably functioned at the tail end of one or other of the Irish bourgeoisies. An illustration is the programme of the Irish Workers' Party (now the Communist Party of Ireland) in the 1960s, nearly half a century after the south's bourgeois revolution: its title—'Ireland Her Own' (!). In this extremely backward situation one primary objective of Irish Marxists must be to detach Marxism from bourgeois ideology and to emphasise its proletarian content. This means drawing upon its distinctive features, rather than passing them over in favour of what it shares with bourgeois or petty-bourgeois thought.

The lack of relevance to contemporary Ireland of 'imperialism' and 'the right of nations to self-determination'; the ideological pertinence of concepts which are distinctively Marxist. These imperatives suggest the employment of concepts which seek a Marxist–Leninist understanding of the relation of class forces and forms of class power in societies relatively indifferent to such problems, i.e. from the point of view of external determinants, for all purposes 'normal' bourgeois societies. In these societies the important secret is not how political and economic development has been 'impaired', but how bourgeois class power has been constituted and maintained. This calls for the application of concepts designed to understand class struggles structured by the unfolding of internal elements rather than abstract and malignant external ones. Such concepts must analyse how in Northern Ireland the local Protestant bourgeoisie gained and held power, how it maintained a bloc or alliance of classes identifying with its rule, and how it divided and oppressed the classes and groups that opposed it.

The *state* is the central Marxist–Leninist concept which makes it possible to elucidate class relations such as these. The state represents the 'condensation' of politics in bourgeois societies. Its content is both the necessary product of the general and specific antagonisms of such societies and the means by which these are moderated to the advantage of the dominant class. The state provides a 'shell' for class rule, lending it a stable and more or less permanent institutional character. Above all the state is the means by which the dominant class subordinates and divides other classes. In the case of capitalist societies it is democracy which serves as the 'best possible shell' (Lenin), since it facilitates the autonomous perfection of the bureaucratic apparatuses on the one hand, together with the distribution of representative power between the various sections of the dominant class on the other.[89] Through this process the oppressed classes are politically emasculated.

The forms of class struggle and their effects on the ruling class were reflected, according to Lenin, in specific forms of organisation of State administration. At the beginning of the twentieth century changes in the class struggle led the bourgeoisie to modify their rule in relation to the oppressed classes.[90] In discussing this question (effectively, that of the 'labour aristocracy') Lenin distinguished class strategies and their embodiment in administrative policies and practices on the one hand, and the state structure on the other. He identified the former as the location of these modifications; the latter was reproduced without substantial amendment.

Later Marxists took this view of how the bourgeoisie holds power further. According to Gramsci it was by maintaining a precarious 'hegemony' over the state, which itself represented an 'unstable equilibrium of compromise' between the various forces in the ruling bloc.[91] The analysis has been systematised and elaborated by Poulantzas, in whose formulation this equilibrium is maintained by the sharing out of different segments of the state structure amongst the ruling bloc.[92]

In acknowledging the suggestiveness and merit of these positions, Balibar has recently qualified them. The bourgeoisie and the ruling bloc indeed have fractions, and some section of the bourgeoisie always dominates the state apparatuses to its own profit. Divisons of the bourgeoisie on politics and in the state do not arise as a result of economically constituted groups struggling for a better division of the spoils of office, however. This is to overlook the essence of the Leninist conception of the state, namely its reproduction of divisions within the subordinate classes. It is this function, which is based upon the class struggle, that generates political divisions within the bourgeoisie, and leads to the materialisation of a particular strategy favouring a specific bourgeois fraction.[93]

Understanding Northern Ireland's politics is in this sense understanding the class struggle in Northern Ireland and the relation of the local state to it. It is understanding the specific class strategies which arose in relation to the class struggle and how these reproduced specific forms of class power. It is also understanding the process by which these strategies were built up, and the effects on the state of the form they took. It should not need saying that it also means understanding the contradictions and crises which became embodied in the dispositions of the bourgeoisie's class power, and how these were affected by certain social changes. The emphasis in the analysis that follows will, in other words, be on the internal relations within the Protestant bloc.

Notes to chapter 1

[1] Engels to E. Bernstein, 22 May 1886, in *Marx and Engels on Ireland* (London, 1971), p. 349.

[2] Cf. Engels to W. Liebknecht, 29 February 1888, *ibid.*, pp. 350–1.

[3] 'The constitutional crisis in England' (1914), in *British Labour and British Imperialism* (London, 1969), pp. 37–9.

[4] 'The English Liberals and Ireland' (1914), *ibid.*, p. 56.

[5] K. Kautsky, *Irland* (Leipzig, 1880).

[6] *Id.*, *Ireland* (1922), trans. and ed. A. Clifford (Belfast, 1974).

[7] *Ibid.*, p. 11.

[8] W. McMullen, 'Introduction' to J. Connolly, *The Workers' Republic*, ed. D. Ryan (Dublin, 1951), p. 24.

[9] 'A plea for socialist unity in Ireland', in Irish Communist Organisation (ed.), *The Connolly–Walker Controversy* (Belfast, 1969), p. 9.

[10] 'Sweat shops behind the Orange flag' (1911), in *Workers' Republic*, p. 96.

[11] 'A plea for socialist unity in Ireland', *loc. cit.*

[12] 'A forgotten chapter of Irish history' (1913), in *Ireland upon the Dissecting Table* (Cork, 1975), p. 44.

[13] *Forward*, 7 June 1913.

[14] *Ibid.*, 28 March 1914.

[15] *Ibid.*

[16] 'A forgotten chapter'. Accounts of the propaganda meetings are given in *The Irish Worker*, April and May 1914.

[17] *Ireland upon the Dissecting Table*, p. 33.

[18] *Ibid.*

[19] *Irish Worker*, 16 May 1914.

[20] Cf. P. Gibbon, *Origins of Ulster Unionism* (Manchester, 1975).

[21] *Ibid.*; P. Buckland, *Irish Unionism*, Vol. II, *Ulster Unionism and the Origins of Northern Ireland, 1886–1922* (Dublin, 1973).

[22] Cf. Gibbon, *Origins of Ulster Unionism*; H. Patterson, 'Conservative politics and class conflict in Belfast in the 1880s', *Saothar*, No. 2 (1974), and F. Wright, 'Protestant politics and ideology in Ulster', *European Journal of Sociology*, XIV (1973).

[23] See H. Patterson, *The Protestant Working Class and the Belfast Labour Movement* (Belfast, forthcoming).

[24] L. Althusser, 'Ideology and ideological state apparatuses', in *Lenin and Philosophy and other essays* (London, 1971), p. 153.

[25] F. Engels, 'Letters from London' (1843), and 'Feargus O'Connor and the Irish people' (1848), in *Marx and Engels on Ireland*, pp. 34–5, 50.

[26] For the most explicit statement of this position see the letter of the Association Démocratique of Brussels to the Fraternal Democrats in London, 13 February 1848, signed by Marx and others. For some reason this letter was not included in the *Marx and Engels on Ireland* collection (Marx and Engels, *Collected Works*, Vol. 6 (London, 1976), pp. 640–3).

[27] This alone was the basis of Marx's formulation that 'the national emancipation of Ireland is no question of abstract justice or humanitarian sentiment, but the first condition of the English working class's social emancipation'. (Marx to Meyer and Vogt, 9 April 1870, *Marx and Engels on*

Ireland, p. 294). Extraordinarily, in 1978 this is quoted by some Marxists in support of the view that support for the Provisional IRA is the 'litmus paper' of true revolutionary principles.

[28] V. Lenin, 'The discussion on self-determination summed up' (1916), in the collection *Critical Remarks on the National Question* (Moscow, 1971), p. 131.

[29] K. Kautsky, 'Die moderne Nationalität', *Neue Zeit*, V (1887); J. Stalin, *Marxism and the National Question* (1913; Belfast, 1971).

[30] See M. Lewin, *Lenin's Last Struggle* (London, 1969).

[31] Lenin, 'The question of nationalities or autonomisation' (1922–23), *Selected Works*, Vol. III, (Moscow, 1970), p. 75.

[32] Lenin, 'The revolutionary-democratic dictatorship of the proletariat and the peasantry' (1905), *Collected Works* (Moscow, 1960–70), Vol. VIII, p. 299. Curiously, in otherwise scholarly works, neither Davis nor Löwy acknowledges this; cf. H. Davis, *Nationalism and Socialism: Marxist and Labour Theories of Nationalism to 1917* (London, revised edition 1973); M. Löwy, 'Marxism and the national question', *New Left Review*, 96 (1976). Nor, in his 'symptomatic' reading, does B. Hindess, 'Lenin and the agrarian question in the first Russian revolution', *Theoretical Practice*, 6 (1972).

[33] 'Critical remarks on the national question' (1913); 'The right of nations to self-determination' (1916); 'The discussion of self-determination summed up' (1916); 'The socialist revolution and the right of nations to self-determination' (1916). These are all conveniently published in the collection *Critical Remarks on the National Question*.

[34] 'The right of nations', in *Critical Remarks*, p. 43.

[35] Lenin, 'The right of nations', p. 49; *State and Revolution* (1917), *Selected Works*, Vol. II, p. 343.

[36] *Ibid.*, pp. 344–5.

[37] Lenin, 'The right of nations', p. 53.

[38] *Ibid.*, p. 48.

[39] Lenin, *Selected Works*, Vol. III, p. 786.

[40] Dublin, 1910; reprinted Dublin, 1967.

[41] 'Sinn Fein, socialism and the nation' (1909), in J. Connolly, *Socialism and Nationalism*, ed. D. Ryan (Dublin, 1948), p. 88.

[42] 'A forgotten chapter', p. 42.

[43] G. D.. H. Cole, *The Second International*, Part I (London, 1956), pp. 70–71.

[44] On the ideology of Belfast socialism, see Patterson, *The Protestant Working Class*.

[45] 'Socialism and Irish nationalism' (1897), in *Socialism and Nationalism*, p. 36.

[46] *Ibid.*, p. 25.

[47] *Ibid.*, p. 24.

[48] Cf. also J. Hoffman, 'James Connolly and the theory of historical materialism', *Saothar*, No. 2 (1974).

[49] Kautsky, *Ireland*, p. 20.

[50] *Ibid.*, p. 2.

[51] N. Bukharin, *Imperialism and World Economy* (1913); London, 1972, p. 17.

[52] Lenin, *Imperialism: Highest Stage of Capitalism* (1916), in *Selected*

Works, Vol. I, p. 682.

[53] Lenin, *Imperialism*, Vol. I, pp. 745–52.

[54] *Ibid.*, pp. 762–3.

[55] *Ibid.*, pp. 747, 749.

[56] *Ibid.*, p. 764.

[57] Bukharin, *Imperialism*, p. 114.

[58] Lenin, *Imperialism*, Vol. I, p. 705.

[59] *Ibid.*, p. 738.

[60] *Ibid.*, p. 741.

[61] *Ibid.*, p. 738.

[62] Lenin, 'The discussion of self-determination summed up', pp. 147–8.

[63] *Ibid.*, p. 124.

[64] Lenin, 'Report on the international situation and the fundamental tasks of the Communist International', *Selected Works*, Vol. III, p. 463.

[65] Mao tse-Tung, 'On tactics against Japanese imperialism' (1935), in *Selected Works*, Vol. I, Peking, 1965, p. 153–62.

[66] For a sustained description see P. Bew, *Land and The National Question in Ireland, 1858–82* (Dublin, 1978), ch. 1.

[67] The Irish agricultural technocrats would have been horrified by the argument of the radical Nationalist journal *The Irishman*, in an issue which Marx seems to have read. 'Every fattened ox that wins his prize at Stephen's Green represents a peasant's levelled home' (28 September 1867).

[68] Marx to Engels, 30 November 1865, in *Marx and Engels on Ireland*, p. 148.

[69] *Ibid.*, p. 149.

[70] Outline of a report on the Irish question to the Communist Educational Association of German Workers in London, 10 December 1867, *ibid.*, p. 136.

[71] *Ibid.*, p. 107.

[72] See *Land and the National Question* on this problem.

[73] Marx to Meyer and Vogt, *loc. cit.*, p. 293.

[74] Marx to Jenny Longuet, *loc. cit.*, p. 330.

[75] Marx to Engels, *loc. cit.*, pp. 331–2.

[76] *Ibid.*, p. 334.

[77] 'Peasant proprietorship and socialism' and 'The land question' (1898), 'Capitalism and the Irish small farmer' (1909), all in *Workers' Republic*, pp. 35–8 and 55–7.

[78] Dublin, 1914.

[79] Lenin described his definitive work on this issue, *Die Agrarfrage* (Stuttgart, 1899), as 'after Volume III of *Capital*, the most noteworthy contribution to recent economic literature', *Development of Capitalism in Russia* (Moscow, 1967), p. 27.

[80] Kautsky, *Ireland*, p. 13.

[81] S. Nolan (ed.), *Communist Party of Ireland Outline History* (Dublin, n.d.), pp. 6–7.

[82] The CPI was dissolved in 1924 (*ibid.*, p. 8).

[83] *Ibid.*, p. 9.

[84] *British Imperialism in Ireland* (Dublin, 1931; reprinted Cork, 1974).

[85] M. McInerney, *Peadar O'Donnell* (Dublin, 1974), pp. 138–9. For a detailed description of the congress see G. Gilmore, *The Republican*

Congress (Dublin, 1934, reprinted 1966). The second edition of this pamphlet (New York, 1935, reprinted Cork, 1974) contains extracts from the congress's agrarian programme (p. 4). For the general background to the congress see Irish Communist Organisation, *The Republican Congress* (Belfast, 1969).

[86] This programme was given its most systematic exposition in a full-length book by Brian O'Neill, editor of the CPI's weekly paper. However, this work was still as far as ever from a detailed analysis. B. O'Neill, *The War for Land in Ireland*, London, 1935.)

[87] E. Rumpf and A. C. Hepburn, *Nationalism and Socialism in Twentieth-century Ireland* (Heidelberg, 1959; Liverpool, 1977), pp. 28–69.

[88] An early example of this tendency was R. M. Fox's *Marx, Engels and Lenin on Ireland* (New York, 1940), in which it is claimed that *Lenin* believed that the 1913 Dublin lock-out meant that 'from now on the struggle in Ireland could only be a struggle for a really independent, really free Ireland, the socialist republic of Irish workers and peasants . . .' and that the significance of the UVF was to 'drown in blood this new movement of Irish workers, which threatened not only to unite Ireland, the shipyard worker of Belfast with the textile worker (*sic*) or docker of Dublin, but also to spread to England . . .' (!) (pp. 21–2). Interestingly, the reverse tendency is to be found in G. Schüller's *James Connolly and Irish Freedom* (Chicago, 1926, reprinted Cork, 1974). This work reads Lenin into Connolly, claiming the latter, for example, to be a champion of 'the union with the peasantry'.

[89] Lenin, *State and Revolution*, pp. 307–9.

[90] Cf. the collection *British Labour*, pp. 42–110. Of course, this process began earlier in Britain (cf. J. Foster, *Class Struggle and Industrial Revolution*, London, 1974).

[91] A. Gramsci, *Selections from the Prison Notebooks* (London, 1971).

[92] N. Poulantzas, *Political Power and Social Class* (London, 1973).

[93] E. Balibar, *The Dictatorship of the Proletariat* (London, 1977).

2

THE CONSTRUCTION OF THE STATE APPARATUSES, 1921–25

The subject of this study, the Northern Ireland state, was born in l921—or, more precisely, between that date and 1925, when the Boundary Commission was finally laid to rest. While the circumstances of its conception, gestation and birth did not wholly prefigure its later development, they made a profound contribution to it. It is only right, then, that they should be examined in detail. The year 1918–19 will be taken as a starting point.[1] Three sets of events together began to dominate the stage of Irish politics in that year. Their conjuncture amounted to a crisis which set the parameters for the formation of both states in Ireland.

First, and most important, British political and military domination of Ireland was broken by the IRA. In response, a shift took place in political relations within the Unionist bloc, a shift which was to have a decisive effect on the spontaneous process of state formation in the north of Ireland. Thirdly, the political representatives of the British ruling class devised a series of new Irish strategies aimed at coping with the situation and ensuring an outcome that would do least injury to British interests. These strategies determined the nature of the external modifications to the spontaneous process of state formation, and in some degree further modified political relations between Protestants.

Most of this chapter will be concerned with the second and, more particularly, the third of these events. Although an analysis falls outside the scope of this work, some prefatory remarks are necessary about the first of them.[2]

The loss of British dominance in Ireland

While it could be argued that any moral hegemony had been dead since the Famine, or at least since the Land War, the political hegemony of the British ruling class remained effectively undisturbed until 1918. Parnell, Dillon and Redmond were by no means its spokesmen, but after 1886 they allowed the British, for all their vacillation, to establish a form of *Pax Hibernica* and to dictate the nature of the Irish question.

From 1913 to 1918 the essence of the *Pax Hibernica* was devolution plus partition. The formula proved resilient because it succeeded in conciliating a violent conflict in the British ruling class as well as one in Ireland, and became a relatively stable reference point for all parties. Equilibrium was disrupted temporarily in 1916 and permanently in 1918–19 by the onset of popular guerilla warfare, the electoral destruction of the UIL, the constitution of the first Dail and other associated changes.

Just as the dissolution of British hegemony led to the decomposition of the *Pax Hibernica*, it led also to a weakening of the internal hegemony of the Irish bourgeoisie in favour of the 'tyranny of the dead'. Like the loss of British hegemony, this accelerated as the military struggle gained ground in 1920. Before 1919 the principal source of the nationalist bloc's disunity had been conflict between constitutional nationalism and the 'physical force' party. By 1920 it was the latter that was in disarray. Like Parnell's party, Sinn Fein and the IRA possessed leaders of strong moral authority; unlike it, they had no strong bureaucratic centres to dictate local policy.

In Belfast, however, the Catholic bourgeoisie largely retained its hegemony over local nationalist politics, as the membership figures for the different nationalist and republican organisations in the city in 1920 make clear(table 1).

Table 1   *Membership of nationalist and republican organisations in Belfast, 1920*

Nationalist	Republican
United Irish League 6,533	Sinn Fein 980
National Volunteers 1,300	Irish Volunteers 500

Source. Patterson, *The Protestant Working Class*.

Even though Joseph Devlin's supporters far outnumbered the membership of other organisations, his influence was diminished by the changing national balance of forces. The faltering of his control over both northern Catholics and southerners who came to fight in the north was discerned by the Unionist leadership, and in a probably more exaggerated way by the British Colonial Secretary, Winston Churchill.[3]

The essence of all these changes was that the traditional nationalist stance of political bargaining and readiness to compromise on partition, which had won grudging acceptance from both the British and the Unionists, now appeared to be suffering eclipse. A resolute determination to destroy British administration forcibly throughout Ireland was now to the fore. Equally significantly, all but those in the British armed forces believed that little could ultimately be done to resist it. The exception was, of course, the Unionists.

The Unionist bloc, 1913–21

The Unionist bloc had been constituted in its contemporaneous form during the opposition to the third Home Rule Bill in the period 1911–13. Previously, while there had been a bloc, it was far from inclusive of Ulster Protestants and even further from being unified.

The basic source of disunity was not the tradition of liberalism among Ulster Presbyterians, as has often been maintained, but the much stronger tradition of autonomous political activity by the Protestant labour aristocracy, urban petty-bourgeoisie and small employers. Dating back at least to 1868,[4] it was complex and heterogeneous in its origins, but possessed a clear and distinct ideology combining militant anti-Catholicism with democratic, anti-landlord and anti-capitalist sentiment.[5] While its political expressions tended to be episodic, they nevertheless modified the development of both conservative politics and the labour movement in the Six Counties.

Independent Orangeism, as it was known, proved most influential in periods when British governments were following conciliatory Irish policies (e.g. 1900–05).[6] Partly in order to circumvent this, the local bourgeoisie in 1905 reorganised itself politically into a force independent of the Conservative party at Westminster. The setting up of the Ulster Unionist Council was a decisive step which neutralised independent Orangeism's rhetoric. The orthodox Orange Order began to expand rapidly soon after.[7] Independent Orangeism's decline was complete by

1913, when the class forces it had represented became integrated into a bloc with Protestant landlords and capitalists, exemplified in the paramilitary UVF. This provided an irresistible focus of popular Unionist opposition to a united Ireland.

There were two consequences of the new integration. The more obvious was that the politics and ideology of the Protestant masses were stripped of their progressive elements. These remained only residually, in the form of a militant lack of deference to bourgeois authority. While the new ideology occasionally accommodated reformist labour views, it found its main expression in a stronger version of the loyalism of the bourgeoisie. The other was that with the establishment of large-scale political and military organisations there emerged a professional political leadership possessing its own relative autonomy from the Unionist bourgeoisie. This was popularly known, after its headquarters, as the Old Town Hall circle. Here the situation rested until 1918.

1918 and 1919 were the years not only of the crushing of the UIL and the development of a militant Sinn Fein challenge to British rule, but of intense economic class conflict throughout Britain, manifested in a large increase in trade union membership and a series of strikes. Locally, the longest and most militant stoppage was a three-week strike of Belfast shipyard and engineering workers. Traditionally well organised, and predominantly Protestant, they defied the national leadership of the Confederation of Shipbuilding and Engineering Unions in demanding a ten-hour reduction in the working week. The strike spread to involve municipal, gas and electricity workers and closed down large sections of industry and commerce. A General Strike Committee assumed powers to issue permits allowing 'necessary' production, published a daily newspaper and generally adopted the attributes of a local soviet. Its activities instilled fears in a section of the Unionist leadership, particularly Edward Carson and R. Dawson Bates, that the class alliance embodied in the old UVF was under threat of dissolution.

Carson in particular appears to have been predisposed to exaggerate the danger of a Bolshevik outbreak in Britain. This notion afflicted right-wing conservatives generally and achieved institutional expression in the activities and publications of the British Empire Union, of which Carson became president in 1918. In Belfast the Unionist leadership had—in the recently created Ulster

Unionist Labour Association—a means of initiating a purge from the local trade union movement of 'Bolsheviks' and (what it saw as the same thing) republicans. Based on some of the most traditionally fervent working-class Unionists in the shipyards, the UULA was first intended as an instrument of Carson's 'New Unionism', i.e. a more 'socially conscious' and 'democratic' Unionist party, designed to stave off electoral losses to Labour in Belfast. In this role it made little progress. 'New Unionism' was opposed by sections of the local bourgeoisie and left the working class cold. The subsequent career of the organisation was to prove more congenial to all concerned. Effectively it involved sounding the counter-revolutionary alarm to 'loyal workers' against the twin threats of socialism and republicanism.

By the beginning of 1920 growing unemployment in the engineering and linen industries and the large numbers of demobilised soldiers still out of work were creating friction within the Protestant bloc. The ex-servicemen, who were comparatively well organised, were a particular thorn in the flesh of the local bourgeoisie. With the latter's encouragement the UULA succeeded in giving the conflict a sectarian twist. It identified the unemployment problem, especially that of Protestant ex-servicemen, with the alleged 'peaceful penetration' of Belfast industry during the war by 'tens of thousands' of Catholics from the south and west.

As the guerilla campaign in those regions intensified, the Unionist leadership increasingly 'exposed' the connection between socialism and republicanism, a process in which it was assisted by the British labour movement's (verbal) support for the national struggle. In the spring and summer of 1920, as the Old Town Hall circle demanded more repression from the British state, its working-class appendage held 'indignation' meetings in Belfast to attack the unions on the other side of the Irish Sea for their 'pro-republicanism' and 'Bolshevism'. The meetings also pledged support for the RIC and demanded more vigorous counter-insurgency measures. After one such gathering in the shipyards in July, attacks began on Catholics and workers identified as Labour party members and socialists. They spread throughout the engineering and some sections of the linen industry to result in over 8,000 expulsions within a week.

As a result of the new national situation the employers and

leading Unionists not only acquiesced in such events but justified them—in sharp contrast to their attitude to previous expulsions (e.g. 1893 and 1912). To the Unionist leadership the reserves of the British government seemed weak, and as a result they were willing to endorse practices which served to consolidate their class alliance and guarantee the social basis for a more authoritarian response to Sinn Fein.

Subsequently in the shipyards, large engineering works and railways, 'Vigilance Committees' were set up to ensure that no 'disloyalist' was re–employed. Most Protestant employers looked on with tacit approval. For the remainder of 1920 popular Protestant domination of Belfast workplaces was ritually celebrated in a series of Union Jack unfurlings and parades, often addressed by members of the UULA. Soon the first signs of Catholic retaliation emerged. Trams carrying shipyard workers were subjected to sniping and bomb attacks. In east Belfast there followed widespread looting and burning of Catholic-owned spirit groceries, and fatal clashes between the British army, guarding Catholic property, and Protestant crowds. Leading members of the UULA became involved in creating an unofficial special constabulary, drawn mainly from shipyard workers, with the task of 'policing' Protestant areas.

A shift in political relations within the Protestant class bloc had taken place. In its anxiety to re-establish a militant basis for resistance to republicanism which could operate independently of the British, the Unionist leadership had been obliged to concede a portion of bourgeois class power to the Orange section of the working class. Having done so, they strove to confer institutional and official status on the arrangement. Popular Protestant practices of workplace exclusivism became linked to the efforts of Carson and Craig to reconstitute the UVF and secure British government approval and funds for it and UULA-based constabularies in Belfast.

One Unionist argument in trying to persuade the British to finance the constabularies was that, unless such organisations were officially sanctioned, wild and enraged Protestants would take the law into their own hands. Since 'the younger and wilder the better' was in some areas a criterion of membership,[8] this was ironic. Although the granting of official status to these bodies had Lloyd George's approval from the beginning, characteristics like this ensured that his approbation was not shared by other important figures in the Irish administration. It was particularly withheld by commander-in-chief of the British army in Ireland, Sir Neville Macready. Macready was even accused of sending enthusiastically nationalist members of the RIC north to lead the UVF into ambushes.[9] In the event he and his supporters were overriden, and official status was conferred upon the Specials in November 1920.[10]

The formation of the state had been anticipated by the formation of one of its most critical apparatuses—an independent paramilitary force whose populist flavour of Protestant self-assertiveness was not to be diminished by its new status. The official endorsement of this spirit was to shape both state formation and Catholic attitudes to it.

The British state and its strategies, 1921–25

At the onset of the Anglo-Irish war the strategy of the British ruling class became once more a subject of dissension. Three main positions emerged. There were those who advocated a new *Pax Hibernica*, involving a predisposition to unity and capitulation to the IRA; opponents of capitulation, who favoured a pragmatic adaptation of the old *Pax Hibernica*; and the rump of the old British unionists, whose motto was 'govern or get out'.[11] These camps were fluid in membership and were spread right across the relevant British state institutions.[12] The result was a degree of incoherence and unpredictability in British policy which increased at least until 1921.

It is evident that until this date efforts were made by successive Cabinets to keep all options open. Temporary restrictions were repeatedly placed for long periods upon the Ulster Unionists' political freedom. It was insisted, for example, that after the treaty the Specials be stood down generally for three months and for a considerably longer period in specific areas.[13] More fundamentally, Lloyd George was still making periodic efforts as late as November 1921 to get Craig to go into a united Ireland as the easiest route to a general Dominion settlement.[14]

Nevertheless, during 1921 two major areas of strategic agreement were reached in ruling-class circles. First, the doctrine that Ulster could not be coerced into a united Ireland by force was finally acknowledged. Lloyd George told Griffith, 'the instrument [the army] would break in our hands if we tried'.[15] It is important to recognise that this did not imply a unanimous endorsement of partition. 'We are pledged not to coerce Ulster,' wrote Tom Jones, Assistant Secretary to the Cabinet, on 10 November 1921. He added, significantly, 'some would confine that to physical force'.[16]

The reason why a united Ireland was still favoured in some quarters related to the second measure of broad strategic agreement that had been reached, as to which of the likely outcomes of the Anglo-Irish war was the most desirable. There was a consensus that the setting up in Dublin of an Irish Republic under de Valera should be prevented, and it was now commonly understood that this meant the promotion and installation of the Free State party. Be that as it may, a serious tactical difference arose on how the objective should be attained.

The Prime Minister, Lloyd George, and his immediate associates (in particular Tom Jones) took the view that successful installation of the Free State party depended upon a hard line being pursued against the Unionists. Only by showing that they could make the British rap the Unionists' knuckles could the Free Staters gain sufficient credibility in the south to persuade people they could bring about Irish unity. It mattered not whether the Free Staters had this power, nor whether they would ever indeed unite the country. It was important only that the impression be given. To that extent the fate of the Unionists was a subordinate concern.

This prognosis was contested by the Colonial Office and its Secretary of State, Winston Churchill. Churchill's position was even more complex than Lloyd George's. In the long run he felt that the best opportunity for the success of reactionary forces in Ireland was an ultimate unity between the most conservative elements, north and south.[17] But for this to be secured, he reasoned, the Unionists had to be convinced of the conservative *bona fides* of 'Cosgrave, Mulcahy and the others'. It followed that the Free Staters should be encouraged to draw 'a clear line between [themselves] and the Republicans'.[18] On this basis Sir Alfred Cope, Churchill's link man in Dublin, 'gave them [the Free Staters] hope of the north coming in on terms provided the Provisional Government won through the present troubles'.[19] While Churchill therefore strongly agreed on excluding de Valera and the Republicans from power, he reversed the order of tactical imperatives formulated by Lloyd George. While he hoped the Free Staters would be installed in power (preferably by civil war[20]) this did not have priority over support for the Unionists.

From December 1921 what differences (as a former Liberal Home Ruler) Churchill had with the Ulster Unionists began to evaporate. Craig's wife recorded that her husband found him the most reliable allay in the British Cabinet.[21] Churchill reciprocated the feeling.[22] He could find the Unionists irritating, believing that they were slow to reach sensible arrangements with Collins.[23] He was also anxious that they remain within the law and seems to have been sensitive to the plight of Belfast Catholics.[24] But in the last resort he was Ulster Unionism's implacable supporter. It was predictable that Sir Henry Wilson, the unionist Chief of Imperial General Staff, should have noted in February 1922 that Churchill's committee had agreed to 'reinforce Ulster as much as she wanted'.[25]

Inevitably the level of British support for Ulster soon became a matter of contention between the Lloyd George group and the Colonial Office. On 17 March 1922 Tom Jones told the Prime Minister, 'we are departing from the spirit of the treaty and will be charged by the world of one more breach of faith if we continue in the present policy of paying for the Special Constables . . . cloaking military force under the guise of a police force'.[26] Churchill cheerfully ignored such warnings and continued to offer Unionism wholehearted support. On 29 April his aide, Sir James Masterson Smith, wrote to Lord Londonderry:

> Sir James Craig was evidently pleased with the talk he had with Winston, and realises that Winston appreciates to the full the difficulties that confront the northern government at the present time and the heavy burden that Sir James Craig and his colleagues are carrying. Early next week Winston hopes to be able to have a meeting at his home with Lord Cavan [Commander-in-chief, Aldershot] and others to explore with care and in detail the requirements for which the northern government press. I think you will find that Winston will be able to go a long way towards meeting Sir James Craig. . . .[27]

It is no surprise to find Craig informing the Ulster Cabinet on 12 May 1922 that the loyalist position was now receiving a much more sympathetic hearing in England.[28] It is hardly surprising, either, to find him reporting that, as far as Irish affairs were concerned, Churchill 'undeniably had the predominating voice where the wider interests clashed with the costs involved'.[29]

The differences between Churchill and Lloyd George came to a head in May, when an unexpected *rapprochement* between Collins and de Valera suddenly appeared likely. Churchill's tactics would have been nullified by such an event. Never a stable man, he now became almost hysterical. He spoke of 'social deterioration going on in many parts which Collins was doing nothing to arrest' and of the need to reconvert the 'English capital' (Dublin) into a new Pale.[30] Meanwhile he transferred troops from Cork to the Six Counties to reassure the Ulster government.[31] Masterson Smith thought him in need of a holiday.[32]

The Lloyd George circle realised the extent to which the situation was slipping from their control. They continued to believe that Churchill's conciliation of the Unionists was undermining the Free Staters. There is some evidence that this was true.[33] Lloyd George further believed that if the northern state continued to be strengthened while Collins and de Valera reached agreement there would be a north–south war. In his view, for this *rapprochement* to be undermined at de Valera's expense it was imperative to weaken the position of the Unionists immediately. He responded to increasing southern complaints about unofficial Protestant violence and breaches of the Craig–Collins pact signed the previous March.[34] With strong support from the Treasury, he informed the northern government of his intention to hold a judicial enquiry into its affairs.

The Treasury's hostility to the Unionists centred on their profligacy' with public funds. It viewed the likely consequence of Churchill's policies as indefinite and unlimited British subvention of forces over which it had no control.[35] 'Of course he does,' scrawled the Treasury controller, Otto Niemeyer, in the margin of a letter from Masterson Smith informing him that Craig preferred to work through Churchill.[36] Niemeyer was a virulent critic of the northern regime who detested Craig's manouevrings and retained a lifelong contempt for him. Like Lloyd George he saw Ulster Protestants as spongers and described Craig's financial demands as 'incredible if they were not in black and white'.[37] Above all, the Treasury deeply resented the setting up of a Joint Exchequer Board to arbitrate conflicts between Belfast and the Treasury, since its very existence constituted a blow to the principle of strict treasury accountability. Its findings were to make the Treasury powerless to resist what O'Nuallain has called 'a consistent line of policy pursued by Sir James Craig and his Ministers ... to extract the maximum, financially, economically and politically, from their connection with Britain, while at the same time endeavouring to whittle down their obligations'.[38]

Had the Treasury objections been sustained in full, life would have been made almost impossible for the Belfast regime. Since this would have run counter to the objectives of both the Churchill and the Lloyd George factions, it was not seriously contemplated. A more interesting question is why a united front of both the Lloyd George circle and the Treasury failed to have any practical effect on the Belfast government's security policies. Craig seems to have attributed it to the strength of Churchill's resolution on the matter, but his strategic position as chairman of the Cabinet committee on the Irish Provisional government[39] was also of great help. Yet it is unlikely that the Colonial Office could have sustained its position for much longer had not a dramatic turn of events occurred in the south.

On 28 June 1922 the battle in the Four Courts started the Civil War in the south: it soon reached the point of no return in its intensity. The whole nature of London–Dublin–Belfast relations was transformed. There was no longer a political constraint on British policy towards the north, the constraint of maintaining Collins's credibility. Subsequent attempts to interfere with the development of the northern state apparatuses were fitful and individualistic rather than the product of concerted government effort. Internal division had prevented such action at precisely the time when it would have counted for most.

Already, though, Lloyd George had shown signs of retreat from an uncompromisingly critical stance towards the Unionists. This is evident from the sequel to the proposal for a judicial enquiry. When the Northern Irish Cabinet first discussed the British government's proposal at the end of May it immediately threatened to resign *en masse*.[40] Bates, now Minister of Home Affairs, was particularly infuriated. On 15 June he wrote to Lloyd George,

> ... it would be impossible to give any explanation as to why, if the occurences in Northern Ireland were to be judicially enquired into, those in the South and West were left unchallenged. In truth the suggested Commission is impossible. You cannot try a Government responsible to a Parliament by a Commission of judges...[41]

The Ulster Prime Minister resolved to travel to London, there to challenge this turn in British policy at its source. A crucial meeting was held at 10 Downing Street on 16 June. Craig argued that a public enquiry could be justified on only two grounds. Either there had to be a strong outcry in Britain against the Ulster government, or the British government must feel the money spent financing security was not justified. Neither of these conditions applied, he claimed. Craig therefore sought instead an inquiry by an official of the British government.

The pressure on Craig began to show in his exaggerated statements and needless provocations. He said a judicial enquiry would destroy the operation of intelligence work in Ulster, but this was not accepted. When Lloyd George muttered a few homilies on the mixture of parties and creeds that made up the British Empire, Craig could not resist a characteristic interjection: 'there was no advantage in that',[42] to which Lloyd George replied 'there was every advantage'. Lloyd George made it clear that he was anxious not to endanger his relations with the southern leaders—'it was most important that we should not appear indifferent to the fate of the [Ulster] RCs'.[43]

Nevertheless, on the decisive point Lloyd George gave in. He accepted Craig's proposal that the enquiry should be secret and be carried out by a public official. The name of S. G. Tallents was agreed on. It was hardly a controversial choice—Tallents was attached to Churchill's Irish committee. Balfour was unhappy about this proposal as the meeting ended. 'A report from Tallents, if public, would have little effect in counteracting propaganda,' he told Lloyd George. Lloyd George replied, 'Sir James had to carry his colleagues with him. A report from Mr Tallents making it quite clear there was a ground for a public enquiry would enable him to do this.'[44]

The decision to appoint Tallents was made at a moment of great importance. Craig had staved off a judicial enquiry which in all likelihood would have destroyed his government. *Either* it would have had to acquiesce in the commission, in which case its relation with the Protestant masses would have been undermined, *or* it would have had to oppose the commission and declare unilateral independence. The decisive factor seems to have been Lloyd George's appreciation that Craig's Cabinet was solidly united behind him. Nevertheless the situation was still unresolved in an important sense. Craig had agreed to accept a recommendation—if Tallents should feel it necessary—to create a judicial commission. Tallents's report would apparently be of great moment.

Tallents arrived in Belfast towards the end of June 1922 and began making enquiries. He quickly made up his mind. Look, for example, at his unflattering portraits of the Unionist leadership. But note his crucial conclusion. Craig he described (somewhat generously) as having 'a great desire to do the right and important thing: not a clever man, but one of sound judgement and can realise a big issue'.[45] Pollock, Minister of Finance, was better informed and 'more intellectual than his colleagues. On any question but politics his word would be taken absolutely.'[46] Bates, on the other hand, was 'a weak man and a political hack. His two chief assistants are also violent partisans.'[47] In general 'Ministers are too close to their followers and cannot treat their supporters as from a distance'.[48] However, any move against Craig would not strengthen a relative moderate like Pollock—rather it would play into the hands of loyalist extremists. The implication was clear. For better or for worse, the British government was going to have to work with Craig.

Tallents placed most of the blame for the failure of the Craig–Collins pact on the IRA. 'I have no doubt that the failure to give effect to Clause 6 of the agreement, which provided for the cessation of IRA activity in the Six Counties, was the major cause of its failure . . .'.[49] Given the level of Republican violence at the time, this conclusion had plenty of evidence to support it.[50]

His recommendation was clear. There was no need for a judicial enquiry. 'Inadvertently it would encourage northern Catholics in their refusal to recognise the Northern government.' He added that if he had to choose a precise wish for immediate fulfilment it would be the kindly removal of the present Minister of Home Affairs to a less responsible post.[51]

Tallents had undoubtedly produced a basically Unionist analysis. Whatever its conclusions, they would have been strategically redundant by the time the Cabinet came to read them though. The political and military miscalculations of the Free Staters and Republicans had seen to that.

State formation—repressive apparatuses

The strategy of class alliance pursued by the Unionist bourgeoisie, together with the diplomatic strategies of the British ruling class, were responsible for the establishment of a Northern Ireland state with a sectarian–populist flavour. It is time now to examine the effects of this pedigree on the general form of the state, which was to acquire its outlines in this period.

If there is one field which exemplifies the specific characteristics of state formation in Northern Ireland it is that of security, that is, the constitution of the repressive state apparatuses. The most important—and the most revealing—event within this area in this period was the Solly-Flood affair, a complex of events which have hitherto been kept secret.

Major-General Sir Richard Solly-Flood was appointed Military Adviser to the Northern Ireland government on 7 April 1922, at the height of the IRA offensive and of official and unofficial Protestant counter-offensives in the north.[52] He was the nominee of Sir Henry Wilson, Chief of the Imperial General Staff and one of the leading Irish Unionists within British ruling-class circles. Wilson, who Craig saw as an important ally, had unofficially been advising the Ulster Cabinet on security for some time. In the spring of 1922 he retired from his military posts to become Unionist MP for north Down.

Neither Solly-Flood nor Wilson was in any sense a supporter of the Lloyd George position. Neither had the slightest idea of ever temporising in the Unionist cause, which Wilson at least saw as a key imperial issue. Even Churchill was obliged to exaggerate the reactionary nature of his position to gain credibility with Wilson.[53] Nevertheless, Solly-Flood was soon to find himself ostracised as a subversive.

Craig presumably requested military advice, through Churchill, because of the incapacity of his own forces to deal with the intensification of the IRA campaign. As Farrell points out, the appointment itself must have been a victory for the Northern Irish government, since under the Government of Ireland Act the Belfast regime was prohibited from raising or controlling a military force.[54]

On the other hand there can be no doubt whose idea the original conception of the Military Adviser was, or what it entailed. In correspondence in September 1920 both Sir Neville Macready and Wilson had agreed that the notion of a 'B' Special Constabulary was a dangerous one. 'To arm those "Black men" in the north without

putting them under discipline is to invite trouble,' Wilson wrote.[55]
An earlier note in his diary was more specific:

> Winston suggested arming 20,000 Orangemen to relieve the
> troops from the North. I told him that this would mean 'taking sides',
> would mean civil war and savage reprisals, would mean, at the very
> least, great tension with America and open rupture with the Pope.
> Winston does not realise these things in the least and is a perfect idiot
> as a statesman.[56]

Both Wilson and Macready saw a need for a new scheme for the
organisation and control of the Ulster security forces. Macready
was later to explain further how the new appointment of Military
Adviser, was to play a key role in this reorganisation. It was to be
backed by a competent staff loaned by the British government and
by a thoroughly effective CID, staffed by officers 'unbiased towards
those political and religious currents which run so strongly in the
North'.[57]

It was this role which Solly-Flood set out to play. He threw himself
into his work with perhaps rather too much gusto. It is clear that in
the eyes of the British government he became linked with various
grandiose and highly expensive schemes.[58] As the nominee of an
ultra-imperialist and ultra-reactionary he was bound to be
unpopular in certain circles anyway. Tallents quite reasonably
requested that a close eye should be kept on his activities.[59]
Unionist apologists have suggested that his eventual removal was
purely an 'economic' decision.[60] In fact, it is certain that Flood was
encouraged by Craig himself to believe in the existence of massive
financial backing.[61]

Flood was given to dramatic gestures. 'He came from explaining
to a meeting a scheme for handing out six to eight revolvers per
factory *for use by tried men under the owner's control*',[62] Tallents
reported after one encounter. He did not even win the trust of
three B Special commandants who had resigned and approached
Tallents with harrowing tales of unpunished murders and other
indications of religious bias in their force.[63] None of this should be
any particular cause for surprise. Sir Henry Wilson's nominee was
likely to pursue the task of defeating the IRA with enthusiasm and,
to some, an irritating flamboyancy.

But it must be insisted that despite his demagogy Flood's course
was a complex and contradictory one. It had a genuinely cutting
edge with respect to certain organs of the newly formed northern

state apparatuses. He was a forceful critic of the B Specials' style of work. He was amazed to find that they had, as far as he could see, no disciplinary code. He drew up a number of critical documents on the force: 'the B Special Constabulary . . . are not only a sedentary force but their ability is greatly impaired by their lack of commanders, discipline and training'[64] is a typical comment. There is clear evidence that he became an object of fear and suspicion to B Special commanders.

He was capable too of winning a limited degree of Catholic approval. Father Murray, one of the 'front line' Belfast priests, declared at a meeting in which Solly-Flood expressed his determination to crack down on Protestant terrorism, 'I wish we had the military in charge; we would be all right comparatively.'[65]

Gradually tensions grew between Flood and the Unionist establishment. At the end of June 1922 his position was greatly weakened by the assassination of his sponsor, Wilson. By 12 September the Cabinet conclusions record the Unionist leadership's determination to centralise the command of security forces in Northern Ireland under one man, the RUC Inspector-General, Charles Wickham. Flood offered his resignation almost immediately, but his staff carried on until the end of the year.

In this period Flood and his staff fought a rearguard action against their opponents. In September the English staff of the CID submitted evidence critical of the RUC and the Specials to a secret British enquiry under Barrington Ward, KC, into the murder of three Catholics in Cushendall in June 1922.[66] As the permanent officials of the Ministry of Home Affairs expected,[67] the subsequent report strongly condemned the Ulster branches of the security forces and was suppressed. His staff also sought to leak embarrassing material concerning the judicial flogging of IRA suspects—a major concern to both British and Irish governments at this time.[68]

But Flood had few allies. His other major sponsor besides Wilson, Macready, was regarded with general suspicion because of his suspected sympathy for moderate nationalism. Flood was believed in Unionist circles to have passed on his criticism of the B Specials to the War Office, and certainly Lord Derby, who had taken over at the War Office following a change of government, became his most important supporter.

Macready complained bitterly about Flood's removal:

Major-General Solly-Flood and the staff he took with him to

reorganise the Police Force in Ulster have without doubt made a very great improvement and the CID branch under Col. Haldane has been mainly instrumental in bringing about the present lull in activities of both Sinn Feiners and Orangemen. It is due to this Department also that they have been very instrumental in stopping reprisals because both officers and agents were entirely unbiassed.

The officers of this Department, I understand, refuse to serve under Col.Wickham who, I am given to understand, is not imbued with the necessity for a strong CID Department, which in my opinion should be maintained even at the expense of the executive police. In addition to this I am quite satisfied that Col. Wickham is quite incapable of organising and commanding a police force such is required at the present time in Ulster. This was also the opinion of Sir Henry Wilson when he suggested to the Northern government that the command of the RUC was the limit of Col. Wickham's capacity.[69]

Tallents 'replied' in a letter to Masterson Smith on 6 December 1922:

There is, I know, though I have not been directly involved in it, a considerable row on about the CID here. This has hitherto been under Solly-Flood who, I understand privately, is now about to leave. He has for many weeks now been a mere ornament, and otherwise than perhaps socially will not be a practical loss. About a fortnight ago the Minister of Home Affairs gave Wickham orders to take the CID over. This much upset G.H.Q., whom I happened to see the same day. This implied that the CID had Imperial interests in their keeping and they would have physically to prevent the transfer after due notice . . .

I have kept outside the discussions, but my sympathies are, I must say, with Wickham and the Northern government. If one twentieth of what I have heard about the CID is true, the sooner it goes the better. I do not see how one can defend an arrangement which makes it difficult in principle for the Military Advisor, an employee of the Northern government, to give control to the police of the same government. And if it be true that it also had military and other work outside the scope of the Northern government, I presume that its fruits on that particular branch appear on the reports which used to be circulated to the Lord Lieutenant, and which seemed to be always a proof of wasted money. I hear that Derby has written to Craig, and that Craig has refused to reconsider the change of control. Macready, as you know, always had a low opinion of Wickham and was, in my opinion, wrong about this as some other Northern questions.[70]

What is significant about Tallents's response is not so much his area of explicit disagreement with Macready—in the assessment of

Wickham and the work of the CID—as the problems he did not mention. These included the original conception of the post of Military Adviser, his unpopularity with the Specials, the Cushendall enquiry, differing attitudes on flogging, and so on. It is impossible to regard his letter as anything but a cover-up.

The true significance—it must be emphasised—is that the Military Adviser and his staff were intended in part at least as a curb on the 'natural' sectarianism of the repressive apparatuses in the north. Macready more than hints that their impartial action against Orange extremists had brought them into disrepute with the regime. It is surely also worthy of note that Solly-Flood's staff refused to serve under Wickham. With the departure of the Military Adviser a curb on the partisanship of the security forces was removed.

It should not be thought that Wickham was blind to the defects of the Specials. His private and public comments on the subject do not admit of such a reading.[71] However, his own personal authority and career were closely linked with the fortunes of the B Specials at this point. He therefore took full advantage of Flood's discomfiture.

The Flood affair left a legacy in the shape of War Office proposals to reorganise the Special Constabulary which plagued the Ulster government as late as 1925. In 1924 the War Office seemed to have returned to the idea of a new Military Adviser. Wickham resisted any erosion of his position in a letter to Spender: 'Any scheme which would place a B man under the control of the Police and a Military organiser would be liable to friction.'[72] In 1923 General Sir Archibald Montgomery carried out an enquiry for the War Office. The Loughgall commandant of the Bs wrote to Spender on 14 December 1925 in response to this visit:

> We have been bothered again with rumours about scrapping the 'B' force or turning it into something else which have disturbed our men. We have traced the trouble to General Montgomery's visit, and as far as I can gather, the expressions used by him in person. We saw the Inspector-General last week and found him in absolute agreement with us on the necessity of keeping up night patrols under the present organisations—and on the type of work. There was a flavour of the late Military Advisor's opinions in General Montgomery we did not like. Any voluntary force like the 'B' force is a delicate instrument needing to be played skilfully not banged on, and whatever their shortcomings, they don't like to be told they are no good and must either be swept or completely reorganised, officers and all![73]

The Solly-Flood affair illustrates some basic tendencies in the new state which were to be of the utmost importance.

First, there is the fact that the Unionist leadership regarded as its principal objective the retention of a military force responsible to it alone, and which the British could never use independently. Had Solly-Flood's proposals been implemented it is probable that the IRA offensive would have been blunted sooner, since the B Specials were notoriously ineffective militarily. In the long run, however, military effectiveness was not the point. Rather, it was that the Unionist bourgeoisie's military independence should receive permanent institutional registration. The maintenance of such an institution was crucial. Its meaning was clear—a signal that Ulster could not be coerced. Because of all this the B Specials were to occupy a position of the greatest importance in the new apparatus.

Second, the affair shows what the Unionist leadership understood as the local condition of maintaining the viability of the Specials. It was no more and no less than retaining the force's essentially 'populist' character. This amounted to a propensity to sectarianism, to a kind of democracy in which unpopular officers were forced out of the force, and to a voracious appetite for public funds. The primacy accorded to the objective of having such a force therefore required as a strategic imperative the retention of a special relationship between the Unionist leadership and the Protestant masses. Not only were the Specials to occupy a significant position within the state apparatuses, but the latter as a whole were to acquire a decidedly populist character.

Third, the affair shows the external condition for establishing such a situation—the acquisition of a large degree of autonomy from Westminster as far as law and order were concerned. Wilson and Solly-Flood were enthusiastic Unionists but were not 'Ulstermen'. They failed to understand that the best allies were not those who tendered Unionism advice, or even apologised for it, but those who shut up. Northern Ireland's viability required not 'good' government but its own government, with as much administrative discretion as possible. Over the years, safeguarding this discretion was effectually to become Unionism's 'foreign policy'.

Conclusion

There are two main trends in the polemical literature on the construction of the northern state apparatus. In the nationalist or republican version British imperialism divided Ireland with the objective of weakening Irish nationalism or even creating a bridgehead for the eventual reconquest of the whole island. No doubt this was made easier by Unionist popular support for partition, but primacy is given to the validating role of the British state. It is sometimes argued in defence of this position that there was even a section of Belfast bourgeoisie which favoured unity and remained cool towards partition. According to George Dangerfield, for example, there was still a viable opposition to Sir James Craig among the Belfast business community in 1921–22.[74] There is reason to believe that this may have been the view of the Lloyd George circle until Tallents's visit.[75] Such views had little foundation, however. The evidence they were apparently based on suggests only that some Belfast business circles saw themselves as moderates, and were worried by what they saw as Craig's excessive reliance on the mobilised popular masses.

Craig acknowledged this in a major speech when he asked for 'closer liaison' with the businessmen and requested a greater, even if 'nominal', participation in the B Specials from them.[76] He admitted that business support had been much greater for the old UVF. The Premier asked the local capitalist elite for £100,000 for propaganda purposes. The response was less than rapturous, as Lord Londonderry explained to Tallents. 'In the old days Carson and the Old Town Hall circle had propagandised the shipyard workers. The business community were not wholeheartedly with them. Craig recently appealed for £100,000 as a minimum propaganda fund, result £13,000, £1,000 from me . . .'.[77]

The Chamber of Commerce continued to press vigorously for 'an end to outrages from whatever quarter'.[78] A clear difference of emphasis is noticeable. Certain sections of the Unionist bourgeoisie undoubtedly felt that the political leadership cultivated unnecessarily close links with the working class.[79] Here is the seed of the division between populist and anti-populist which—once the threat to the state's very foundation had been removed—was to appear within the state apparatus itself. At this stage, however, the conflict remained muted and subordinate, and was to remain so for some time.

In the Unionist version the critical aspect is the determination of the Ulster Protestants not to accept a united Ireland. At best many of the British political leaders were seen as unreliable allies. In this account the role of the British state is of secondary importance compared to the weight of pressure within Ireland itself. As for the shape of the state, this was dictated by Catholic nationalist ideological hostility, north and south.

It is time this last proposition at least was heavily qualified. It is now possible to reconstruct the attitude of the key nationalist political elements towards the northern regime. The anti-treaty forces under de Valera were, of course, uncompromising opponents of the Craig regime. They had little influence in Ulster, however, and were regarded with contempt by the more representative northern leaders.[80] This did not, of course, mean that they were unable to maintain a certain capacity for aggravative and protective violence—as the pro-treaty IRA did. The two most important northern leaders were Joseph Devlin, the constitutional Nationalist MP, who still retained the support of most of Belfast's Catholics, and Bishop Joseph MacRory, a supporter of Michael Collins and Sinn Fein, who spoke for the militant Sinn Fein spirit to be found in the Catholic areas closer to the border. Throughout the spring and summer of 1922 Devlin's prominent supporters (particularly in the Belfast Catholic business—as opposed to professional—community) contrived to give the impression that they favoured immediate recognition of the regime.[81] MacRory was torn between accepting this view and listening to the more aggressive councils of Michael Collins.[82] Collins told him in January that southern non-recognition of the northern Parliament was necessary 'otherwise they would have nothing to bargain with Sir James Craig'.[83] He committed himself to the support of schoolteachers and local bodies who refused to recognise the Ulster regime. MacRory noted that 'if the policy of non-recognition was adopted, the people of the North would have to fight alone'.[84] The bishop was caught on the horns of a dilemma. He sought to follow Collins but he seems to have been pulled in the direction of support for Devlin. In May, for example, with a show of reluctance he conveyed Devlinite pressure on the subject to Collins.[85] At the end of June he told Tallents that he favoured an 'absolutely free Ireland' but saw it was 'not practical politics'.[86] He offered recognition of the northern regime if it agreed to co-operate with the south on certain broad general questions.

During this period Michael Collins, as the leader of the Provisional government, was the decisive figure around whom the others were dancing. Throughout 1922 the Cabinet records report him as being committed to a 'peace policy'[87] towards the Unionists, but the term covered a wide variety of practices—some of which were not exactly peaceful. He supported northerners who refused to recognise the state. He reminded his Cabinet when—perhaps symptomatically—it appeared to be forgetful of the necessity of drawing up schemes of non-co-operation with the loyalists.[88] In early March he was to be found arguing that the Sinn Fein line should be insistence on confronting uncompromising Unionists with a boundary commission followed by a tariff war against those portions which still remained outside the Free State.[89]

By the end of March 1922 such militancy was also compromised by the pact with Craig, which obviously involved a degree of *de facto* recognition. The paramount obsession of Belfast Catholics was a reversal of the expulsions and evictions, and this had undoubtedly been conveyed to the Free State government in strong terms. By the end of May Collins was furious that Craig had failed—in his view—to keep the terms of their personal agreement. He warned the British government that its support for Loyalism was endangering its broad agreement with him. He continued to send arms to the north, and it is certain that broad groupings in the IRA continued to have confidence in him.

By June, however, the militancy of the Free State government had waned somewhat. The anti-treaty IRA's offensive in the Belleek triangle of County Fermanagh was reversed early in the month by British troops. The affair seems to have greatly alarmed the Free State regime, which reaffirmed its commitment to a 'policy of peaceful obstruction' on the north and resolved 'that no troops from the Twenty six Countries either those under official control or attached to the executive should be permitted to invade the Six Counties'.[90] This commitment undeniably helped to spark off the subsequent civil war in the south. At the end of June Collins publicly stated the new position:

> I think any attitude towards Ulster which is the attitude of the government is not understood. There can be no question of forcing Ulster into union with the Twenty-six Counties. I am absolutely

against coercion of this kind. If Ulster is going to join us it must be voluntary. Union is our final goal, that is all.[91]

The beginning of the civil war was soon followed by further indications of a slackening of interest in reunification. Early in July Cabinet hints were already being dropped that the policy of paying the salaries of northern nationalist teachers should be abandoned.[92]

Collins, however, retained a strong if inconsistent personal involvement in Ulster. On 2 August, as commander-in chief, he called a meeting with the northern leaders of the pro-treaty IRA. According to Seamus Woods, the O C of the 3rd Northern Battalion (Belfast),

> The late Commander-in-Chief outlined the policy we were to adopt—the non-recognition of the Northern government and passive resistance to its functioning. At the same time from the military point of view we were to avoid as far as possible coming into direct conflict with the armed forces of the Northern government; any action on our part would be purely protective. The late Commander-in-Chief made it clear to us that the Government in Dublin intended to deal with the Ulster situation in a very definite way, and so far as the Division was concerned, every officer present felt greatly encouraged to carry on the work which we had policy to pursue and an assurance that the Government would stand by them.[93]

A few days later he seemed to give a different impression in a letter to Churchill when he noted, 'The Nationalists of the North East stood out *for the time being* to prevent the carving up of their country.'[94] Nevertheless on 22 August, when Collins was killed in the course of the civil war, the militant northern nationalists felt they had lost their most significant supporter on the Free State side. Seamus Woods wrote at the end of September pointing out that the Free State government now appeared to favour recognition of the Unionist state. 'Owing to the position that has arisen in the rest of Ireland [the civil war] I take it the Government feel that they are not equal to the task of overcoming the Treaty position with regard to Ulster.'[95]

In November, accepting the logic of its position, the Free State withdrew financial support for those northern teachers who had been refusing to recognise the regime.[96] Some months later Cosgrave told Craig that for the southern leader the only significance of the Boundary Commission was the need 'for a political cry etc., . . . at the coming elections'.[97]

Such collusion seems to date from 12 September 1922. On that date Craig wrote to Churchill:

> I am delighted to see that the Provisional Government really seems to be taking a firm line and I have received unofficial representations from them that we should assist in rounding up certain agitators who make a practice of crossing the border into Northern Ireland whenever the pursuit in the South of Ireland becomes too hot. This forms an additional reason that we should maintain our force at a high state of efficiency.[98]

The matter of Nationalist attitudes towards the foundation of Unionist government is therefore of some complexity. As far as the Free State faction in government was concerned, the summer and autumn of 1922 appear to have marked phases of retreat from support for even peaceful forms of resistance in the north. Key Ulster Catholic leaders seem to have favoured some form of recognition of Craig's regime. On the other hand, in certain moods Collins had been sufficently belligerent to create genuine Loyalist fears as to what the real meaning of the 'peace' policy was. Moreover Catholic opposition in border areas where there was a Nationalist majority tended to be strong.[99] On balance it seems difficult to suggest that the Nationalist pressure was sufficently coherent or united to explain *ipso facto* the form of the state. For example, there is no evidence to suggest that Belfast Catholic non-recognition of the regime was automatic.

The history of the Belfast Catholic Recruiting Committee, set up to investigate the possibility of recruiting Catholics into the Specials, is instructive in this respect. It has been pointed out that two of its members were arrested, while three others were put on the 'wanted' list.[100] Even so, the committee continued to meet and to discuss the principle of Catholic involvement in the security forces. There was no question of outright Catholic rejection of the idea. Father Laverty, the most important 'political' Catholic priest in Belfast and a supporter of Collins, claimed to have prevented personally the resignation of fifty Catholic members of the RUC. The overwhelming impression that emerges is that Catholic involvement in the Specials depended on a cessation and reversal of the expulsions of Belfast Catholics from their jobs and homes.[101] In other words, the Belfast Catholic attitude to the Northern Ireland State was a product of a specific conjuncture of events rather than simply the expression of a deep-seated ideological attitude.

The major strand in the Unionist viewpoint has the merit of stressing the *dominant* importance of forces inside Ireland. That of the nationalists has the merit, on the other hand, of stressing the role of an important external force—even if British policy is accorded a unity it did not always possess. However, a correct analysis of the situation cannot be produced simply by supplementing these strands. For in fact both Unionist and nationalist accounts share a common deficiency. They do not pose the connection between the formation of the Northern Irish state and the class relations inside either the Unionist or the nationalist blocs. In this chapter primacy has been given to the analysis of these relations. The action of external forces was effective only in so far as it fused with forces thrown up by these relations.

In particular, the expulsions of the summer of 1920 marked a critical phase of class relations within the Unionist bloc, a crisis which permitted the development of the B Specials and gave the Unionist state apparatuses a particularly repressive aspect from the Catholic point of view. Yet although the Unionist political leadership's dependence on the B Specials (which worried at least some sections of the bourgeoisie) was already marked in the period 1920–22, it did require external British support—and here the nationalist account is correct—to underwrite this relationship.[102]

British policy vacillated and was subject to internal divisions but in the outcome, the pressure on the Ulster security forces evaporated.[103] The combination of developments inside the Unionist class bloc with the principal strategy within the British state produced a particular form of state. Subsequent personal attempts to reduce its sectarian paramilitary aspect were easily thwarted. Full Catholic recognition, which in the first instance had been negotiable, receded into the distance.

The result was, of course, disastrous for the Catholic community. They did not contest the gerrymandering of the local government election boundaries by the electoral commission under the control of Bates's nominee, Sir John Leech, K.C. The 1924 election revealed the vital importance of the committee's work. As Farrell notes, 'Some of the results were bizarre. In the Omagh Rural Council area with a 61·5 per cent Catholic majority, the Nationalists had won the Council in 1920 with 26 seats to 13. After Leech's endeavours the Unionists held it with 21 seats to 18.'[104] The Nationalist boycott of the Leech commission gave the Unionists a ready-made excuse. In the course of a British government investigation Tallents told Sir Alexander Maxwell, 'The Northern Ireland government will no doubt contend that they have every desire to be fair and that if any unfairness in the distribution of districts has taken place, it is due to the fact that the Nationalists did not appear before the Commission.'[105] In fact, in later years, the Home Office itself—to the irritation of the Dominions Office—offered precisely this explanation for what had happened.[106] The gerrymandering naturally increased opportunities for discrimination in local government employment. As one official admitted, 'there can be little doubt that in those areas where there was a Protestant majority in the councils, in practice posts do not often go to Catholics'.[107]

The Unionist leadership, perhaps significantly, was not totally united on this issue. Sir Wilfrid Spender hoped (and claimed that Sir James Craig did too) that it would be possible to induce some of the councils to use their powers of co-option for the purpose of securing a better representation of minorities.[108] Spender also opposed discrimination against Catholics by local government agencies.[109] But such doubts and reservations within the Unionist bloc were to prove of little significance in the absence of a systematic Catholic attempt to utilise them.

It was not that Nationalists were unaware of these divisions—they simply lacked a strategy for exploiting them. Seamus Woods, commanding the 3rd Northern Battalion of the IRA, pointed out how intra-Unionist conflicts had led to shooting incidents between different sections of the security forces. In the summer of 1922 he noted, 'a desire for peace became popular amongst the better classes and the Northern government took up the task of restoring order in good faith'.[110] This led to violent conflict with the extremist District Inspector Nixon's followers—whom Woods compared with the irregulars in the south. (Woods ought to have been well informed: the IRA had stolen all the files from the RUC headquarters and from Solly-Flood's office!) However, Woods merely noted these developments and made no comment on their implications, if any, from a nationalist point of view. Some months later Collins's intelligent assistant law adviser, Kevin O'Shiels, commented on a mid-November speech of Craig's, 'It will be noted that he is now suffering from the danger of unlawful and irregular action among his own disappointed supporters ... behind the veneer of calmness ... There are grave rumblings of discontent which may do much to drive the Northern premier to seek accommodation with us.'[111] Again, beyond the expression of pious hope there is nothing here in the way of a political strategy.

In 1940 'Ultach' published in the *Capuchin Annual* a paper entitled 'The Persecution of Catholics in Northern Ireland'. Arguably it is still the most eloquent and concise condemnation of the discriminatory and oppressive features of the Unionist regime. Stormont paid the author the compliment of banning his sequel. In the storm it provoked one crucial feature has been ignored: 'Ultach' did not argue, as so many Nationalists have done, that the oppression of Catholics was an inevitable product of partition. He wrote: 'I do not regard the present intolerable position of Catholics in the partitioned area as being a necessary consequence of *partition as such,* but rather the result of a *particular form of administration.*[112] This chapter has sought to detail the processes, at the level of the British state, the Dublin government and, most important of all, relations within Ulster itself, that determined this outcome, the outlines of this 'particular form of administration'.

Notes to chapter 2

[1] The important works covering the genesis of Unionism are: Buckland, *Irish Unionism,* Vol. II, *Ulster Unionism;* Gibbon, *The Origins of Ulster unionism;* and Patterson, *The Protestant Working Class.*

[2] Two major works on this subject are: F. S. L. Lyons, *Ireland since the Famine* (London, 1971), and Rumpf and Hepburn, *Nationalism and Socialism.*

[3] PRONI Cab. 4/14/11; PRO C.O. 906/25 (meeting of Churchill and Belfast Catholic businessmen, 2 June 1922).

[4] Cf. Gibbon, *Origins,* pp. 87–111.

[5] Cf. H. Patterson, 'The Independent Orange Order: a crisis for Unionism?' (forthcoming).

[6] H. Patterson, 'Refining the debate on Ulster', *Political Studies,* XXIV (1976).

[7] Between 1908 and 1913 the Order's membership in Belfast more than doubled, rising from 8,834 (Patterson, *The Protestant Working Class*) to 18,800 (S. Baker, 'Orange and Green', in H. Dyos and M. Wolff (ed.), *The Victorian City* (London, 1973), Vol. II, p. 808. It was to remain around this figure in the 1920s—an estimate of 20,000 was given in the *Belfast Newsletter,* 7 January 1924.

[8] W. Clark, *Guns in Ulster* (Belfast, 1967), p. 9.

[9] Spender, *Financial Diary,* October 1943, PRONI D715.

[10] P. J. Buckland (ed.) *Irish Unionism, 1885–1923: a Documentary History*

(Belfast, 1973), p. 442.

[11] For an analysis of the leading figure in this group see K. Jeffrey, 'Sir Henry Wilson and the defence of the Empire', *Journal of Imperial and Commonwealth History*, V (1977).

[12] The Irish Office concentrated these divisions. In 1919 Haldane spoke of 'some 36 departments, many of them hardly on speaking terms with each other' (T. J. Jones, *Whitehall Diary*, Vol. III, *Ireland*, London, 1971, p. 12).

[13] They remained excluded from the Bone area of Belfast in January 1922 (*Belfast Newsletter*, 21 January 1922).

[14] St. J. Ervine, *Craigavon: Ulsterman* (London, 1949), p. 444.

[15] Quoted in N. Mansergh, *The Irish Question, 1840–1921* (London, 1975), p. 31.

[16] Jones, *Whitehall Diary*, p. 160.

[17] Churchill to his wife, 14 August 1922, in M. Gilbert, *Winston S. Churchill* (Companion Vol. IV, Part 3, London, 1977, p. 1957. (All remaining references are to Part 3 of this volume unless otherwise stated.)

[18] Churchill to Cope, 24 August 1922, in *ibid.*, p. 1964.

[19] Cope to Masterson Smith, 4 August 1922, PRO C.O. 31.

[20] Gilbert, *Churchill*, pp. 1891 (PRO Cab. 23/30), 1947–8.

[21] Ervine, *Craigavon*, p. 473.

[22] Churchill to his wife, 10 February 1922, in Gilbert, *Churchill*, p. 1766.

[23] Uncirculated draft Cabinet memo, 11 February 1922, in *ibid.*, p. 1847.

[24] PRO C.O. 906/25.

[25] Diary of Sir Henry Wilson, in Gilbert, *Churchill*, p. 1774.

[26] Jones, *Whitehall Diary*, p. 194.

[27] Churchill papers, 22/12, in Gilbert, *Churchill*, pp. 1879–80.

[28] PRONI Cab. 4/41/10.

[29] Craig to Baldwin, 28 November 1922, PRO T. 160/150/5814/1.

[30] Jones, *Whitehall Diary*, p. 201.

[31] Cab. 23/30, in Gilbert, *Churchill*, p. 1893.

[32] Jones, *Whitehall Diary*, p. 200.

[33] Lyons, *Ireland*, pp. 454–5.

[34] The pact was signed in view of the growing 'anarchy' north and south. Its formal objective was co-operation in pursuit of peace. The significant clause of the pact concerned security. An advisory committee of Catholics was set up to recruit Catholic specials to patrol Catholic areas. Many Unionists feared that if such provisions were implemented the force would be destroyed.

[35] 'Sir James Craig rather humorously says that the last thing in his mind is to escape the obligations of the 1920 Act. But under that Act the *whole* obligation for the Specials is on the Ulster exchequer.' (Niemeyer's note, 26 May 1922, PRO T. 163/6; g 256/049.)

[36] PRO T. 163/6; g 256/049 (9 May 1922).

[37] Niemeyer to the Chancellor, 22 November 1922, PRO T. 160/150/5814/1.

[38] L. O'Nuallain, *Ireland: the Finances of Partition* (Dublin, 1952), p. 44.

[39] Gilbert, *Churchill*, p. 1706.

[40] PRONI Cab. 4/46/2.

[41] PRO C.O. 906/29.

[42] PRO C.O. 906/26. Minutes of Downing Street meeting.

[43] *Ibid.*

[44] *Ibid.*

[45] PRO C.O. 906/24. The Tallents papers are to be published in full by Kevin Boyle.

[46] Pollock had quite a reputation as an intellectual. He had lectured an amazed Irish Convention in 1917 on Parnell's views on economics. Lord Charlemont, a Cabinet colleague, regarded his opinions on education as 'close to those of the leaders of the Soviet Union' (Ervine, *Craigavon*, p. 524).

[47] PRO C.O. 906/24.

[48] *Ibid.*

[49] PRO C.O. 906/30.

[50] M. Farrell, *Northern Ireland: the Orange State* (London, 1975), p. 57.

[51] Tallents to Masterson Smith, 4 July 1922, PRO C.O. 906/30.

[52] For details see Farrell, *Orange State*, pp. 39–65.

[53] C. P. Scott, Diary, quoted in Gilbert, *Churchill*, p. 1681.

[54] Farrell, *Orange State*, p. 54.

[55] G. F. N. Macready, *Annals of an Active Life* (London, 1924), Vol. II, p. 488.

[56] Wilson papers, 26 July 1920, in Gilbert, *Churchill*, Companion Vol. IV, Part 2, p. 1150.

[57] Macready, *Annals*, Vol. II, p. 629.

[58] Jones, *Whitehall Diary*, p. 198.

[59] Tallents to Masterson Smith, 4 July 1922, PRO C.O. 906/30.

[60] A. Hezlett, *The 'B' Specials* (Pan edn., London, 1973), p. 102.

[61] Cf. Craig to Churchill, 19 September 1922, PRO T. 160/150/5814/1.

[62] Documents of June 1922, PRO C.O. 906/27. See also Ricardo's notes.

[63] Undated document, probably early July 1922, PRO C.O. 906/27.

[64] Guiding lines of plans for the defence of Ulster, 20 September 1922, p. 17, PRONI 7G/25.

[65] Belfast Catholic Recruiting Committee, 31 March 1922, PRO C.O. 906/25.

[66] Sir Arthur Hezlet has written, 'Cushendall was the ambush of A Specials on 23 June in which four IRA were killed' (*B Specials*, p. 92). The report of Barrington Ward reads a little differently: 'My conclusion is that no one except the police and the military even fired at all . . . I am unable to accept the evidence of the Special Constabulary from Ballymena. I am satisfied that they did not tell me all they knew about the circumstances in which three men died, and in view of the reports made by the military officers at the time and the evidence given by them before me, I do not believe that none of the police entered any of the houses . . . Major Ross-Blundell was ready to assume responsibility for the acts of the Special Constabulary under his temporary command: but I am bound to say that I do not see how any steps could be taken to prevent what happened . . .' (Secret report of Barrington Ward, Cab. 24/138 CP 4193).

[67] Megaw to Craig, 4 September 1922, PRONI Cab. 7B/47/1.

[68] Megaw to Craig, 1 September 1922, *ibid.*

[69] Secret S.F.B. 69, 2 September 1922, PRO Cab. 43/2.

[70] PRO C.O. 739/1.

[71] Macready, *Annals*, Vol. II, p. 609. In a passing-out parade speech at a Specials training camp Wickham 'asked them, and the others with whom they worked and lived, to maintain control over themselves and put a stop

finally to the outrages which had occurred in the past' (*Belfast Newsletter*, 30 September 1922).

[72] Wickham to Spender, 19 November 1924, PRONI Cab. 7A/4/3.

[73] PRONI 7G/26.

[74] G. Dangerfield, *The Damnable Question: a Study in Anglo-Irish Relations* (London, 1977), p. 347.

[75] Cf. the reports from Cecil Litchfield (a senior Ulster civil servant) that Belfast businessmen were prepared to hold a joint economic conference with the south (Jones, *Whitehall Diary*, p. 195).

[76] Speech, 3 April 1922, PRO C.O. 906/23.

[77] PRO C.O. 906/24.

[78] *Belfast Newsletter*, 4 April 1922.

[79] Cf. recollections of Sir W. Hungerford, first secretary of the Unionist party, in Buckland (ed.), *Unionism*, pp. 441–2.

[80] S. G. Tallents, memorandum on talk with Bishop MacRory, 1 July 1922, PRO C.O. 906/26.

[81] Tallents to Masterson Smith, 4 July 1922, PRO C.O. 906/30.

[82] See the tone of his letter to Collins, 7 May 1922, in SPO S1801a.

[83] SPO, Cabinet conclusions, Vol. I, meeting of the Provisional Government, 30 January 1922, North East Ulster Policy. (Hereafter PG.)

[84] *Ibid*.

[85] MacRory to Collins, 7 May 1922, SPO S1801a.

[86] Talk with Bishop MacRory, 1 July 1922, PRO C.O. 906/26.

[87] SPO, Provisional Government Cabinet conclusions, 1 February, 3 June 1922, etc., 19 August 1922, p. 1.2.1922.

[88] SPO, Provisional Government Cabinet conclusions, PG12, 4 May 1922; see also PG17.

[89] SPO, Provisional Government Cabinet conclusions, 6 March 1922.

[90] SPO PG27, 3 June 1922.

[91] *Belfast Newsletter*, 30 June 1922.

[92] SPO PG56, 11 July 1922.

[93] S. Woods to Commander-in-chief in the South, 29 September 1922, SPO S1801a.

[94] PRO C.O. 906/31. Emphasis added. Collins to Churchill.

[95] S. Woods to Commander-in-chief in the South, 29 September 1922, SPO S1801a.

[96] SPO PG57a, 8 November 1922.

[97] PRONI Cab. 4/84/9, 30 July 1923.

[98] PRONI Fin. 30/FC/9. We are indebted to Philip McVicker for this reference.

[99] This problem might have been reduced by a different boundary line.

[100] Farrell, *Orange State*, p. 54.

[101] Minutes of meeting, 31 May 1922, PRO C.O. 906/23.

[102] To the tune of £6·78 million of a total cost of £7·5 million in the period 1921–25 (Farrell, *Orange State*, p. 79).

[103] Cab. 23/30, 3 August 1922, in Gilbert, *Churchill*, Companion Vol. IV, p. 1948. Here the decision not to prune Belfast's paramilitary forces is explicit.

[104] Farrell, *Orange State*, p. 84.

[105] 'The local elections in Northern Ireland', 25 April 1924, Sir A. Maxwell, PROD.O. 35/893.

[106] Dominions Office comment on Home Office views, Sir Henry

Batterbee, 18 November 1938, PRO D.O. 35/893.

[107] *Ibid.*

[108] Tallents told this to Maxwell ('Local Elections in Northern Ireland'), PRO D.O. 35/893.

[109] *Financial Diary*, latter half of October 1934.

[110] He claimed that Nixon was currently threatening to shoot Wickham. For this matter see his document in SPO 81801a.

[111] Notes in SPO S1801/C.

[112] Page 161. Emphasis added.

3

POLITICAL FORCES AND SOCIAL CLASSES, 1925–43

Existing characterisations of the Northern Ireland state, whether they derive from nationalist or unionist ideologies, or from the ideologies of political science, have shown a common tendency to what might be called a check-list' approach. Various institutions have been listed and described, and then compared with abstract types of parliamentary democracy, fascism or 'divided regimes'. The state itself has been evaluated accordingly. Like the method, the consequent characterisations have been highly abstract, moralistic and often uninformative.

As a result of this concern with classification the question of *why* the state took its peculiar form has been ignored. Why, for example, did Sir James Craig feel compelled to continue to insist upon its 'Protestant' character long after any republican military threat had receded? Why did it seem to remain so remote from the British model? Why was no effort made to build a consensus upon which it could rest? These are the real questions of the inter-war period.

There are a number of ways of answering questions of this kind: in terms of the political and psychological make-up of the principal protagonists, for example, or in terms of common 'ideological survivals', whose effects were the same. These will be considered in the course of the analysis. The route chosen here will be different, however. It will involve seeking to trace and identify the connections between class relations in the dominant social bloc and their effects upon the state.

The state apparatuses, 1925–43

A first necessary stage in this route, and one which will occupy a substantial part of the analysis, concerns the clarification of the actual sets of political activities or practices effective within the Northern Ireland state apparatuses during this period. These must be established independently by empirical investigation, since any attempt to deduce them directly ('respectively') from given social classes would imply reductionism.

An examination of the public records of the inter-war period generates an unexpected picture of the politics of the ruling class in Ulster. While the Northern Ireland state apparatuses, singly and wholly, presented a basic unity in 1925, it was not to last long. Significantly, in a greater or lesser degree they were all to become arenas of conflict between two identifiable groups, striving to effect very different sorts of procedures and decisions. The opposition between these groups leaps from almost every file in the archives.

One group centred around Sir James Craig; the Minister of Labour, John Andrews; and the Minister of Home Affairs, R. Dawson Bates. Broadly speaking, this group sought to generalise to the state as a whole the relation between Protestant classes epitomised in the B Specials. This relationship was characterised by a combination of sectarian and 'democratic' practices, and by a high consumption of public funds. As a matter of shorthand, it will here be called 'populist'. Another group, centred on two of the regime's Ministers of Finance, Hugh Pollock and John Milne Barbour, and the head of the Northern Ireland Civil Service, Sir Wilfrid Spender, opposed this tendency. They strove instead to press the state along a *via Britannica* of a pre-Keynesian kind.

Particularly instructive were the tensions between these forces in four major areas: the construction and composition of the Northern Ireland Civil Service, the role of the Ministry of Finance, the question of social service expenditure and most importantly, the status of the Northern Ireland state itself.

The civil service

The Northern Ireland Civil Service has most frequently been cited by Unionist apologists as a bastion of bureaucratic practices, corresponding to liberal parliamentary democracy.[1] In fact, it and its composition were the centre of a struggle over the attenuation of such criteria. At first sight this may not appear convincing. It is well known that a number of Catholics were appointed to senior posts, for example Bonaparte Wyse and Samuel Sloan.[2] Moreover in 1925–26 Sir Russell Scott of the Treasury gave the NICS machine a fairly clean bill of health in terms of efficiency, though he did feel it necessary to warn against 'the influence of politics'.[3] Further confirmation of the optimistic view of the NICS would be found by some in the fact that five per cent of the original staff were British, and that the proportion was much higher in most senior grades.[4]

Yet clear instances of discrimination against well qualified Catholics occurred from the beginnings, and over sixty appointments were made without normal selection procedures being observed at all.[6] Spender, who became head of the NICS in 1925, felt that these nominees were a long-term handicap to the service and on his appointment decided to institute examinations of equivalent standard to those in the British and Indian civil services.[7] The results of Spender's efforts were modified by other pressures, though. At the Ministry of Home Affairs, Bates refused to allow Catholic appointments.[8] In 1926 the Minister of Labour, John Andrews, found two 'Free Staters' in his Ministry when he returned from holiday. He immediately initiated a tightening of regulations to disqualify such candidates automatically.[9] In 1927 Edward Archdale, the Minister of Agriculture, boasted that there were only four Catholics in his Ministry.[10] While Unionist politicians were included on civil service appointment boards, nationalist requests for this privilege were ignored.[11]

As the years passed, evidence emerged of Orange Order surveillance of Catholic civil servants and even civil servants married to Catholics. Prominent and respectable Unionists like Sir Robert Lynn (editor of the *Northern Whig*) and Sir Charles Blackmore (Cabinet secretary) were the messenger-boys for the Order in these matters.[12] Craig's attitude was at best ambiguous.[13] Predictably, the number of Catholics in the higher ranks of the NICS dropped consistently throughout the late '20s and early '30s.[14]

The group around Pollock, Milne Barbour and Spender fought the trend. Milne Barbour was in favour of having a sizeable number of Catholics in the NICS, 'though it may be a risky thing politically to say'.[15] Pollock reminded the Cabinet in 1927, 'it is our policy to maintain our civil service as far as possible on [British] . . . lines'.[16] Populists derided him for his self-image as 'father of the civil service'.[17]

Under the premiership of John Andrews populist attenuation of bureaucratic procedures increased further. In 1943 Andrews informed Spender of his doubts about employing Catholics in the NICS, claiming that the hierarchy's attitude made it impossible for them to be loyal. Spender thought Andrews's views unfair and alarmist, pointing out that in any case none of the Permanent or Assistant Secretaries was Catholic. Andrews refused to be consoled and demanded the compilation of a register of Catholic civil servants.[18]

The strongest evidence of the modification of bureaucratic by populist practices comes from critical comments on the NICS by senior members of other civil services. In 1933 Sir Richard Hopkins of the Treasury threatened Spender with a general inquiry.[19] Spender fended this off, but in 1934 a retired senior cadre of the Indian Civil Service named Anderson unexpectedly called on Spender and gave him

> a somewhat lurid picture of the province, stating that he could not understand the attitude of our officials, who seemed bent on encouraging increased expenditure rather than reducing expenditure ... in this respect, as in many others, the officials of Northern Ireland acted quite contrary to the traditions he was accustomed to in the Indian Civil Service ...[20]

For reassurance Spender wrote to his old friend Sir Ernest Clark. Clark had effectively founded the NICS during his days as Assistant Under-Secretary at the Irish Office and was now Governor of Tasmania. 'Your service,' Clark replied, 'both in its recruitment and management, is not strictly on Civil Service lines, because the political element has entered ... into your appointments. If you don't mind me saying so, you are yourself an instance of this ...'[21]

The Ministry of Finance

Bureaucratic procedures were also markedly modified with respect to the position of the Ministry of Finance, which as has been indicated was the main base of the anti-populists within the state. Contrary to the conventional view, the position of the Ministry in relation to other state apparatuses was in no way comparable to that of the Treasury. While its formal status was equivalent,[22] its real control of other departments fell far short of its British equivalent. Spender himself wrote in 1932:

> It was much more difficult for a government which was so close to the people to resist demands made upon it, than it was for a government of a larger country ... we [i.e. Spender and Pollock] endeavoured as far as possible to follow the high British standards but I had to admit that owing to our own peculiar local circumstances

pressure was sometimes brought to bear on the Ministry of Finance by the Prime Minister and others in a way that would not happen in . . . the Treasury, and . . . on this account we did not have the same Treasury control that obtained in Britain . . .[23]

Far from exercising control, 'overzealous' Ministry of Finance officials, when transferred to other departments, were hounded out of the civil service.[24] When the Ministry opposed Craig's populist policy of 'distributing bones'[25] to Unionism's supporters it was frequently ignored. It found in one remarkable instance, that of the Ulster Transport Board, that the Ministry of Home Affairs had greater weight in what was basically a matter of economic policy.[26]

Social service expenditure

The Spender–Pollock–Milne Barbour group disliked much expenditure on social services. Pollock expostulated, 'I am not sorry to see that strong pressure is coming from important blocks in Parliament to force the government to undertake reductions in social services.'[27] An exaggerated fear of idlers exploiting the dole led the inappropriately named Spender to suggest the drawing up of a black list.[28] Craig specifically condemned this kind of attitude.[29] However, the anti-populists received praise and support on this score at least from Sir John Anderson, a key figure in the British civil service. Anderson was delighted, for example, when he found Northern Ireland failing to implement costly British social reforms, particularly in the field of education.[30] The issue is of critical importance and lies near the heart of the populist–anti-populist divide. For in a curious way, on this issue at any rate, it was the populists who took a 'greater British' and the anti-populists a 'little Ulster' stand. It must be understood, of course, that these terms bear no relation to their later connotations in the Unionist crises of the 1970s.

The status of the Northern Ireland state

The disagreements between the populists and anti-populists are encapsulated in the maiden speeches of Craig and Pollock in the Northern Ireland House of Commons. Craig dwelt not so much on the legislative powers given to the new parliament as on the administrative powers which local government now possessed. He opened up the prospect of a new type of regime for Ireland—one deeply responsive to local pressure. Pollock, however, was more interested in the constitutional aspects of devolution. He claimed that Northern Ireland was 'an autonomous state with a federal relationship to the United Kingdom'.[31] His stress on autonomy went hand-in-hand with an emphasis on strict financial housekeeping.

While Pollock opposed the automatic extension of British social reforms to the Six Counties, the populists regarded the doctrine of parity or 'step by step', that is, the maintenance of an equivalent level of social services, as an article of faith. From this point of view the essential advantage of the ('Colwyn') financial arrangements agreed with Britain in 1925 was that Northern Ireland services could be ranked as a first charge on the area's revenues. The main question of devolution was whether Britain could be persuaded to replace the imperial contribution by a payment making parity possible. Even after this position had in effect been reached, owing to the implementation of a separate agreement (1926) subventing Ulster's employment fund, the populists continued to argue for a general British payment.

The debate reached its climax in the early '30s. Pollock's view of the situation was supported by the Attorney General, Sir Arthur Quekett, who argued that the Colwyn Committee's purpose was not to revise the Government of Ireland Act but to find workable arrangements within the outline of its provisions.[32] The main populist spokesman was Andrews.

> I think [he observed] there is a very general confusion in the mind of many people with regard to the constitutional position of Northern Ireland. Statements are often made which assume that Northern Ireland is autonomous or in the position of a Dominion . . . in fact . . . it is no more than a subordinate authority . . . to which the sovereign legislature for its own convenience has devolved certain limited functions in respect of local services . . . This being so, it seems to me unanswerable in equity that these measures of limited devolution are accompanied by those standards which are regarded as necessary and proper for the whole of the United Kingdom.[33]

Craig supported this view against Pollock's.[34] Divisions on this issue were severe enough to lead the anti-populists to weigh in on the side of the Treasury when the latter challenged populist arguments about equal standards, or tried to insist upon Northern Ireland bearing the burden of the cost of equalisation.

For example, the Treasury felt that the over-generous mode of derating[35] in 1929 and (for a considerably longer period) underrating in Northern Ireland were irregularities that ought to be rectified. As early as 1925 G. C. Upcott was noting:

> In Great Britain 44 per cent of education expenditure and 50 per cent of police expenditure are borne by local rates, in Northern Ireland the local charge for these services is negligible . . . If Northern Ireland claims that she is entitled to maintain her services on the standard prevailing in this country we are, I submit, justified in replying that they should raise the burden of local rates to the same level.[36]

The anti-populists accepted the logic of the Treasury position, and the scene was set for a conflict with those populists, in particular Craig, who did not. Craig at first dealt with the problem by denying its importance—despite clear warnings over at least three years, it was not until December 1933 that he admitted the depth of the crisis in Stormont–Treasury relations.[37] Even then he was to claim repeatedly that through personal contact with Whitehall he had won dramatic concessions. These concessions were invariably products of his for once enlarged imagination.[38] As Hopkins explained to the Chancellor of the Exchequer, 'Lord Craigavon in discussions of this kind is very inclined to assume that decisions are in his favour, unless it is made unusually clear to him what the decisions are.'[39]

Spender and Pollock, on the other hand, fought hard to gain acceptance of the Treasury line in Northern Ireland. Spender even went so far as to alert the Treasury on his own initiative if Craig showed signs of 'forgetting' his commitments.[40] The rating proposals of 1934 signalled Craig's defeat in this area.[41] He was effectively excluded from London–Belfast financial affairs until the Anglo–Eire negotiations of 1938 permitted a rather less than glorious return to the stage. In his absence financial matters were dealt with mainly by the permanent officials in an atmosphere of increasing confidence.[42]

While they had lost one battle the populists were to win the war, in this as in other fields, over both the anti-populists and the Treasury. The latter had reopened discussions in 1931 with the intention of reversing the Colwyn Committee award's advantages for the Northern Irish. 'We started these discussions,' the Treasury official Brittain recalled, 'on the general principle, first, that it is not right that the Imperial contribution should in effect rank after all local expenditure in Northern Ireland.'[43] The discussions came to an inconclusive end, he added, when the Treasury's whole attention became concentrated on the economic measures of September 1931. As Ulster's economic position continued to weaken markedly in the 1930s it became impossible to raise the matter in the same terms again.

As Hopkins—who replaced Niemeyer as Controller in 1927—was to put it near the end of the decade,

> When the Northern Irish government was set up it was expected that their revenues would be sufficient both to meet their expenses and to provide a substantial contribution to Imperial services (defence, debt, &c.) This expectation was realised at first fully and later in a diminishing degree. Since 1931 Northern Ireland has been in effect a depressed area. So far from receiving any large Imperial Contribution we have invented a series of *dodges* and *devices* to give them *gifts* and *subventions* within the ambit of the Government of Ireland Act so as to save Northern Ireland from coming openly on the dole as Newfoundland did'[44]

Hopkins's note implies that the general position of Britain and Northern Ireland within the world economy was not subject to control by the northern government. Other documents make it clear that this was in fact his view and explain his willingness to resort to what he later described as 'wangles' and 'fudges' to help the regime.[45] 'The fact is that they copy all our legislation and that therefore we set their general standard, for better or for worse. In times like these, that standard means bankruptcy for a small community which is suffering terribly from unemployment.'[46]

Political forces and social classes

A purely political explanation?

The content of the 'Protestantism' of Craig's 'Protestant State' is now somewhat clearer: in essence it amounted to a combination of patrimonialism, 'responsiveness' and a practical 'Keynesianism'. It was modified by liberal democratic practices, rather than the other way round. The extent to which this happened was a result of the presence of anti-populists within the state apparatus. The question is then as to the basis—if any—of the conflict, and how populism apparently prevailed. A purely political explanation is possible. Such an analysis would stress the differing political motivation of the two principal figures involved in it, Sir James Craig and Sir

Wilfrid Spender.

In the case of Craig there can be little doubt that British indifference to the chaos in Ulster in the period of state formation affected him profoundly. He frequently stated that it was his intention to make the British government pay the 'debt' it owed Ulster on this account. On one occasion Spender charged him with pressing for advantages over and above those given to other British regions. Craig, Spender reported, merely smiled to himself in an amused fashion.

Spender's obituary saw the Prime Minister as having become the epitome of 'little Ulsterism', over-responsive to almost any non-Catholic pressure-group in the province, whilst remaining more or less indifferent not simply to the Treasury but to wider Greater British and Imperial concerns.[47] Other Irishmen have wasted their talents through profligacy. Craig's great talent *was* profligacy. During the Anglo-Eire negotiations of 1938, for example, he literally asked only to be 'bribed' with armaments contracts to give his acquiescence to a London–Dublin deal.[48] He displayed little interest in the broader strategic considerations (the Irish ports, for example) which so concerned Spender.

On the other hand, Spender adhered to very different political traditions. He was an English army officer who had adopted the Ulster Unionist cause primarily on the grounds of imperial security. He saw Pollock, his Minister, as the soundest imperialist in the Cabinet. In retrospect he even presented Pollock's championing of the Loans Guarantee Act (which did so much to make Belfast shipbuilding viable) not so much as an aid to regional employment but as the necessary condition for building some of the ships so badly needed for the coming world war.[49] Nor was this a matter of Spender projecting his own obsessions on to Pollock. The latter's first budget speech made the point 'we are the children of the Empire, we Ulster people'.[50]

It is tempting therefore to regard a purely political stress on differing 'world views' as a complete explanation. This is certainly the position of conventional political scientists and their advocates.[51] Richard Rose, for example, has committed himself to the view that the divisions in the Unionist bloc from 1921 onward can be explained simply by reference to the division between those who owed full allegiance to the British state and those who did not.[52] Is it not a simple matter to suggest that the fully allegiant group is that which has been described as anti-populist, and the ultra-loyalists or non-allegiant (in Rose's terminology) are those we have called populists ? The idea assumes further credibility when it is considered how Rose deepens his account of this central division. The fully allegiant group accepted the ultimate sovereignty of the British government. The 'ultras', however, rejected it when it conflicted with the principle of maintaining Protestant dominance. On this basis it is a relatively easy matter to accept 'fully allegiant' as a characterisation of the Ministry of Finance group and 'ultra' as an adequate assessment of the Craig–Bates–Andrews circle.

Yet it is at this point that Rose's account runs into a paradox. The supposedly fully allegiant or anti-populist group had a more exalted conception of the Northern Irish parliament and state than the 'ultras'. It is the anti-populist group that talks of Stormont's autonomy in all fields, of its 'federal' relation with the UK. On the other hand, it is the 'ultras' who use phrases like 'subordinate regional authority'. In other words, great care is necessary to ensure that the analysis of inter-war Unionist divisions is not derived by projecting back in time an ideological reading of the dissensions of 1968–72.

While it is beyond doubt that differing political attitudes did play a critical role in determining the nature of intra-Unionist conflicts in the 1920s and '30s, they are not wholly explicable at this level. Recourse has to be made to an examination of the relationship between these attitudes and differing class forces.

Economic explanations: divisions within the local bourgeoisie

Many recent writers have stressed the political significance of divisions in the inter-war European bourgeoisies. In particular, the division between monopoly and non-monopoly capital has been underlined.[53] Can such an analysis throw light on Ulster in the same period ?

Both the interests of monopoly capital in the shipbuilding industry and the main bastion of competitive capital, the linen industry,[54] were well represented at the political level—the shipbuilding industry because of the state's heavy financial and political interest in its fortunes. Linen too had direct representatives in the shape of men like Andrews and Milne Barbour, who were not even required to give up their directorships when they became Ministers. There was some grumbling on the part of linen interests that the Loans Guarantee Act ought to have been extended to their sector, but it was of marginal significance. The Cabinet as a whole tended to reflect the consensus of the linen trade that protection rather than a reorganisation and amalgamation of the many rather inefficient units was the answer to secular decline. Andrews, while accepting that some consolidation was inevitable, wrote to Craig, 'It is not competition among ourselves that is the trouble, so much as competition under quite unfair conditions overseas.'[55] Sir Gilbert Garnsey, a London accountant called in by the Ministry of Commerce, merely confirmed the view that the linen capitalists would resist any move towards combines. It was probably with relief that Craig replied to Andrews, 'I am quite prepared to set on one side any possible reorganisation of the trade.'[56]

To approach the problem from a different angle: it is difficult to present the anti-populist grouping's policies as a reflection of the specific interests of any particular fraction of capital against any other. While continuing to receive support for certain basic objectives from competitive capitalist bodies such as the Belfast Chamber of Commerce,[57] the anti-populists were also the architects of the Loans Guarantee Act, which was clearly in the interests of monopoly capital. It should be observed that the implementation of Pollock's views on 'sound finance' was in fact necessary for the smooth functioning of the Act.

If there was a politically significant economic division in the domestic bourgeoisie it arose not from monopoly v. non-monopoly capital but rather from the resentments of that group commonly called Ulster's minor or miscellaneous capitalists against the domination of the state by shipbuilding and linen interests.[58] This group, which the Ulster Industries Development Association attempted—with no great success—to represent, was engaged mainly in producing for the home market. 'Buy Ulster Goods' was its slogan. Craig offered the Association some support, particularly in the early '30s, but it was markedly unpopular with the Ministry of Finance. In his last Stormont speech in 1935 Pollock gave vent to years of private misgivings. 'I have no sympathy with the theory which seems to be shouted on all occasions "Use only Ulster goods".'[59] It is also important to note that this group—particularly through its links with Unionist critics of the government—was involved in the successful agitation of 1937 for a greater state role in the economy. The anti-populist Minister of Commerce, Milne

Barbour, had reluctantly broken with the *laissez-faire* tradition of the Ministry in November 1931 to propose a scheme for attracting industry to the province by offering free sites and other inducements.[60] The scheme succeeded in creating very few jobs, and Milne Barbour was anxious in November 1936 to let it lapse.[61] However, within a period of just over a year the government was forced not only to keep the legislation alive but to expand its provisions substantially.[62]

Apart from this the UIDA was effectively marginal to political decisions and divisions. Its main grievance, after all, was that it did not get enough consistent support at the heart of the state apparatus.

Class forces and the British state

The fact that the nature of the divisions in the state (and consequently the nature of the state itself) cannot be explained by a reduction to divisions in the local bourgeoisie need not rule out a Marxist perspective. In his recent interpretation of the classical Marxist theory of the state Etienne Balibar has argued that unity or disunity in the state, the conflict of and dominance by particular bourgeois fractions, etc, arises not from organic internal divisions of that class but from the state's relationship to the proletariat and *its* divisions.

According to this interpretation the fundamental purpose of the state is *to maintain the conditions for the exploitation* of the proletariat. In this light 'the basic function of the state is to hinder the class unity of the proletariat, a function which is also the basis of its contradictions'.[63] Balibar is not denying the importance of divisions within the bourgeoisie, nor the existence of dominant 'fractions' of this class, nor even the fact that the state apparatus is always turned to the profit of such a fraction. The point is rather that these fractions are constituted in the process of the political subordination of the proletariat.

To explain the reason for the remoteness of the Northern Irish from the British state is therefore in this interpretation to specify the different conditions under which the British and Ulster working classes could be divided and ruled. To explain the *social basis* of the forces which dominated these territories' respective states is to specify the content of another process. *The force which is dominant is that whose leading role is most conducive to class peace.*

Consider in this connection the contributions of Robert Skidelsky and John Foster to the analysis of class conflict and economic development in Britain between the wars. Skidelsky's central concern is economic stagnation. His explanation of it is illuminating. The conflicts and changes necessary to generate economic development could never occur, since the dominant political trend was the minimisation of conflict. 'The Baldwin–MacDonald politics of decency and consensus were designed to dissipate [the threat of class war] and they succeeded remarkably well. Unfortunately, the consensus created was based on mass unemployment and the dole, rather than full employment and growth . . .'[64] He quotes A. J. P. Taylor: 'the very forces which made Great Britain peaceful and stable prevented her from becoming the country of the New Deal'.[65]

Minimisation of conflict on a *societal* scale was made possible by the survival of economic internationalism and minimal government as the twin political watchwords. These policies, promoted by Baldwin, together with the mass unemployment they caused, effectively split the working class into a 'constitutionally educated' wing following the Labour party on the one hand, and a tiny and isolated Marxist wing following the Communist party on the other.[66] The alternative was the more belligerent strategy of Churchill in 1926: a vigorous class mobilisation of the frightened provincial employers, which would have turned society into a battleground.

In this interpretation, the economically ascendant section of the ruling class owed its dominance in part at least to the fact that policies which favoured it economically were those which divided the working class in a fashion amenable to the maintenance of class peace. As Foster has shown, from this section's viewpoint they happily also coincided with policies which retarded the development of rival economic groupings. The acceptance of the Baldwin line implied the postponement of something that would have been concretely required by the Churchill line—a political organisation of productive capital on a national scale.

Despite its failure to develop a significant base in monopoly industry, banking capital was still dominant and still profoundly distrustful of the potentially protectionist ambitions of domestic industry. The inner core of the governing establishment had hardly changed at all [since before the First World War] and it was, of course, these men who previously cemented relationships between the urbane economic imperialism of the London bankers and the party politicians . . .[67]

The Baldwin–MacDonald 'politics of decency and consensus' thus implied a continued hegemony for finance capital. The MacDonald government of 1929–31, for example, rejected the alternative of exploiting the differences between industry and the City as these had been outlined[68] in what Tom Nairn has recently called 'the major document of the era',[69] the Macmillan *Report on Finance and Industry* of 1931. The idea of promoting economic recovery through deficit budgeting (as, for example, in the United States, Germany, France and Sweden) was turned down. So too was the positive use of public works and other Keynesian suggestions. By and large, those who sought to make unemployment and domestic industrial development the central concerns of British policy—Lloyd George in 1929, Keynes and Mosley—were pushed to one side.

In Britain, according to this view, the political standing of economic groups did not depend on considerations of relative economic strength. On the contrary, the economic content—the 'social basis'—of the dominant and subordinate political forces was dictated by the economic implications of the dominant and subordinate bourgeois political lines, drawn up to deal with the class struggle.

Class forces and the Northern Ireland state

In this light, consider again the problem of the social identification of political forces in the Northern Ireland state apparatus. A new direction of analysis has been suggested: from the nature of the class struggle, to a reclarification of the principal political lines, to the social basis of those lines.

In Britain the alternative political lines gained their coherence from their inscription in a class struggle of a particular sort: a forceful challenge to the state apparatus by the masses. Two options open to the political representatives of the bourgeoisie were to try and give this challenge a voice it controlled (the Labour party), while emasculating its militancy through unemployment; and (Churchill's line) to bludgeon it into the ground. In Northern Ireland the class struggle was completely different. There was no comparable challenge by the masses, and in this sense emasculation and 'education' of an already united working class were redundant. On the contrary, given the historical make-up of Unionism, a secular 'constitutionally educated' working-class mass was undesirable. The clue to the nature of the Local class struggle is the historically exaggerated dependence of the bourgeoisie upon the Protestant masses. Its object was the unity/disunity of the working class, Protestant and Catholic, *at any level,* even the most economistic, reformist, 'educated'. Disunity between the Protestant and Catholic working classes was Unionism's *sine qua non.* Populism was a strategy which made sense only in this context. Its 'solution' to the danger of a united working class was to weld ever more tightly the links between the Protestant bourgeoisie and the Protestant masses, to the visible exclusion of the Catholic masses. Like any such political strategy, it had economic consequences, among which was the perpetuation of a certain 'social basis'.

But what of anti-populism ? If the unity/disunity of the working class at this elementary level was the essence of the class struggle, what was anti-populism's relation to it? In what way did anti-populism represent a strategy for class struggle? The fact is that in this respect it had *no independent practical implications.* It was concerned not with the class struggle itself but with the conditions and limits of the populist mass line. In this sense, with all that it implies, anti-populism was not a strategy at all but a rhetoric located critically at the heart of another, real strategy. *Its aim was to save the populist position from its own excesses.* In short, its coherence was entirely parasitical upon the populist position, and it was thus doomed all the while to remain a minority force within the state apparatuses. In suggesting that a position like Ulster anti-populism was not a developed one *vis-à-vis* the class struggle, Balibar's interpretation effectively *solves* the problem of anti-populism's social basis. Because it existed in no fully implementable form, anti-populism could not of itself represent the interests of any particular fraction of capital. It had no independent social basis in this sense, and was not tied to the economic interests of a specific group. To appreciate the meaning of this view it is necessary to return for a moment to the evaluation of the dominant populist strategy.

In scope the populist strategy departed considerably from 'consensus and decency' and its forms of implementation. The tying of the Protestant masses to their political leadership above all required a different approach to the problem of unemployment from that in Britain. It required an approach that was in essence 'productivist', protectionist and, in a *purely practical* way, Keynesian. As it happened, the regional economy's profound handicaps meant that this sort of policy would have had to have been pursued to a degree incompatible with membership of the United Kingdom if a complete solution was to have been found. Nevertheless, it was followed as far as possible and was expressed most clearly in the Loans Guarantee Acts and expenditure on public works. The latter was seen specifically as the proper lesson of the 1932 Outdoor Relief riots,[70] and was pressed on with long after Ministry of Finance entreaties demanded it should stop.

Why, it may be asked, was it necessary to go this far ? Why could not Orangeism alone suffice ? Its practice might even have been consistent with acceptance of the dominant British political watchwords, and the consequent avoidance of inter-state conflict. The problem of Orangeism, however, was that its support amongst Protestant trade unionists was considered to be weak. The Orange Order was obviously a historical asset. Nevertheless Craig made perfectly clear his view that the Order was not up to the task. He stressed instead the role of the UULA. It—and not the Order—he insisted was the 'most wonderful organisation in Ulster'.[71] When the Orange Grand Master, Sir Joseph Davidson, protested at his institution's unwonted demotion Craig was unrepentant. The UULA won the 'cream' of the working class and 'so many influential trade union leaders' to Unionism. Without irony, he observed there was nothing like it anywhere in the world.[72]

The effect of these policies was to maintain the dominance of industrial capital. Craig was quite prepared to make his preference for this fraction, as against banking capital, explicit:

> He had been spending the bulk of his time recently in consultation with the heads of the great business concerns in Ulster, whose advice he always liked to take in preference to that of banks or stockholders, and although it might seem to be impertinent of him to say so, if Britain had obtained advice from the manufacturers, a great deal of misfortune might have been avoided.[73]

It was this division, rather than that between monopoly and non-monopoly capital, which was articulated by the political lines developed in the local bourgeoisie with respect to the local class struggle.

In both a local and national context, the reproduction of populism and of the ascendancy of industrial capital which was its consequence had certain implications.

An unfettered mass line. Generally speaking, particularly with respect to home affairs, an unflinchingly populist mass line was pursued in the '30s. In 1932, after widespread attacks by Protestant mobs on pilgrims travelling south for the Eucharistic Congress, Bates arranged with the Attorney General and Chief Crown Solicitor that the Protestant offenders should be treated leniently.[74] Events like this induced delusions of grandeur in Orange quarters. In 1935 Bates, at Orange insistence but without notifying Pollock, who was acting Prime Minister, lifted a government ban on Orange parades.[75] The result was massive inter-communal violence.[76]

Keynesianism. As has been indicated, the pursuit of policies that effectively approximated to a crude Keynesianism generated considerable conflict with the Treasury, until the latter itself turned Keynesian. Andrew's demands on public works for example, were claimed by the Treasury to be typical only of left-wing socialists in Britain (with all that this implied).

To say that a policy was unpopular with the Treasury is to imply equal disfavour from the City of London. It is certain that many of the officials involved in the critical dialogue with the Northern Irish government had the closest links with the City. Sir Richard Hopkins is a good example[77] and Sir John Anderson an even better one.[78] The opposition of Hopkins, the Treasury controller, and Anderson, the government's unemployment 'expert' in the '30s, to the populist group is clear.

This was in the last resort as dangerous as mass inter-communal violence, since, as Spender was fond of saying, the chairman of the Midland Bank stood in the same relation to the Ministry of Finance as the Governor of the Bank of England to the Treasury. The Midland was the Northern Ireland state's exchequer bank and an important force in the boardroom of Harland & Wolff. On an inner directorate of five it had two members. Of the remaining three, one represented the other banks, one the Ministry of Finance and one the Treasury—reflecting more or less accurately the extent of these bodies' investment. Sir Ernest Clark, the Ulster government's representative, later recalled having 'to face the Midland Bank every month to beg for enough to carry on in the bad times'.[79] At one point in 1936 the Midland even threatened to let Sir James Lithgow, the Scottish shipbuilding magnate, gain a controlling interest in the firm. Lithgow was well known as a fierce critic of the Belfast yard, holding that it was operated at over-capacity. He had indeed already used his influence at the Board of Trade against the 'unfair' advantages given to Belfast shipbuilding by the Loans Guarantee Act.[80]

In these respects, *even for the reproduction of industrial capital*, the populist line had to be checked. It is here that the positive function and the true meaning of the anti-populist position may be appreciated. The anti-populists were extremely sensitive to the need to employ financial methods approved by the banks. Spender wrote to S. D. Waley at the Treasury that Andrews might well benefit from a trip to London if he learned thereby 'of the co-operation that he is likely to get from the financial magnates in London if our government adopts *sound methods of finance*'.[81] The Midland Bank, to take the obvious case, had an important interest in certain shipping lines (e.g. Union Castle) as well as in the Belfast yard. The greatest care was needed in Loans Guarantee operations—which became even more substantial in the '30s—and clearly such projects had to be copper-bottomed by the creditworthiness of the Northern Ireland state.[82] The Midland was naturally a strong force in support of orthodox financial methods. The anti-populists' sensitivity to the bank never went as far as servility, but they did use it to make the government face up to what they saw as 'the basic facts of life'.

The 'social basis' of the populists was local industrial capital; the anti-populists had no such basis. They represented, if anything, the necessary forms of accommodation of industrial to other forms of capital, which allowed their line in the class struggle to be implemented. The anti-populists did not represent 'financial capital' or any other independent force. Had their general policies been implemented, they would not have been a basis on which the bourgeoisie could have won the class struggle. Had their financial policies alone been implemented, not even finance capital would have been reproduced. Anti-populism's parasitism on populism became demonstrable as the political line of British finance capital itself changed. In the later '30s and early '40s Spender was to grow more and more afraid of 'creeping socialism'—often working through such unlikely protagonists as Lord Reith.[83] Simultaneously he became less in touch with the changing paradigms of British economic policy. Sir Richard Hopkins, a firm anti-Keynesian in 1930[84] and such an important figure for Spender, was an ardent Keynesian by 1940.[85] It was too much for Sir Wilfrid. 'I think the world quite mad . . . my views on economics are quite too old-fashioned for modern conditions,' he wrote to the Treasury on 12 January 1939, adding, in an attempted sting, 'and I am even fool enough to believe that one ought to live on one's own income.'[86]

Nevertheless the contribution of the anti-populists to the reproduction of the Unionist class alliance was to become more and more crucial as the years passed. This was because Craig's populism (and that of his successor, Andrews) was to become increasingly frivolous and unrestrained as time passed. He frequently perambulated the province on the most extraordinary tours. In the process he visited almost every Unionist local authority. These waited upon him with a list of projects and complaints for his attention. At Portstewart, for example, a case was made out for classifying the road to the golf links as first -class.[87] Almost invariably his response to such trivia was favourable. In 1937 he demanded that money be poured into the renovation of Musgrave Street police barracks, Belfast, because a raw ex-public school RUC officer cadet complained of conditions there.[88] Had such expenditure been implemented *carte blanche* it would have exasperated the Treasury beyond self-control. There was only one thing as dangerous for the local bourgeoisie as a unified working class—a unified opposition of Catholics and the British state.

Conclusion

The most systematic Irish nationalist attempt to grasp the nature of the state was produced by 'Ultach' in 1940. It was a rigorous attempt to demonstrate in a precise analogical way that the Northern Irish statelet was totalitarian. 'I should like it to be understood here that I am not indulging in the emotional exaggerations of political propaganda.'[89]

In this endeavour he drew on certain features of an already burgeoning theory of totalitarianism which insisted on the essential similarity of the Soviet and Fascist regimes. In this perspective the Soviet, Nazi and Orange systems required a state of political high tension to keep the masses in movement.[90] All three presented measures of coercion as, in fact, measures of self-defence against dangerous enemies.[91] The Unionists, it is true, had permitted elections, but only those they were sure to win. 'Ultach' argued that the abolition in 1929 of proportional representation for parliamentary elections had been designed to enforce a false unanimity of opinion among Unionists. The abolition of PR and gerrymandering in local government served to remove any possible focus of opposition from Nationalist local authorities. He even claimed—less convincingly, perhaps—an analogy between the Unionist practice of allowing criticism of the government by extreme Orangemen with the Soviet practice of 'self-criticism'.[92] Above all, however, 'Ultach' explicitly insisted that in the totalitarian regimes, as in Ulster, the state had to be conceived as the 'instrument' of the party.[93] This theme is frequently reiterated in the most recent study of the subject.

In general terms it may be observed that 'Ultach's' borrowed methodology tended to give a falsely monolithic impression of the state apparatuses under consideration. Baldly instrumental conceptions—whether the subject wielding the instrument is said to be a class or a party—make it difficult to perceive the state as a set of relationships shot through by conflicts of the sort analysed in this chapter. Hardly surprisingly, 'Ultach' was at a loss to explain the 'liberal' features of the regime—why, for instance, if it was in the fullest sense totalitarian, it allowed a strong Nationalist press to function with considerable (if not total) freedom.[94]

The method employed in this chapter has not been that of 'Ultach'. It has been to study the Northern Irish state in relation to the class forces inside the Unionist bloc and to the relevant class forces within the British state; above all, the aim has been to examine the state with reference to the reproduction of divisions within the popular classes in Ulster. We have found not unamity but fissures and divisions.

The stress on the populist/anti-populist division has been intended to break down the view of the Unionist state as an undifferentiated entity. It has been argued that this division contributed to the resilience of the state: in particular, the anti-populists acted as a curb on certain populist practices which invited conflict with the British government.

'Ultach' was correct in diagnosing the regime's vulnerability : 'Its weakness lies in the fact that it can be removed when England wishes.'[95] However, he was unable to explain why 'democratic' England should continue to support 'totalitarian' Unionism.

Near the end of the inter-war period, clear proof of our thesis is provided by the outcome of British government enquiries into allegations by the Eire government of maltreatment of the Catholic minority in Ulster. The Dominions Office and the Home Office both prepared minutes on the subject.[96] In general, the tone of the Dominions Office comment is rather critical of the Ulster regime, while that of the Home Office is predominantly defensive.

Sir Henry Batterbee of the Dominions Office would, in particular, have liked to have seen more information on, for example, 'the charge that the government service is practically closed to Catholics. Could not the figures be given... The Head of the Education is an exception, but is he the exception which proves the rule?'[97] The Home Office countered by claiming that Catholicism was in general the religion of the masses in Northern Ireland, while Protestantism was that of the classes.[98] It was hardly surprising that Protestants predominated in jobs requiring a certain educational level.

However, the decisive factor in warding off the Dominions Office concern was the attitude of Sir Wilfrid Spender. Spender expressed himself pleased by the way in which in the late 1930s an increasing number of Catholic applicants were coming forward to join the NICS. He tried to show that entry was not decided on sectarian criteria—in so far as he could control it.[99] There is little doubt that Spender's obvious sensitivity on the question greatly reassured the British civil servants.

It was felt that it was enough simply to register a certain concern about the situation. Batterbee wrote:

> To sum up, except as regards gerrymandering, the Home Office [in defence of Ulster] put up a fairly good case. There is no reason to suppose that there is a deliberate injustice to Catholics on the part of government. But, as Mr. Stephenson (of the Home Office) points out in his minute, the bias of the Northern Irish authorities is bound to be in favour of those who are supporters of the present regime; it is everywhere inimical to good and impartial administration where Government and Party are as closely united as a Northern Ireland. In the South, Mr. de Valera was at one time largely dependent on the IRA for support, but he has been able to throw off his dependence on that body in a way that the government of Northern Ireland have not been able to throw off their dependence on the Orange

Lodges.[100]

This passage is a fairly accurate representation of Dominions Office views. Certainly it was felt that the original Catholic boycott of the Leech commission was no excuse for sustained gerrymandering in local government. On the other hand, Spender had reassured his British colleagues about the conditions in government service. In general, it was sufficient to hope that the Home Office had now been alerted to the fact that there were real problems and that it would not continue to allow the situation to drift. This relatively mild and hopeful conclusion demonstrated the fundamental importance of anti-populism for the survival of the Stormont regime. As long as the crucial people in the British state apparatus felt that strategic figures in the Northern Irish administration were attempting to implement British methods they were unlikely to respond to 'Ultach's' demand for strong British intervention to secure 'normal conditions'[101] in Ulster.

Notes to chapter 3

[1] Cf. R. J. Lawrence, *The Government of Northern Ireland* (Oxford, 1965).

[2] Sloan was Establishment Officer of the NICS. Whilst born a Catholic, he did in fact lapse. Shortly before his death in February 1940 he reverted to his religion. This fact leaked out and intensified Orange pressure on the NICS (Spender to Gramsden, 28 August 1940, PRONI D715).

[3] Cf. Scott to Spender, 24 October 1925, PRONI Cab. 7Q/7.

[4] Fifty-three of the 1,012 appointments of the first eighteen months were British—thirty-eight of them in Labour and twelve in Finance (*Belfast Newsletter*, 24 December 1922).

[5] Cf. paper by J. McColgan read at the Institute for Irish Studies, 1977. Also P. J. Gannon, 'In the catacombs of Belfast', *Studies*, Vol. II (1922), App. V, p. 295, is significant for the background. H. P. Boland, for example, brought to his interview with Sir James Craig in late June a strong recommendation from his Treasury superiors: 'There is every probability that you will find a man of this type indispensable,' it was said. However, Sir Ernest Clark replied that 'the answer of the Northern government is "Thank you very much, but no." I believe you know why.' Boland was southern Irish and Catholic. John McColgan's fascinating research is now to be found in 'Irish Government administration: British administrative policies in Ireland, 1920–22', University College, Dublin, unpublished Ph.D., 1977. Gannon appears to establish a pattern of discrimination in Belfast Corporation appointments.

[6] *Belfast Newsletter*, 24 December 1922.

[7] Spender, *Financial Diary*, 30 May 1938, PRONI D715. At first this had the effect of making a majority of administrative grade appointees British.

[8] *Irish Times*, 4 May 1967, and Spender, *Financial Diary*, 5 June 1941. In a rare moment of candour Dr John Oliver, who enjoyed a wide-ranging career within the NICS, gives a glimpse of Bates's general style of work: 'For example, I was told that in the very earliest days of the Ministry of Home Affairs the Minister decided to meet a request from the Inspector General of the Royal Ulster Constabulary for motor tyres for the police fleet by telephoning the managing director of a business firm in Belfast and placing an order. Why not? ... Why bother to go through a long rigmarole of tiresome civil service procedure, advertise, receive sealed tenders, open them, pick the lowest tender, only to find the tenderer turns out to be an unreliable, inexperienced supplier who lets you down?' (J. A. Oliver, *Working at Stormont*, Dublin, 1978, p. 46.)

[9] PRONI Cab. 4/182/25; cf. Cab. 4/182/24. The 'Free Staters' had good British army backgrounds. It should be added that Andrews justified his position by referring to the Irish language qualifications for jobs in the Irish civil service. Indeed it is true that, while the Irish government even under de Valera 'in general' saw no need for a nationality clause in the civil service, the language requirements were a good substitute (SPO GC2/36, 20 December 1938). However, de Valera was prepared to allow a probationery period in which a civil servant could acquire this proficiency (SPO GC 1/6, 28 January 1938).

[10] Farrell, *Orange State*, p. 90.

[11] *NIHC*, Vol. VIII, c. 667.

[12] Spender, *Financial Diary*, 7–22 December 1935. There was even a case of a Catholic gardener at Stormont who was dismissed—despite a good army record and a reference from the Prince of Wales (!)—following Orange Order pressure on Craig (*ibid.*, 15 January 1934).

[13] In 1927 he resisted the extension of Whitley Councils to the NICS by claiming that it was necessary to prevent any further outbreak of that 'public hostility' to the service which had marked the early days of the regime. Craig had then been prepared to resent this pressure (PRONI Cab. 4/200/6). 'Then again they were charged that they employed Englishmen in their civil service ... it made him blush to hear such statements' (SPO S4743). Five years later he seemed prepared to use such sentiments as a means of controlling the service.

[14] Spender, *Financial Diary*, 7–22 December 1935. This was Spender's personal impression. To be fair, by the late '30s Spender believed that Catholics were presenting themselves for civil service examinations in relatively high numbers—though not quite in proportion to their share of the population (PRO D.O. 35/893, Spender comments included in Sir E. J. Harding's report, 18 November 1938). They dropped in the RUC too, from 541 in 1924 (*Belfast Newsletter*, 4 January 1924) to 489 in 1935 (PRONI Cab. B236) and 454 in 1944 (quoted in G. L. Dobbie 'Partisans and protectors: the police in Northern Ireland, c. 1920–70', unpublished paper).

[15] *NIHC*, Vol. VIII, c. 667–8.

[16] PRONI Cab. 4/200/18.

[17] J. W. Nixon, *NIHC*, Vol. XVIII, c. 2464–5.

[18] Spender, *Financial Diary*, 29 March 1943. The register was compiled, but Brooke did not use it.

[19] *Ibid.*, 5 May 1933.

[20] *Ibid.*, 4 January 1934.

[21] Clark to Spender, *ibid.*, 6 December 1935.

[22] It controlled the NICS establishment and regulations, was the largest Ministry, had accounting officers attached to other Ministries and the Parliamentary Draughtsman as one of its officials, etc. As late as June 1941 Bates even used the excuse of the wartime emergency to temporarily break the Ministry of Finance's formal control in this area (Spender, *Financial Diary*, 5 June 1941).

[23] *Ibid.*, 5 March 1932.

[24] *Ibid.*, notes of a discussion, 9 January 1934; diary, 30 June 1934.

[25] Quoted in P. J. Buckland, 'The unity of Ulster Unionism', *History*, 60 (1975).

[26] PRONI Cab. 4/333/16, Cabinet memorandum, 5 January 1936.

[27] Pollock to Craig, 15 June 1932, PRONI Cab. 7F/57/1.

[28] Spender to Blackmore, 25 March 1930, PRONI Cab. 7A/3/1.

[29] Craig's speech to the UULA, 2 January 1937, PRONI Cab. 8PF/22.

[30] Record of an interview at the Treasury, 24 July 1930, PRONI Cab. 7A/3/1.

[31] G. C. Duggan, *Northern Ireland: Success or Failure?* (Dublin, 1950), p. 4. The maiden speeches are in *NIHC*, Vol. I, c. 33–7, 45–62 (Craig), and c. 119–34 (Pollock).

[32] Quekett memorandum, 2 April 1930, PRONI Cab. 7A/3/1. Also A. Quekett, *The Constitution of Northern Ireland* (Belfast, 1928), Vol. I, pp. 48–50.

[33] Andrews memorandum, 18 November 1930, in Cab. papers, 1 May 1933, PRONI Cab. 7A/3/1.

[34] Secret and confidential Cabinet conclusions, 19 November 1933, *ibid*.

[35] Especially in agriculture.

[36] Upcott to Craig, 3 August 1925, PRO T. 160/269/111999.

[37] Spender, *Financial Diary*, Conference on the General Financial Position of the Province, 12 December 1933.

[38] *Financial Diary*, 2 November, 4 December 1933, 20 January 1934.

[39] Hopkins to the Chancellor, 16 May 1933, PRO T. 160/550/F6563/021/1.

[40] PRO T. 160/550/F6563/021/1. Cf. the correspondence of Hopkins to Spender, 12 October 1933, and of Spender to Hopkins, 20 October 1933, which is clearly the result of a warning by Spender. See also *Financial Diary*, 25 April 1932. Support for the Ministry of Finance line was expressed consistently by the Belfast correspondent of *The Economist* from 1927 to 1929.

[41] Lawrence, *Government*, p. 58.

[42] Spender, *Financial Diary*, 12 August 1935, May 1936.

[43] Formulae for the Northern Ireland contribution, 16 March 1933, PRO T. 160/550/F6562/021/1.

[44] Hopkins's document for Sir F. Phillips, 8 February 1939, in PRO T. 160/1138/15586. As early as 24 November 1930 Bewley wrote to Waley, 'Any honest statement of the position cannot help pointing out the fact that we now subsidise Northern Ireland to the tune of £1 million a year or more,' PRO T. 160/430/12302.

[45] Hopkins to the Chancellor, 16 May 1933, PRO T. 160/550/F6562/021/1.

[46] Hopkins to the Chancellor, 10 May 1933, *ibid*.

[47] Spender, *Financial Diary*, 28–30 November 1940. See also the retrospective undated addendum for May–October 1943.

[48] As D. W. Harkness (in *History and the Irish*, Belfast, 1976, p. 13) has pointed out, the language is indeed explicit. On 22 March 1938 Hopkins wrote to the Chancellor of the Exchequer, 'the position at the moment . . . is that Lord Craigavon said he would be forthcoming if he were bribed' (PRO T. 160/747/14026/04/2). Spender noted, 'I should perhaps make it clear that although my general views coincided with those of Lord Craigavon, they were coloured by a different background. Where he was determined to make the interests of Northern Ireland the great purpose of his life, I was still obsessed with questions of the defence of the UK' (*Financial Diary, loc. cit.*).

[49] *Ibid.*, August–September 1936. See also May–October 1943, pp. 208 ff.

[50] *NIHC*, Vol. II, c. 626.

[51] See the defence of the empiricist view of politics by B. Hindess, 'The concept of class in Marxist theory and Marxist politics', in J. Bloomfield (ed.), *Class, Hegemony and Party* (London, 1977).

[52] E.g. in R. Rose, *Northern Ireland: a Time of Choice* (London, 1976), p. 16.

[53] Cf. N. Poulantzas, *Fascism and Dictatorship* (London, 1974).

[54] In 1922 the Ministry of Commerce estimated that 340,000 of a population of 1·24 million were 'nominally engaged' in the linen trade ('Memorandum on the Linen Trade', PRO T. 172/1287).

[55] Andrews to Craig, 23 July 1928, PRONI 7F/67/1.

[56] Craig to Andrews, 25 July 1928, *ibid.*

[57] Belfast Chamber of Commerce *Journal*, 19 May 1932.

[58] Delegation of UIDA to meet Craig, 31 May 1937. Also Cleland to Milne Barbour, 26 November 1937, PRONI Cab. 7F/108/2 and 7F/126/3.

[59] *NIHC*, Vol. XIX, 18 March 1937, c. 643. For some nationalist comments on Craig's views, see *ibid.*, Vol. X, c. 109. It was the view of the Ministries of Finance and Commerce that the intended beneficiaries of this campaign did not seem to benefit by it. These were firms producing biscuits, meal, furniture, hosiery, ink, matches, pickles and sauces, preserves, footwear, soaps, etc. ('UIDA, note of its establishment and functions', PRONI Cab. 7F/108/1).

[60] Memorandum dated 6 November 1931, PRONI Cab. 7F/126/3. In 1923 Craig had argued that industrial undertakings 'should be left to the initiative of the great commercial magnates' (PRONI Cab. 4/70/7).

[61] Milne Barbour to Craig, 13 November 1936, PRONI Cab. 7F/126/3.

[62] *Belfast Newsletter*, 5 and 26 November 1937.

[63] Balibar, *Dictatorship*, p. 231–2.

[64] R. Skidelsky, 'The reception of the Keynesian revolution', in M. Keynes (ed.), *Essays on John Maynard Keynes* (Cambridge, 1975), p. 101.

[65] *Ibid.*

[66] M. Cowling, *The Impact of Labour, 1920–24* (Cambridge, 1971), pp. 407–8.

[67] J. Foster, 'The state and the ruling class during the General Strike', *Marxism Today*, May 1976, p. 142.

[68] Skidelsky argues that this was an objective possibility (*Politicians and the Slump: the Labour Government, 1929–31*, London, 1967, pp. 387–8).

[69] T. Nairn, *The Break-up of Britain: Crisis and Neo-nationalism* (London, 1977), p. 50.

[70] Spender, *Financial Diary*, 9 January 1934. The outdoor relief riots of 1932, though short-lived in their impact on working-class politics, had seen the most significant moment of proletarian unity in Belfast since the state had been created. Craig claimed 'the agitation had got so serious that he believed that they might have found themselves confronted with wilful damage which would be out of all proportion to the £300,000 paid away on Relief schemes'.

[71] Craig to Davidson, 12 January 1933, PRONI Cab. 8PF/32.

[72] *Ibid.*

[73] *Belfast Newsletter*, 19 November 1931.

[74] Bates to Craig, 26 July 1932; Craig to Bates, 28 July 1932, PRONI Cab. 7B/200. British Home Office interest in such matters—as both publicly and privately expressed—was slight; see D. Harkness, 'England's Irish Question', in G. Peele and C. Cook (eds.), *The Politics of Reappraisal* (London, 1975), p. 61, and P. Bew, 'The problem of Irish Unionism', *Economy and Society*, 6 (1977), p. 107, n. 16.

[75] Farrell, *Orange State*, p. 138.

[76] PRONI Cab. B236; 'Disturbances in Belfast', *Financial Diary*, first week in June 1936.

[77] M. Beloff, 'The role of the higher civil service', in Peele and Cooke, *Reappraisal*, p. 213.

[78] Skidelsky, *Politics*, p. 217. Anderson rejected the advice of Keynes and others and declared, 'everything must wait upon the forces of nature'. He had studied the problem for seven weeks.

[79] Clark to Spender, 12 November 1943, *Financial Diary*.

[80] Note on visit by Sir J. Lithgow, 17 October 1933, PRO M.T. 9/2560/8426.

[81] Spender to Waley, 6 December 1938, PRO T. 160/1138/15586.

[82] Spender to Blackmore, 11 October 1930, PRONI Cab. 7A/3/1.

[83] Spender, *Financial Diary*, 20–25 July 1942.

[84] S. Howson, *Domestic Monetary Management in Britain, 1919–38* (Cambridge, 1975), p. 143.

[85] S. Howson and D. Winch, *The Economic Advisory Council, 1930–39* (Cambridge, 1977), p. 152. Cf. the Keynes–Hopkins conflict on public works described in D. Winch, *Economics and Policy* (Fontana edn, London, 1972), pp. 120–1.

[86] PRO T. 160/1138/15586.

[87] Cf. an itinerary, PRONI Cab. 7B/136.

[88] Spender, *Financial Diary*, 26 September 1936.

[89] 'The persecution of Catholics in Northern Ireland', *Capuchin Annual*, 1940, p. 162.

[90] *Ibid.*, p. 165.

[91] *Ibid.*, p. 164.

[92] *Ibid.*, p. 163.

[93] *Ibid.*, p. 162.

[94] *Ibid.*, p. 163.

[95] *Ibid.*, p. 174.

[96] See PRO D.O. 35/893/XII/123, 'Treatment of the Catholic minority in Northern Ireland'. Cf. also D.O. 35/893/XII/251, UK/Eire, political and

constitutional relations: allegations made by the Eire government as to the maltreatment of the Catholic minority in Northern Ireland arising out of partition.

[97] PRO D.O. 35/893/XII/123, Sir H. Batterbee minute dated 7 November 1938.

[98] *Loc. cit.*, Minute by Stephenson, 13 March 1938.

[99] PRO D.O. 35/893/XII/251, notes by Sir E. J. Harding *c.* 7 November 1938. Harding was Permanent Under-Secretary of State for Dominion Affairs.

[100] PRO D.O. 35/892/XII/251, Dominions Office comment on Home Office views, Sir Henry Batterbee, 18 November 1938.

[101] 'The persecution of Catholics', p. 175.

4

WAR AND WELFARISM: THE TRANSFORMATION OF POPULISM AND ITS OPPOSITION, 1943–51

The Second World War had important political and ideological effects on British society, and Northern Ireland could not stay immune. It involved a substantial increase in state planning and economic management. As its most recent historian has pointed out, these developments were associated with a significant change in the dominant ideology, towards acceptance of a 'managed' economy and the 'welfare state'.[1] They also owed much to the implicit political pressure of the working class, which as Hobsbawm points out 'injected a deliberate element of social equity into public policy, such as had been notably absent in the First World War.[2] The effects of these developments on the ruling class in Ulster were to be of particular significance because of the clear divergence between its main political strategy after 1921 and that pursued by the British ruling class. The latter was Baldwin's one of 'educating the Labour party', of integrating it into responsible, constitutional politics. It was necessitated by the massive post-World War I increase in unionisation and militancy, and the associated decline in the political and ideological significance of the labour aristocracy as a mass agency of ruling-class control.[3] The ruling class in Ulster was saved the problem of developing a fresh strategy by the intensification of the national struggle in 1920. This enabled it to disarm the working class by branding its leadership as 'Bolshevist Sinn Feiners'. The local labour movement suffered severely in the expulsions of 1920 and the subsequent 'cleansing' of Belfast workplaces of 'alien elements'. The consequent disorientation, pogroms and repression, followed by two decades of severe unemployment, provided the local ruling class with sufficient leeway to continue with business as usual. Foster has pointed out that it was the bankers who favoured the strategy of 'educating labour' in Britain. Industrial capital, particularly in the provinces, was equivocal or hostile, tending instead towards the Churchillian alternative of class mobilisation 'to defeat labour, discredit its leaders, attack its trade union base and decisively reassert the class values of the existing order'.[4] In Ulster banking capital did exist, but it did not act as a decisive element. The dominance of the representatives of industrial capital within the state machinery, together with the weakness of the labour movement, meant that the war acted on a ruling class whose traditions were not such as to produce a 'British' type of flexibility.

This chapter examines the progressive de-insulation of the economy, politics and ideology in Northern Ireland during and immediately after the Second World War. Four aspects of this de-insulation, each with very different effects, will be examined. Each exemplifies the limitations on the manoeuvrability of the ruling class implied by its traditional political inflexibility. Together they illustrate the solution to de-insulation adopted by the bourgeoisie's political representatives, and the restrictions on future options which it embodied.

Industrial mobilisation, post-war reconstruction and the fall of Andrews

The issue of post-war reconstruction first emerged in 1941, when the British government committed itself to a far-reaching programme and the discussions began which led in 1942 to the Beveridge report. In a letter to the Chancellor of the Exchequer in August 1942 John Andrews, who had succeeded Craig as Prime Minister in 1940, outlined the political problems such plans created for the Unionists.

> In numerous public utterances of responsible people the minds of our people have been directed more than ever before towards what is called a 'new order' or a 'fair deal', the 'scandal that poverty should exist' and the 'horrors associated with the slums'.[5]

He feared the emergence of political difficulties if the Unionists appeared to be prepared to do less than the British government:

> 'our people frequently chafe at their feeling of inability to exercise any sort of initiative in their desire for reform. For a very considerable time a very definite and sustained demand has been pressed upon me that I should give a real lead as regards the government's intentions on social problems in future years. We cannot maintain the necessary interest in our parliamentary institutions if we are not allowed to exercise some initiative.[6]

The background to Andrews's concern was rising public

dissatisfaction with the local ruling class's performance in industrial mobilisation. Long after Dunkirk, when there was an acute labour shortage in Britain, unemployment remained high in Northern Ireland.[7] It appears that the change-over to war production was considerably hindered by the hostility of government Ministers and the bourgeoisie to the integration of the province into the UK structure of area boards, set up by the Ministry of Supply.[8] Such decreases in local unemployment as there had been was largely accounted for by the export of labour.[9]

Dissatisfaction with the government had manifested itself in two Stormont by-election defeats. An independent Unionist had won North Down, while Harry Midgley of the NILP had taken Belfast Willowfield.

Shortly before his correspondence with the Treasury, Andrews had raised the issue of post-war reconstruction at a Cabinet meeting, pointing out the extent to which many social services in Ulster were inferior to those in Britain. Sir Basil Brooke, who had been widely expected to succeed Craig and who was now Minister of Commerce, made it clear that a public commitment to make up such 'leeway' would require Treasury clearance.[10] As a result it was agreed to set up a Post-war Planning Committee chaired by Brooke and composed of the Minister of Finance and the Permanent Secretaries for Home Affairs, Agriculture, Labour and Commerce. Spender, who was a member, thought the committee would be a check on Andrews's populism. 'I think that both the chairman and the secretary will act upon sound principles and prevent as far as possible any stampeding of our government into premature action.'[11]

Despite this, and apparently without Treasury approval, Andrews proceded to commit the government to its own programme of reconstruction in a Stormont speech at the end of July. He promised slum clearance, a housing programme, educational expansion and large-scale extension of water, sewage and electricity to rural areas. He emphasised that the programme was his own government's concern, though it would be related to British plans.

The speech provoked an extremely hostile reaction at the Treasury. In an internal communication, an official wrote:

> Mr Andrews has chosen to disregard not merely the financial responsibility of his government towards ours, but even the element

of inter-government courtesy [a reference to the fact that the speech
had been made before the Treasury received a copy of it]. Mr
Andrews appears to be trying to establish the principle that whatever
tune Northern Ireland calls, the Imperial Government will pay the
piper.[12]

In a message to Spender, Compton of the Treasury spelt out his
department's main objections:

> It seems to commit your government to specific services on a very
> generous scale and without any prior consideration as to whether
> they can be met out of the available resources in the post-war years.
> Further, it pays no regard to the maintenance of parity of services
> between your government and ours. In this connection surely the
> sentence in para. 6 [Andrews's reference to the programme as a
> domestic concern] is misleading . . . We are concerned, just because
> you may be proclaiming standards which conflict with our policy,
> secondly because there is evident danger of your being committed
> to a programme which would imperil the financial structure of your
> government.[13]

The British Chancellor of the Exchequer, Kingsley Wood, himself
wrote to Andrews on 6 August. He emphasised the dangers of
capitulation to contemporary tendencies to consider social
reforms independently of their financial consequences, and the
implications of this for Belfast–London relations. In particular, no
programme could be endorsed which threatened parity.[14] The
same message was conveyed in stronger terms still by Wood to
Maynard Sinclair, Parliamentary Secretary to the Ministry of
Finance, when they met at the Treasury.

> The Chancellor admitted that there was a similar demand in Britain
> but this came mostly from the Socialists . . . in Northern Ireland it
> comes principally from our own supporters; he [Wood] feels that a
> reconstruction programme of any kind, and particularly one
> showing substantial advances in our social services, will be difficult to
> achieve and will not be possible in the immediate post-war period.

In recording this in his diary, Spender echoed the Treasury position
and criticised Andrews's behaviour:

> I am quite convinced in my own mind that the best interests of
> Ulster will be ensured by the closest co-operation with the British
> government and that any attempt to make political capital by
> forestalling the British post-war measures will not be to the
> advantage of our province. In the end I believe that it would also

prove disastrous to our present government if such a policy was pursued for purely political reasons . . .[15]

Sinclair revealed the Treasury position to the second meeting of the post-war planning group, adding that he had assured Wood that the government's only intention was to make up 'leeway'.[16] This same line was taken by Andrews in his reply to Wood. By now, however, it was too late. The Treasury viewed Andrews as a dangerous demagogue.

The difficulties were accentuated by general doubts, both locally and in Britain, about Andrews's competence. These sealed an alliance in Ulster between Brooke, the civil servants on the planning committee and Spender. For the latter, disquiet was mainly financial in character. An existing anti-populism had been reinforced once more by the Treasury. Wood and his department were the proponents of a traditional policy on government expenditure and were to be the major opponents of the Beveridge report.[17] Brooke did not entirely share their views. For him, the articulation of this position was strictly subordinate to political considerations. He did not oppose populism as such, but rather its degeneration into a rhetoric detached from practical possibilities. As the degree of Treasury opposition became known, Andrews stood condemned not as a populist but as an inept—and in this sense a dangerous—one..

In fact Andrews continued to enrage the Treasury. In a speech at Stormont at the end of the war he claimed that in September 1942 he had secured agreement from the Chancellor that Ulster could incur extra expenditure to make up 'leeway', her backwardness in basic infrastructure and social services.[18] While he did in fact claim as much at the time, the Treasury view was that this was a 'dangerous doctrine' on which he needed to be corrected.[19] In a letter to Andrews, Wood did assure him that the case for making up leeway was being sympathetically received, but added, 'The times are now such and will be after the war that both of us must have regard to the financial situation as a whole'.[20] Yet Andrews in his reply interpreted this too as an acceptance of his position. Compton, one of the main Treasury officials concerned, commented, 'Andrews naively notes the points on which obligations rest on the Imperial Treasury and ignores the points on which obligations rest on Northern Ireland.'[21]

Other problems too continued to be encountered. Alongside

Brooke's planning committee, the government had appointed a planning consultant, W. R. Davidge, to report on the preparation of a town plan for Belfast.[22] In his preliminary report in September 1942 Davidge recommended a reconstruction plan for the city and a large area round it, a plan for the city and county of Derry, and plans for the improvement and development of Armagh, Tyrone and Fermanagh. On his recommendation, and with the support of Andrews and Bates, a Planning Advisory Board was created. Brooke's group reacted with hostility and refused to meet until there was a clear division of powers. This was apparently not forthcoming, and in December the Brooke committee was disbanded.

The issue of industrial mobilisation meanwhile continued to attract public criticism. Owing to the intervention of another independent Unionist, the government lost the Westminster seat of West Belfast to a Labour candidate in February 1943. This was the first time it had passed from their hands since 1922.

The Andrews initiative was in ruins. Brooke had emerged as the champion of 'responsible' government. It was only a matter of time before he became Prime Minister. This would not represent the eclipse of the dominant populist practices of the '30s , but rather a tactical adjustment in the aftermath of an unsuccessful attempt to extend them. Andrews had allowed his fears of the criticisms of the Unionist war effort to stampede him into a piece of demagogy which had endangered relations with the section of the British state apparatus whose goodwill was essential to the financing of increased government expenditure. Internal political pressures had moved him too far ahead of the existing balance between reformism and orthodoxy in Britain. Brooke's line, on the other hand, acknowledged that in the context of the political and ideological transformations brought about by the war, traditional tactics were insufficient to reproduce the class alliance and the power bloc. Promises of 'bones' in the future, especially when made so patently under the pressure of political criticism, were no substitute for the obvious inadequacies in the government's handling of industrial mobilisation. Andrews, clinging to his geriatric Cabinet, was stumbling from expedient to expedient. Just as they failed to win the Treasury's approval, they failed to win approval at home. Ironically, by the end of the war British orthodoxy had accommodated a degree of interventionism and welfarism sufficient to create the conditions for just the sort of developments that Andrews wanted in 1942.

For the present, events conspired to ensure that he was incapable of producing the style of active leadership required to offset the national unpopularity of the discredited Conservative appeasers of the '30s. In 1943 the threat from the NILP had not yet assumed the dimensions it was to acquire in the last two years of the war. Brooke was able to take advantage of the internal divisions between partitionists and anti-partitionists in the party (which had culminated in Midgley's resignation to form the Commonwealth Labour Party in December 1942) to give his incoming government a coalitionist, 'national' flavour. Midgley was brought into the Cabinet.

Economic policy

Apart from Midgley and his party, the forces Brooke gathered behind him to implement the realignment of the populist position indicated in the clearest possible way that it would provide only a little more flexibility than its predecessor. Particularly in his struggle against the Andrews line, Brooke had depended considerably upon a revival of residual anti-populism. Although the discrediting of Andrews should not be seen as a victory for this force within the Northern Irish state apparatuses, certain critical changes had occurred in its position which now made it a more substantial, if less coherent, entity.

The first and most important of these was that its views on public expenditure had come to be increasingly articulated by a section of the (previously largely populist) industrial bourgeoisie. Linen capitalists, who had been identified with this group at least in their protectionism, appear to have become alarmed at the tendency of industrial bourgeoisies generally to emphasise productivist and Keynesian views. While retaining their close links with the members of the Cabinet and the parliamentary party, the linen bourgeoisie now provided the backbone of opposition to proposals involving 'extravagance'. A second and more deep-seated change in anti-populism was that it became divested of its broader non-partisan implications, and ceased to be associated with general attempts to institutionalise the *via Britannica* locally. While the basis of this transition is unclear, it was obviously tied in some respect to the change in allegiance of the linen bourgeoisie.

Newly circumscribed anti-populist proposals, and the linen bourgeoisie's views generally, increasingly found a voice through the previously ineffective Ministry of Commerce. As Minister from 1941 to 1943 Brooke generally followed them on industrial matters. As a result of his own developing influence, they became part of the state's industrial policy. While acknowledgeing the problem of industrial mobilisation, pro-Brooke Unionists departed from Independent Unionists and the NILP in attributing it solely to Andrews, and not to the linen industry's failure to adjust to the war situation.

In January 1943 Brooke appointed a committee to consider post-war problems for the industry and such measures as might be necessary for it to overcome them.[24] Of its eleven members, ten were directors of linen firms.[25] Its proposals were basically conservative,[26] and were welcomed by the industry.[27] But to the industry's critics they simply served to make more unlikely the reforms in its structure which were regarded as a necessary condition of its survival in the predictably unfavourable post-war situation.

One such critic, writing in 1944, pointed out that although the inter-war period had seen an increase in the degree of vertical and horizontal integration, the industry was still dominated by a large number of small or medium-sized firms. Large-scale 'rationalisation' was necessary if the generally low level of efficiency and associated high costs of production were to be eliminated. 'Rationalisation' would greatly improve the quality of management. Many small, uneconomic firms were able to stay in business only by paying low wages or accepting very low returns on capital.[28] The industry had failed in the 1930s to adopt any measures of rationalisation comparable to those in shipbuilding and cotton. The consistently *laissez-faire* line of both Andrews and Brooke had clear effects on the war effort.[29]

Thus it was that the implementation of the linen bourgeoisie's line within the state apparatus ensured a policy towards the industry that was bound to increase the government's political difficulties as Labour and independent Unionists criticised its handling of the war effort.

Populism and the 'fifth column'

In considering the events discussed so far, their most important characteristic should not be overlooked. While together with their effects they represented modifications of the traditional populist strategy, these were essentially marginal. Neither of the modifications discussed effaced the core element of populism—the relationship between the Protestant bourgeoisie as a whole (through the state) and the Protestant masses. The new administration of Brooke, while in part the result of an anti-populist reaction to the policies of the Andrews regime, in no way diverged in its principal strategy. This is clearly illustrated in the continuity of concern demonstrated by both administrations on the issue of the importation of southern workers.

Here the determinant aspect was the reimposition of a form of sectarian articulation on a potential class issue: unemployment. Throughout 1942 the Independents and later Midgley had consistently raised the issue of the persistence of serious unemployment. However, the issue was raised within a predominantly populist framework which made it relatively easy to deal with. In February 1942 at Stormont Midgley accused the Unionists of 'solving' the problem by encouraging workers to move to British industrial centres.[30] The notion that the Andrews administration was 'exporting' Ulstermen was taken up by Independent Unionists (e.g. W. Henderson and J. W. Nixon, the MPs for Belfast Shankill and Belfast Woodvale). The latter linked this claim to the accusation that the government was allowing workers from Eire to get jobs in the north. Henderson claimed, 'There are more Fifth Columnists in Northern Ireland than in any other country in Europe and they are still being brought in here.'[31]

Because of the conditions under which the state had been born, the issue was of great significance. The question of the bourgeoisie's attitude to the 'peaceful penetration' of the First World War had been a major source of conflict within the Protestant bloc from 1918 to 1920. It had been resolved by bourgeois acquiescence in explusions and the Vigilance Committees, and by the institutionalisation of this position in the B Specials and, to a lesser extent, the state apparatuses generally. The state became acutely sensitive to working-class and petty-bourgeois grievances of this kind. In the '30s the anti-populist group had attempted to put into perspective the usually fanciful and lurid accounts of 'Eirean' infiltration which Craig sometimes received from local Unionists. After the collapse of the Pollock–Milne Barbour–Spender circle there was no attempt made to curb this aspect of populism. Rather, it was indulged by both Andrews and Brooke in a successful attempt to hegemonise opposition over unemployment.

Owing to the enlistment of skilled workers and an increased demand for certain types of skilled labour, the Ministry of Labour had brought in some skilled southerners. In response to criticisms it was pointed out that no unskilled workers were imported under Ministry auspices, although some private employers had done so independently.[32] Efforts were initially made to control this, but by the beginning of 1942 Andrews was pressing for more action. The possibility of an order under DORA regulations to make it compulsory for all employers to engage workers through employment exchanges was rejected, and it was agreed to set up a joint Ministerial committee (Home Affairs, Labour and the new Ministry of Public Security) to investigate alternative methods of restriction.[33]

The progress of the committee was slow, and Andrews became increasingly agitated. By April he claimed to have evidence of 'increasing public criticism of the ease with which workers from Eire could obtain employment in Northern Ireland'.[34] At his suggestion it was agreed that the Minister of Home Affairs should arrange to see the British Home Secretary to secure his approval for some sort of restrictive measure.

In September 1942 the British Cabinet, in keeping with the vigour of its war effort, agreed to Belfast's proposals for a 'Residence in Northern Ireland Restriction Order' by which the period of an immigrant's residence would be controlled by permit.[35] Andrews and his Minister of Labour, J. F. Gordon, were still dissatisfied. Their anxiety to deflect their supporters' disquiet, no matter how trivial its basis, was demonstrated in subsequent events. In January 1943 Andrews reported receiving a complaint from the Downpatrick district that local building trade workers were being dismissed from from a contract while men from Eire were being retained.[36] Gordon promised to make immediate enquiries, stating that in his own view the existing measures were still insufficient. The Cabinet agreed that he should draw up proposals to strengthen the order.

The fall of Andrews and his supporters—including Gordon—had nothing to do with this issue. It continued to be a matter of the greatest importance for the Brooke Cabinet. The only criticism of Andrews on this score was of the degree to which his Cabinet's fixation on it had led to other wartime problems being ignored.

Its significance for Brooke may be illustrated simply. In July 1944 a Protestant clergyman made a speech in which he alleged that the Belfast government had complete discretion in issuing residence permits, with the implication that the order would be used to exclude southern Catholics. Brooke became concerned that if the government was to be attacked in the future for being soft on southerners it should be made clear that it was not its own master in this area. He discussed the speech with his Minister of Home Affairs, William Lowry: it was agreed that a statement should be issued denying that the administration of the Act was solely a Northern Irish matter, and pointing out that the Home Office had to be consulted. The statement referred to the fact that permits could not be issued on a confessional basis.

The rest of the Cabinet reacted strongly:

> there was considerable discussion as to the wisdom of emphasising too strongly that the Order could not be administered on the basis of the religious persuasion of the applicants. It was recognised that the Minister of Home Affairs was responsible to the Home Secretary for the manner in which the Order was administered and that there could not be any process of selection on a sectarian basis. On the other hand, the repetition of this principle . . . was like trailing one's coat and seemed in the view of the Cabinet to be unnecessary and particularly undesirable at the period of the 12th celebrations.[37]

Lowry's defence of the statement was in the same liberal spirit.

> . . . he thought it essential as a matter of policy to indicate quite clearly that discrimination according to religion was beyond the powers of the government, although he was fully in sympathy with the view that unless some steps were taken to ensure the Protestant Ascendancy, the future of Northern Ireland was in jeopardy.[38]

In his Minister of Public Security (later to become Minister of Labour), Harry Midgley, Brooke had as staunch a populist as Gordon, but a more perceptive one. From mid-1944, when the government becan to anticipate the problems associated with demobilisation and reconstruction, Midgley emphasised that the real issue in this area would be that of Eire ex-servicemen obtaining work in post-war Northern Ireland. A veteran of the First World War and an organiser of an ex-servicemen's group in the '20s, he seems to have feared a repeat of the mass Protestant working-class disaffection with Unionism in 1919 and 1920, which in its sectarian mode attacked the local bourgeoisie for employing Catholics from 1914 to 1918. Midgley was particularly worried that the implementation of the Beveridge proposals in Northern Ireland would lead to a 'deluge' of southerners, who apart from increasing competition in the labour market and arousing loyalist hostility would 'gravitate to the disloyal element in our population and increase our political difficulties'.[39]

Brooke took note, and at a Cabinet meeting in February 1945 announced that he planned to meet Churchill to discuss inter-state relations, as 'there might be several areas on [sic] which Northern Ireland's constitutional powers needed strengthening',[40] particularly, of course, control over southern immigration. Later in the month Maynard Sinclair, Minister of Finance, reported that at several recent political meetings he had found 'very strong dissatisfaction about the number of Eire workers employed in Northern Ireland, and still coming here while so many of our own people were unemployed'.[41]

In March, Midgley reported a critical situation developing, as some trade unions were claiming that when workers became redundant Northern Irish dilutees should be paid off before skilled southerners. There was Cabinet agreement that in such cases the residence permits should be withdrawn even if it resulted in a strike.[42]

Brooke duly travelled to London to discuss the employment situation with British Ministers, raising the topic of control of Eire immigrants and 'the difficulties which were likely to arise in Northern Ireland in the absence of any statutory power to control entry after the war'.

No attempt was made to verify empirically the hypothetical deluge of Eire workers, nor to gain even an impressionistic estimate of the 'danger'. Rather, concern seems to have been directly related to the expression of alarm by groups and organisations considered influential with the Protestant masses. Early in 1946 Brooke reported that the British Legion had made representations to him about the large number of civilians employed in some establishments run by imperial Service departments like the Air Ministry. The Legion asked the government to have such people replaced by ex-servicemen. For once, a cursory investigation of the situation was made, and Midgley found that of five and a half thousand in-post employees, only two thousand were ex-servicemen. Worse still, a considerable proportion of the civilians came from Eire. Imperial government regulations made no provision for preferential treatment of former members of the forces, but Brooke nevertheless insisted that the imperial departments removed the southerners.[43]

Despite the important changes in the political and ideological climate brought about by the war, the ruling class's principal traditional strategy of dividing the masses was retained. The important questions concern the social basis for this continuity and the new tactics developed in relation to it.

Welfarism

A fourth issue involving the de-insulation of Northern Ireland was that of the welfare state. While enthusiasm for welfarist legislation was evidently strong amongst the Protestant working class, and was expressed in the growth of the NILP, its major effect was to continue the process of redivision of the ruling class which had begun during the dispute in 1942 over post-war reconstruction.

The major aspect of this realignment was the final transformation of anti-populism from its original status as a non-partisan critical force whose most important allies were in the British state apparatus (especially the Treasury). By the late '40s this element remained anti-populist only in its parsimony. Not only had it ceased to be non-partisan and non-sectarian, but it had become associated with a section of the Orange Order. It developed an obsessive concern with 'socialistic' British legislation and, as Keynesian thinking on budgetary control became dominant, lost its allies in the Treasury. Populism, on the other hand, was reproduced with only minor modifications. It pragmatically absorbed welfarism in its stride, as it had relief works in the '30s.

While these were important changes, they should not divert attention from the most fundamental one of all in these years, implicit throughout this chapter. In the process of the political redivision of the ruling class, differences between populists and their opponents descended from a strategic to a tactical level. While anti-populism had never been a comprehensive bourgeois strategy for prosecuting the class struggle in the way populism had, it nevertheless contested the basic aim of dividing the working class along Catholic–Protestant lines, and not simply the tactics for doing it. Promoting such a division had not previously been part of anti-populism.

By 1950, however, this was no longer so. Both populists and their opponents took for granted the overall objective of tightening the bond between Protestant bourgeoisie and masses. They differed not on this, but on the degree to which the Northern Ireland state could secure welfarism whilst resisting the erosion of its autonomy by other aspects of Westminster legislation.

Another significant change was that, unlike earlier divisions, the new ones were not reproduced within the central state apparatuses themselves. These appear to have been united in their defence of the government's populist policies against critics both at Stormont and in the constituencies.

Many of the government's critics were bourgeois, and many of the arguments the government used against them were justified by reference to the demands of the working class. This was evidence not that the state was becoming neutral to class forces, but that the populists' relative independence was made necessary by the implementation of a line which would perpetuate the subordination of the masses.

At least partly as a result of its alliance with traditional anti-populists against Andrews's post-war reconstruction speech, the Brooke circle's original reaction to the Beveridge proposals had been cautious. Brooke argued:

> I do not see how any government could possibly commit itself until it knows what the financial position is going to be after the war ... If you deprive industry, whether socially owned or privately owned, of its means of producing work and wealth, then those magnificent schemes put forward by Sir William Beveridge must fall to the ground for lack of funds ...[44]

At the same time it was clearly recognised that the maintence of the Unionist class alliance required not merely a sectarian position on an issue like Eire workers but action of some sort on social and economic issues.

In 1943 the NILP concentrated on the backwardness of local health services—Ulster had the highest infant mortality rate in the UK, and the position was similar with deaths from tuberculosis, facilities for the treatment of which were, like the maternity services, pathetically inadequate.[45] On the industrial front, the winter of 1942 saw strikes at Short's and other engineering works and the development of a militant Belfast shop stewards' committee.[46] Further strikes and prosecutions under DORA regulations followed in 1943, and in 1944 the NILP began for the first time to form industrial groups, the first being in the shipyard. The number of trade unionists affiliated to the party increased sharply.[47] In March and April 1944 a strike of engineering workers at the yard, the aircraft factory and some of the largest engineering plants led to a conflict with the state when five shop stewards were arrested. The shop stewards' committee ordered a mass walk-out from Belfast factories, which forced the release of the men and a favourable settlement of the original wage claim.[48]

While the degree to which the Beveridge proposals could be implemented depended on the results of the forthcoming post-war British election the government in Northern Ireland could only adopt a strategy of piecemeal accommodation to popular pressure. In March 1944 a new Ministry of Health and Local Government was created. Brooke had also reformed a post-war reconstruction committee under Sir Ronald Nugent.[49] However, it was recognised that in lieu of a national scheme its activities would be cosmetic.[50]

The Unionists fought the general election on a strong anti-socialist platform. They emphasised the dangers to local industry of Labour's commitment to nationalisation and planning.[51] However, in the same campaign they also committed themselves to introduce whatever social reforms were passed in Britain.[52]

At the Stormont election the same year the NILP nominated eight candidates in Belfast, and although they captured only two seats (Oldpark and Dock) all their candidates won substantial votes. If it is remembered that the Protestant oppositional vote was split by six Midgley-ites, it is clear that the government's post-election strategy towards the masses had to acknowledge the demands of Protestant workers as articulated by the NILP.[53]

What, then, would be the relationship of the government in Ulster to Labour's implementation of Beveridge ? In his analysis of

Protestant politics A. C. Hepburn has argued:

> ... perhaps the main reason for the Unionists' effortless
> maintenance of power lies in the ultimate insignificance of the local
> parliament. Once a working agreement was reached between
> Westminster and Stormont on the financial aspects of devolution ...
> social progress could be maintained, with no additional effort or
> expense, simply by reproducing Westminster legislation.[54]

The introduction of welfarism to Ulster was not such a frictionless
process as this implies. The implementation of 'socialistic' laws
threatened not only to produce disunity within the ruling class but
possibly to encourage the Protestant masses to reconsider their
relationship to the local state. In December 1945 the Cabinet
discussed a memorandum drawn up by Brooke on a proposal by
BBC Northern Ireland to broadcast a series of talks called 'The
Week in Stormont', to be given by back-bench MPs in proportion
to party strength. Although Britain already had a similar
programme about Westminster, Brooke argued that in the Six
Counties 'there are special circumstances which make such a
programme of talks highly undesirable'. These naturally included
the fact that 'the Nationalist members are aiming at the destruction
of our Constitution', but also and more interestingly, that

> ... our parliament meets on only one day in some weeks, and the
> business may be of a relatively unimportant character. In such a week
> there would be very little material ... the radio talk would create the
> impression that our Parliament (as some of our opponents are
> constantly saying) is of little importance ... and talks of the character
> proposed should impress the public with the value and prestige of
> our parliament.[55]

The threat to the state's dominance over the Protestant masses
arose from the fact that a government which Unionism had
identified as a major enemy of Protestant interests was introducing
a series of significant improvements in everyday life. The problem
was solved by the outbreak of ruling-class division, which enabled
the Brooke Cabinet to present itself as the champion of popular
interests.

Once the Cabinet began to consider the legislative programme
of the Attlee government, concern with both its 'socialistic' nature
and its implications for the existing division of powers between the
two governments became evident. In September the Supplies and
Services (Transitional Powers) Bill was discussed. Under it, orders

made by Northern Irish departments using delegated powers would have to be laid before the British Parliament. Brooke argued that although it might be administratively convenient for control to be exercised from London, it would be a mistake to 'allow them to take over our legislation'. Nugent, the Minister of Commerce, commented on the 'deterioration' of the situation since the British election: 'whereas it was the desire of the last government to have controls removed as soon as possible, the present government was showing a tendency in the other direction'.[56]

Eventually it was decided that the Bill did not threaten Stormont's powers, and it was accepted. The issue was raised again in October over another Westminster Bill, however—the Investment (Control and Guarantees) Act. Maynard Sinclair pointed out that certain clauses dealing with investment control related to a transferred service.[57] Although the close links between local and national banks and insurance companies were obvious grounds for central control of capital issues, a major policy issue was at stake:

> My own feeling is that we should take no step which would in any way weaken the constitutional position of the parliament and government of Northern Ireland . . . [Although the present issue was not vital] I can forsee a circumstance in which any precedent which might indicate our readiness to allow the Imperial Parliament to legislate in respect of a transferred service might prove embarrassing . . .[58]

As a result, separate legislation was introduced in Stormont.[59]

In November Brooke referred to the investment Bill as an index of what was now seen as a potentially serious threat to existing relations between Stormont and Westminster:

> The adoption of some of the measures which were being passed by the present government at Westminster could be justified on the grounds that they were an unavoidable part of the aftermath of war, but as time went on more extreme socialistic measures may be introduced which on account of the financial relationship between Northern Ireland and Great Britain, would have to be followed here. At any time the government might have to face a situation in which the measures they considered they had no alternative but to introduce would be unacceptable to members of the Unionist party, and if the government could not rely upon their support chaotic conditions would result . . . he was extremely uneasy on this score and had been considering whether any changes could be made to avert such a situation. The possibilities were Dominion status or a

return to Westminster.[60]

In Cabinet discussions in January and February 1946 Nugent and Brian Maginess, Minister of Labour, submitted memoranda favouring Dominion status. It appears they were considered seriously by the rest of the Cabinet. Both Ministers took as their starting point the following characterisation of the UK:

> Britain seemed to have shifted significantly leftwards, and governments, Labour or Conservative, would hereafter assume much tighter planning and control, irksome to Ulstermen used to 'independence'.[61]

They both stressed that the new status should not militate against the introduction of welfare legislation—'our industrial, though not our social, legislation can no longer run on parallel lines' (Maginess). It was necessary to request 'a greater degree of responsibility and at the same time ask for continued financial assistance' (Maginess). Dominion status was rejected if it meant Ulster having to live within its own resources. 'It might mean that our present standards might have to be lowered, [which] would tend to lessen the difference to the worker between Northern Ireland and Eire and therefore by so much would weaken one of our most telling arguments against Union with the country . . . on the political side it would present the Labour Party here with the best election platform they could ever hope to have . . .' (Maginess).

Brooke and Sinclair made speeches throughout the winter of 1945–46 emphasising that the relative autonomy of Stormont remained intact even when it implemented measures for which Westminster was financially responsible. On one occasion Sinclair managed to combine this with a typically populist blast:

> Family allowances would cost more per head of population in Ulster than in the rest of the UK. He did not think this was due to the Unionist population. He rather thought there was another reason . . .
>
> Ulster would always be able to make her budget balance and make an Imperial contribution because she was going to be in a more prosperous condition than after the 1914–18 war . . .[62]

In his budget speech he denied that 'parity' and 'step by step' meant that Ulster should 'slavishly follow' the whole pattern of life in Britain. 'We should preserve in the administration of our services the greatest possible degree of flexibility.'[63] In December 1945, speaking at an Orange meeting, Brooke read out a letter from an English Tory attacking the Labour government and thanking heaven for a bastion of conservatism at Stormont. Brooke went on to forecast difficult times ahead in relations with Westminster.[64]

It was soon to become clear, though, that feeling within the Cabinet was for playing this down. As early as November the Minister of Home Affairs, Edmond Warnock, made a speech arguing that Labour represented no threat to Ulster's constitutional position and that, although it differed in some principles, the party's social programme was 'not unlike our own'.[65] In fact the Cabinet was coming under attack from the right for importing too much 'socialistic' legislation. Brooke's speech had been partly motivated by the need to defend Unionism's conservative credentials.

In December William Grant, Minister of Health and Local Government, introduced a Bill to create a public house-building authority—the NIHT. It was bitterly attacked by local builders' organisations. Grant pointed out that it departed from the British pattern by providing subsidies for private builders.[66] Nevertheless at the UUC in February 1946 he was attacked as an opponent of private enterprise, and a resolution demanding more concessions to private builders was adopted.[67]

The criticisms of the government by back-benchers and the constituency organisations were to increase in 1946, culminating in a campaign for Dominion status to save Ulster from 'creeping socialism'. By then, however, there was little Cabinet support for it.*

In a series of agreements with the Treasury from 1946 onwards the Unionist government was able to obtain the financial guarantees that would underwrite the reforms Andrews had promised in 1942.[68] Apart from the fact that they fully integrated the province into the welfare state, they enabled the domestic exchequer to put money into local services at the expense of the

---

*Mr Denis Norman has drawn our attention to important Cabinet memoranda which were not available at the time when our research was being carried out. As part of his research into the O'Neill period he has intensively investigated the role of the Ministry of Commerce. He points out that Nugent as Minister of Commerce was expressing hostility to Westminster policies and arguing for Dominion status until 1948: Cabinet memoranda by Nugent on 10 November 1947 (Cab. 4/730/17) and 11 November 1948 (Cab. 4/772/5).

Imperial Contribution. This had become particularly important in the area of capital expenditure, where Northern Ireland could have found it difficult to make up 'leeway' without getting into debt. From 1947 the Treasury permitted the Ministry of Finance to divert revenue from the imperial contribution to a Capital Purposes Fund for industrial development and other projects. At the same time Westminster made it clear that these concessions were incompatible with an increase in devolution.

Equally significantly for the Cabinet's change in attitude was the fact that by the summer of 1946 Brooke and his colleagues had become convinced of Attlee's goodwill towards them on partition, and had acquired a more balanced view of the actual extent of his proposals for nationalisation.[69] As Rumpf and Hepburn put it, 'It became clear at quite an early stage that no one in the Attlee Cabinet was inclined to upset the Unionist applecart.'[70] The Home Secretary, Chuter Ede, rebuffed the attempts of both the NILP and the 'Friends of Ireland' group of back-bench Labour MPs to raise issues such as electoral law and practices, discrimination and the Special Powers Act in Ulster.[71]

Nevertheless, an important section of the local bourgeoisie remained more concerned with the province's integration into an enveloping system of 'socialist control' than with the problem of perpetuating the political and ideological conditions for maintaining their class rule. Their discontent was clearly influenced by the increases in taxation during and since the war, which were regularly denounced by Unionist back-benchers as 'death-blows' to local enterprise.[72] Their increasingly bitter reaction to the main lines of Unionist government policy threatened to provoke major conflict within the Unionist party. The issue that crystallised the opposition was the government's attempt in 1946–47 to introduce a Statistics of Trade Bill.

In November 1946 the Attlee Cabinet announced its intention of introducing legislation to empower the Board of Trade to collect figures from employers on numbers employed, wage rates, value and ownership of fixed capital, stocks and subsidies from central and local authorities. The Northern Ireland Ministers concerned—Sinclair and Nugent—observed that similar legislation would have to be introduced at Stormont, since the statistics were an element in the formation of national policies from which they hoped the province would benefit. At the same time Sinclair raised an important objection: 'there is a natural reaction of the business community against disclosing all these particulars . . . I feel we may wish to operate something far less drastic . . .'.[73]

Nugent replied that it was imperative the legislation be similar, citing the general benefit of existing economic and financial relations:

> The main object in collecting these statistics is to provide the Imperial government with a sound foundation of facts and figures on which to base their policies of full employment. We are committed to a similar policy in Northern Ireland and stand to gain considerably by the prosecution of that policy on the part of the Imperial government. It would be difficult to substantiate our claim to be treated as a development area in the government's policy with regard to the distribution of industry if we are unable to provide up-to-date information on trade and business [here].[74]

The government agreed with Nugent.

When this became known in September 1947, opposition was substantial. Unionist back-benchers were already attacking the Health Services Bill, the NIHT, and the creation of a Northern Ireland Transport Board (which involved the nationalisation—on generous terms—of the almost bankrupt local railway system). In the furore over these measures the demand for Dominion status to save Ulster from socialism was for the first time given public prominence.[75]

Unionist Ministers were now forced to defend the Attlee government, emphasising its defence of Ulster's constitutional position.[76] Brooke praised Chuter Ede, and argued that, as a subordinate assembly, the Ulster government had no alternative but to introduce some of the legislation being adopted.[77]

The Belfast Chamber of Commerce and various other industrial and commercial bodies passed resolutions against the Statistics of Trade Bill.[78] In Unionist constituency parties, capitalist pressure resulted in similar resolutions being accepted. As opposition mounted (supported by the *Belfast Newsletter*) Nugent told a specially convened UUC Executive Committee meeting that he had decided to invite 'representative businessmen' to form a committee to examine the Bill. He gave an assurance that a second reading would not take place until it had reported.[79] The eventual result was complete government capitulation and the introduction of an emasculated Bill in March 1949. While this represented a defeat for Brooke, he was able to profit by it. The local bourgeoisie's hysterical outcry against 'socialism' provided him with a means of completing the incorporation of welfare measures into the structure of dominance over the Protestant masses.

In a series of speeches in late 1947 he represented the government as the champion of a humane, progressive middle way between two extremes:

> In a modern democratic state, the government must assume responsibility for a wide range of activities in the interests of the community, but the indiscriminate charge of 'socialism' is unjustified and absurd ... there is a need for a middle course between the extreme philosophy of *laissez-faire* and the fetish of socialisation ...[80]

The demand for Dominion status was singled out for attack in a speech to a Unionist rally in Larne, where he combined an appeal to fear of nationalism with an open avowal of the significance of welfarism for the reproduction of the Unionist class bloc:

> To attempt a fundamental change in our constitutional position is to reopen the whole Irish question. The government is strongly supported by the votes of the working-class who cherish their heritage in the Union and to whom any tendency towards separation from Britain is anathema ... The backbone of Unionism is the Unionist Labour party. Are those men going to be satisfied if we reject the social services and other benefits we have had by going step by step with Britain?[81]

By now it was evident that although most of those who advocated Dominion status were critics of 'socialisation', not all anti-socialists were proponents of Dominion status. Thus J. M. Andrews, who was unsympathetic to the government, made an extended attack on McCoy which was welcomed by the *Newsletter*.[82] The *coup de grâce* was probably a speech in favour of the idea by an anti-partitionist Labour MP, Jack Beattie.[83] By the end of 1947 it found support only on the wilder fringes of the party.[84]

Although it proved possible to use a division within the ruling class to present the state as the progressive guarantor of parity with the new standards of British welfare, there was no fundamental change in relations between populist and anti-populist practices. The relatively full employment of the post-war period, together with the Brooke circle's defence of the welfare state, seemed to the correspondent of *The Round Table* to offer the prospect of evolution toward a more normal type of regime:

> One result of the last three years has been a certain realignment of the Unionists themselves. The lessening of the threat of constitutional change which so long strengthened the right wing has enabled the party to regain more of liberal tradition. The Prime Minister has not deferred to the older and more diehard element in going ahead with social reforms. It is too soon, perhaps, to see the effects of this broadened outlook on relations with the minority, but notably in the new educational system inspired by the Butler act, Unionist dissidence was safely risked in order to make concessions to the Roman Catholics . . .[85]

Yet within two years the Minister of Education who proposed these concessions had been forced to resign in the face of another sordid capitulation to pressure from the Protestant Churches, the Orange Order and many MPs.[86] Later, in 1951, a Public Order Act was passed to enable the RUC to suppress 'inflammatory' nationalist marches more effectively.[87]

If these manifestations of the 'Protestant' nature of the state confounded the hopes of optimistic liberals, there was a tendency to see them as a natural reaction to the victory of a new coalition in the southern elections of 1948. The coalition included a social-republican party, Clann na Poblachta, and within a year it had taken Ireland out of the Commonwealth, changed its name from Eire to 'Republic of Ireland' and launched an all-party Anti-Partition Campaign which financed candidates in the general election Brooke called in January 1949.[88]

The argument that liberalising tendencies fell victim to events in the south betrays a fundamental misconception of the nature of the Unionist class alliance and of bourgeois dominance over it. Dominance was achieved by the strenuous efforts to reconcile practices that were often discrepant and sometimes conflicted. There was disagreement within the ruling class about welfarism only because one bourgeois section saw that Protestant working-class disaffection was bound to arise if British legislation was not put into effect. In no way did this imply any liberalisation of the state's attitude towards Catholics. A commitment to some form of welfare state was to become an integral part of post-war British Conservatism and was compatible with many elements of traditional Conservative ideology.[89] In Ulster, Brooke and his circle made it clear that welfarism involved no threat to the indigenous bourgeoisie, whose industrial policy they continued to implement. It was a politically and ideologically neutral development both in Britain and in Ulster. Such significance as it had was determined by *existing* political and ideological practices: in Britain, those of a bureaucratised social democratic party; in Ulster those of an exclusivist Unionism. The Unionist leadership clearly saw welfarism as a necessary element in maintaining domination over the Protestant masses. This is not to say that other practices which had secured domination in the past were redundant. Precisely because the welfare measures were politically and ideologically indifferent they had to be integrated with the existing machinery of dominance. The Cabinet's reaction to the proposed BBC programme mentioned above makes it clear that even before anti-partitionism intensified in 1948 the primary attitude of the state towards Catholics was still exclusivist. Farrell also cites a speech of Brooke's in February 1947 to the City of Derry and Foyle Unionist Associations in which he applauded a fund they had set up to prevent Catholics buying Protestant-owned property, and further restrictions on the local government franchise the previous year.[90] The anti-partition campaign simply allowed the ruling class to merge welfarism into populism with greater ease. Welfare benefits were presented as the fruit of the British connection and Catholics stigmatised as two-faced intransigents for accepting the benefits while continuing to reject the legitimacy of the state.

The effects of the political, ideological and economic deinsulation of the province from 1940–45 had been weathered successfully by Brooke and his circle, certainly in a fashion apparently beyond Andrews's limited resources, cerebral or otherwise. The 'solution' was a series of tactical modifications to populism, during which anti-populism briefly revived and then collapsed beyond recognition as a political force.

For all the formal changes in the state (new Ministries, policies and general administrative expansion) its nature and its inflexibility remained much as they had been. Indeed, it could be argued that the recent changes had diminished its flexibility. By commiting itself to welfarism and 'step-by-step' the Unionist bourgeoisie was redefining its dependence on the Protestant working class and the British state in potentially dangerous ways.

Notes to chapter 4

¹ P. Addison, *The Road to 1945* (London, 1975).
² E. J. Hobsbawm, *Industry and Empire* (London, 1972), p. 245.
³ J. Foster, 'The state'.
⁴ *Ibid*., p. 140.
⁵ PRO T. 160/F 14464/043/04/1327.
⁶ *Ibid*.
⁷ In 1939 the unemployment rate was 22 per cent; in 1941 it was still 12·3 per cent (*Ulster Year Book*, 1947).
⁸ J. W. Blake, *Northern Ireland in the Second World War* (Belfast, 1956).
⁹ O'Nuallain, *Finances*, pp. 131–2.
¹⁰ PRONI Cab. 4/513/7.
¹¹ Spender to Brooks, 8 July 1942, PRO T. 160.
¹² PRO T. 160.
¹³ *Ibid*.
¹⁴ Wood to Andrews, 6 August 1942, *ibid*.
¹⁵ Spender, *Financial Diary*, 15 August 1942.
¹⁶ PRONI Com. 7/6.
¹⁷ Addison, *Road*, pp. 229, 237.
¹⁸ Lawrence, *Government*, p. 70. Harbinson refers to this illusory agreement as Andrews's 'most abiding memorial' *The Ulster Unionist Party, 1882–1973*, Belfast, 1973, p. 140.
¹⁹ Comments on Andrews's letter, 30 August 1942, PRO T. 160.
²⁰ 14 September 1942, *ibid*.
²¹ *Ibid*.
²² PRONI Com. 7/6.
²³ PRONI Com. 7/4.
²⁴ Summarised in A. Maltby, *The Government of Northern Ireland, 1922–72: a Catalogue and Breviate of Parliamentary Papers* (Dublin, 1974), p. 64–5.
²⁵ *NIHC*, Vol. XXVI, c. 607.
²⁶ The report suggested a refund of 20 per cent of excess profits tax and the provision of low-interest government loans for modernisation of plant and machinery. Flax and linen research should be under unified control and the industry should have the determining voice on proposals for investment. On internal structure, reference was made to the recommendations in 1928 of four representatives of the principal branches of the industry that as an ultimate object the whole industry be amalgamated into one unit. This was felt 'impractical', and instead a policy of vertical integration was advocated.
²⁷ Brooke to Dalton (Board of Trade), PRONI Com. 7/36 PW55.
²⁸ A. Beacham, 'The Ulster linen industry', *Economica*, November 1944. Almost identical views had been expressed by a local linen capitalist, W. J. Larmour, in a lecture in Belfast in 1929 ('Northern government accused of masterly inactivity', *Belfast Newsletter*, 23 February 1929).
²⁹ 'The resources of the textile industry were not utilised to the fullest possible extent—the logic of total war demanded maximum production from the working part of the industry, the closure of the remainder and the transfer to other work of the labour released . . . but no attempt was made'

(Blake, *Second War*, p. 394).

[30] *NIHC*, Vol. XXV, c. 21.
[31] *Ibid.*, c. 161.
[32] *Ibid.*, c. 198.
[33] PRONI Cab. 4/496/5.
[34] PRONI Cab. 4/507/7.
[35] PRONI Cab. 4/525/8.
[36] PRONI Cab. 4/533/12.
[37] PRONI Cab. conclusions, 4/592/2.
[38] *Ibid.*
[39] PRONI Cab. 4/597/7.
[40] PRONI Cab. 4/614/9.
[41] PRONI Cab. 4/615/5.
[42] PRONI Cab. 4/618/6.
[43] PRONI Cab. 669/12.
[44] *NIHC*, Vol. XXVI, c. 65.
[45] Lawrence, *Government*, p. 136; J. F. Harbinson, 'A history of the NILP, 1881–1949' unpublished M.Sc. thesis, Queen's University, Belfast (1966), p. 149.
[46] Farrell, *Orange State*, p. 173.
[47] Harbinson, *NILP*, p. 159.
[48] *Ibid.*, p. 169; Farrell, *Orange State*, p. 174.
[49] Spender, *Financial Diary*, 13 April 1944.
[50] *Ibid.*, 20 April 1944.
[51] In one speech in Oldpark, Brooke proclaimed, 'Once they started nibbling the biscuit of socialism, before they knew where they were their children would be tied hand and foot.' Grant, the Minister of Labour, attacked the Labour Party commitment to full employment more floridly still: 'There never had been a time when there was full employment in this country, full employment was a fallacy' (*Belfast Newsletter*, 6 June 1945).
[52] Speech by Sinclair, *Belfast Newsletter*, 30 May 1945.
[53] Harbinson, *NILP*; Farrell, *Orange State*, p. 190.
[54] Rumpf and Hepburn, *Socialism*, pp. 179–80.
[55] PRONI Cab. 4/646/5.
[56] PRONI Cab. 4/635/14.
[57] PRONI Cab. 4/636/9.
[58] *Ibid.*
[59] PRONI Cab. 4/678/7.
[60] PRONI Cab. 4/642/9.
[61] This and other quotations from memoranda are from an account of the discussion by D. W. Harkness, *Irish Times*, 16 November 1977.
[62] *Belfast Newsletter*, 12 November 1945.
[63] *Ibid.*, 22 November 1945.
[64] *Ibid.*, 13 December 1945.
[65] *Ibid.*, 30 November 1945.
[66] *Ibid.*, 22 December 1945.
[67] *Ibid.*, 9 February 1946.
[68] Lawrence, *Government*, pp. 78–81.
[69] Cf. the Harkness article, *Irish Times*, 16 November 1977.
[70] Rumpf and Hepburn, *Socialism*, p. 202.

[71] *Ibid.*, pp. 202–3.
[72] O'Nuallain, *Finances*, pp. 109–10.
[73] PRONI Cab. 4/690/5.
[74] PRONI Cab. 4/694/3.
[75] By W. F. McCoy, Unionist MP for South Tyrone (cf. *The Round Table*, XXXVII, 1947).
[76] Cf. W. Topping's speech, *Belfast Newsletter*, 29 September 1947.
[77] *Belfast Newsletter*, 21 September 1947.
[78] *Ibid.*, 29 October 1947.
[79] *Ibid.*, 5 November 1947.
[80] *Ibid.*, 14 November 1947.
[81] *Ibid.*, 27 November 1947.
[82] *Ibid.*, 22 November 1947.
[83] *NIHC*, Vol. XXXI, c. 2894.
[84] E.g. T. Lyons and the Rev. G. McManaway, Unionist MPs for North Tyrone and Derry City.
[85] *The Round Table*, XXXVIII (1948).
[86] Farrell, *Orange State*, p. 196.
[87] *Ibid.*, p. 200.
[88] *Ibid.*, pp. 183 ff.
[89] Addison, *Road*.
[90] Farrell, *Orange State*, p. 181.

5

THE ORIGINS OF O'NEILLISM, 1952–64

This chapter is concerned with the problems of analysing the relationship between economic changes in Northern Ireland from about 1950 to 1963, and the political crisis that manifested itself at the close of the period as Terence O'Neill became Prime Minister. Like the conflict within the Unionist party some years later over civil rights, the crisis has been widely interpreted as an outcome of tension between 'traditionalists' and 'modernisers'. The modernisers were successful in installing O'Neill, but not in maintaining him in power.

This type of analysis has dominated the left and has been forcefully restated by Michael Farrell, who posits a direct relationship between the difficulties of the economy, which became acute in the late '50s, and the emergence of this division at the political level. The government's response to the growing difficulties of the traditional staple industries was 'complacent and lethargic'. In reaction to the defection of Protestant workers to the NILP in the 1958 election, it made a conventional appeal to sectarianism. In evidence Farrell quotes a prominent Unionist, A. B. Babington, who advocated that the party should keep registers of unemployed Protestants from which employers could recruit.[1] Since the idea was repudiated in Stormont by the Minister of Labour, it cannot bear the significance Farrell attaches to it.[2] His other main source for the characterisation of 'traditional' Unionism—O'Neill's autobiography—is also suspect if it is seen as anything more than a contribution to the political struggle which must be deciphered before its ideological products can be evaluated.

Such analyses, having postulated the traditional–modernist division, attribute it to economic tension between local capital, said to maintain its power by according sectarian privileges to Protestants, and external capital, said not to do so. As this argument was originally applied to the events of 1968 and has subsequently been projected back a decade, fuller discussion of it will be postponed until the next chapter. Nevertheless a few words on its strictly theoretical implications, and its characterisation of 'traditional' industry, are in order here.

The main theoretical defect of this approach is its economistic reduction of a political crisis to a conflict between two forms of capital. It reduces questions that can be posed only at the level of the state and its relationship to the Protestant masses to the 'needs' of different sectors of industry. The role of the state in capitalist society—as the factor of cohesion and class dominance—is completely ignored. The Marxist–Leninist theory of politics attributes primary significance to the state as an objective of political action because, in the words of Marx, '. . . the political state represents the table of contents of man's practical conflicts. Thus the political state, within the limits of its form, expresses . . . all the social conflicts, needs and interests . . .'[3]

As a result of ignoring the significance of the state in the crisis, Farrell is reduced to a species of psychologism. Certain 'real' pressures are outlined–the changing economic structure in the north, British capital's need for good political relations with the south as the latter becomes an increasingly important market and sphere of investment, etc.[4] These pressures push O'Neill into a series of reforms which enrage the Unionist bloc's traditional base. O'Neill is seen as a mouthpiece of the multi-nationals, while the traditional bourgeoisie is regarded as a spent force ('the Ulster-based industries had all but disappeared'[5]). The Unionist backlash is explained in terms of the disruptive effect of 'modernisation' on the collective psyche of the Protestant masses:

> The Orange ideology was too deep-rooted to be dispensed with overnight, especially at a time of change and confusion when new industries were replacing old ones, threatening small businessmen and established skilled workers, when new blocks of flats were replacing old slums, new towns replacing old villages. Orangeism provided stability and status in a changing world and defended jobs and positions.[6]

Orangeism is treated as a set of prejudices and dispositions 'in the heads' of Protestant workers, activated by the economic crisis and the 'stresses of modern living'. A side-affect of this social psychologising is the obliteration of secular and progressive working-class reactions, when they were actually the dominant ones.

In Marxist–Leninist theory the question of ideology is posed in a way that breaks with all varieties of psychologism. It treats ideology as a specific level of society, which has the effect of constituting and individualising persons as 'subjects'.[7] A materialist theory of ideology necessitates the recognition that 'an ideology always exists in an apparatus and its practice or practices'.[8] Hence a consideration of the ideological aspects of the crisis must examine the central and local organisations which embodied different aspects of Unionist and Orange ideology.

The previous chapters have argued that the key role in perpetuating the Protestant class bloc was played by the state. However, this should not be taken to imply that the state was a privileged autonomous entity which could impose, at will, particular ideological formulae on the subordinate classes. Its crucial role as a force for cohesion and hegemony did not mean that the dominance of the ruling class could be imposed without some form of mediation. Rather, its function was to epitomise and give a specific articulation to the contradictions within society in such a way as to ensure 'class peace'. Thus, for example, the ideology of triumphal sectarian exclusivism associated with the expulsions of 1920 was no bourgeois tactical device but a result of the endorsement and hegemonisation by the bourgeoisie of relatively independent sectarian traditions. Throughout its subsequent history the state's endorsement of sectarian activities remained an important element in the reproduction of the class bloc. The backtracking on education in 1950, the passing of the Public Order Act and the flags and emblems legislation were all post-war examples.

Yet if this was an important element in the maintenance of ruling-class hegemony, it was not the only or even the dominant one. The really essential basis for the reproduction of the class bloc was the state's sensitivity to the political impact on the Protestant masses of changes in their material conditions.

Once this is recognised, the real problem of the 1950s is seen to be not a combination of structurally generated bourgeois dissension and the need to overcome ideological backwardness, but Northern Ireland's autonomy within the United Kingdom at a time when the main parties in Britain were committed to full employment and were recognising the 'regional problem' for the first time. The political crisis of the early '60s can be understood only if it is recognised that a large proportion of the Protestant working class were not the dupes of Orangeism in their reaction to local economic decline but were influenced by a secular ideology of opposition to regional deprivation, articulated by the NILP.

By effectively ignoring the state, or treating it as an epiphenomenal expression of the economic interests of different sections of capital, writers like Farrell and Boserup[9] fundamentally misinterpret the history of the '50s and early '60s. The ironic consequence is that both end up crediting O'Neill with the intention of reforming sectarian structures (although his attempts are then dismissed as feeble). In fact he had no such reforming zeal. The belief that he had is the other side of the coin to the view that the bourgeoisie 'created' sectarianism, that is, it sees sectarianism as a *tactic* to be now adopted, now dropped.

Historical analysis has shown that, far from being a product of the needs of capital, support by a large section of the bourgeoisie for exclusivism in the workplace was mixed, and dependent upon specific political and ideological conditions.[10] Another study of the structure of the Protestant class bloc in its classic period has demonstrated that its organisation involved the assimilation of the practices of exclusivist Orangeism to a much wider coalition of social forces, which included the secular social imperialist ideology of the labour aristocracy and the explicitly anti-Orange (if antinationalist) ideology of liberal Unionism.[11] A ruling class wedded simply to exclusivist practices would have been incapable of winning the struggle against Home Rule, and the preceding chapters have demonstrated that that once the state was created, dominance was maintained only by a combination of different strategies.

Sectarianism was neither a 'tactic' nor unequivocally tied to the needs of the local bourgeoisie. It was a set of institutions and practices which acquired significance in the context of the *state's* relations with the Protestant masses. The failure of existing analyses to understand sectarianism is symptomatic of their failure to comprehend this general relationship. In this connection Farrell's analysis of the interaction between economic problems and the political crisis of the '60s is mistaken. The 'modernisation' associated with the change-over from Brooke to O'Neill was a product not of the economic decline of the traditional bourgeoisie but rather—as Farrell partly recognises, without attributing it its full significance[12]—of a specific political problem. This was the potential loss of control over key sectors of the working class as persistent high unemployment assumed the dimensions of a political issue by contrast with full employment and a bipartisan commitment to the elimination of regional disparities in Britain.

In its attempts to deal with the problem the O'Neill administration became formally associated with a national move to more vigorous forms of regional economic planning. This had specific effects. Notably it posed a threat to certain local apparatuses of Protestant domination, and meant a shift in the central state machine towards more power for the bureaucracy and a 'presidential' style of politics. There was certainly a backlash, but it was a localised one whose most significant effects were within the parliamentary and constituency Unionist parties. Not until after the development of the civil rights movement did it involve significant sections of the Protestant working class. It is also important to note that initially it had nothing to do with opposition to civil rights-type reforms, since O'Neill made no attempt to introduce any.

The economy in the 1950s

In 1950 the dominant aspects of the north's economic structure were the continued pre-eminence of the two traditional staple industries, and the high proportion of the workforce (by UK standards) engaged in agriculture. Of the total number of workers in manufacturing, 30 per cent were in textiles and linen and 20 per cent in shipbuilding, engineering and vehicle repair.[13] Agriculture accounted for one sixth of the gainfully employed and almost a quarter of gainfully employed males.[14]

1951 was the last year of the post-war boom in demand for manufactured products, which had allowed the linen industry, for example, to enjoy conditions unknown before the war.[15] By the summer of 1952 production had declined in a number of industries.[16] In the three years up to June 1954 linen employment fell by 15 per cent.[17]

Although general economic conditions improved in 1954 and 1955, the linen trade now entered a long period of rationalisation and contraction. As the textile industries of the advanced capitalist countries faced increasing competition from low-cost ex-colonial producers, linen was confronted with the additional problem of the expansion of the synthetic fibre industry. With government assistance (see below), a programme of re-equipment and modernisation was initiated to increase productivity. As a direct result there was a large-scale reduction in employment. Between 1954 and 1964 the number of jobs in plants employing 25 or more (the great majority) fell from 56,414 to 33,957. The number of plants fell from 298 to 200.[18]

Rationalisation was accompanied by concentration. The importance of vertical and horizontal integration increased. So too did the proportion of total capacity controlled by 'combines'—firms owning plants engaged in all processes from spinning to making-up, and disposing of their intermediate products solely to other departments of the same organisation. Even in 1954 combines had controlled over 30 per cent of spinning and weaving capacity. By 1964 there was a much greater degree of integration, and the bulk of employment was in the control of a few large organisations.[19]

Government assistance was crucial in this process. Little direction seems to have been exercised over the disbursement of funds to specific firms, and as a result a number of modernised plants went bankrupt in the slump of 1958. These were acquired by combines, who proceeded to strip their assets.[20]

By concentrating solely on the gross decline of employment in the linen industry Farrell is led to accept a distorted view of this process. It was not simply a case of the decline of the linen bourgeoisie. Although significant numbers of small and medium-sized firms closed in the period, a linen complex still existed at the end of it. Moreover the industry was now dominated by a small number of firms who had clearly benifited from the decade of rationalisation. The decline of employment in a classic staple should not be seen as an index of the virtual disappearance of the traditional bourgeoisie. As the Hall Committee was to point out, the 1950s saw a strengthening of the industry in some respects. Productivity had increased, research into the use of new fibres and fabrics had intensified, and new materials were being used on a limited scale.[21] A process of concentration had occurred and the bourgeoisie had been pruned. It was still far from an insignificant force, though.

The important feature of the history of shipbuilding in the same period was not so much decline itself as its timing. In 1950 more than a tenth of Ulster's manufacturing jobs and about a fifth of those in Belfast's were to be found at Harland & Wolff. Employing 21,000 in four yards and eighteen berths on the Queen's Island, it was the largest single localised shipbuilding complex in the world.[22] Until about 1955 its main problem was a shortage of steel due to the rearmament programme. By that date, however, the building programme had caught up with the post-war backlog of demand. From then on, the international market became increasingly competitive. British firms came under increasing pressure from Continental and Japanese yards, which as a result of the war had been obliged to undergo more substantial re-equipment. By 1958 the number of ships afloat exceeded requirements. UK shipbuilding output fell back to its 1954 level in 1959, and by 1960 it was 22 per cent below its post-war peak.[23]

In Belfast, although there had been some lay-offs in the late '50s, the major decline occurred over a very short period. Between 1961 and 1964 employment in shipbuilding and repairing and marine engineering dropped by 40 per cent (11,500).[24] The compression of such a substantial decline into such a short period, and its concentration in Belfast, had critical political repercussions.

Agriculture in the post-war period also experienced an intensification of the process of amalgamation, the elimination of marginal holdings and an advance in mechanisation.[25] An increase in output of 80 per cent was achieved between 1938 and 1960, despite a declining work-force. Between 1950 and 1960 total agricultural employment fell by nearly a third (28,000).[26]

The contraction of the staples was reflected in a high level of unemployment throughout the decade. In the manufacturing sector, a small decrease occurred in total numbers employed between 1950 and 1960. Although new industry was attracted by various government inducements, the employment it created did not cancel out the effect of the decline in the staples. There was an increase in service employment of 18,500, due mainly to government investment in education and personal and public health. But the contraction of agriculture and a relatively high birth rate meant that throughout the decade unemployment never fell below 5 per cent and averaged 7·4 per cent. This was four times the national average.[27] If it was nothing like the figures of the '30s, the fact remained that it was now taking place in the context not merely of full employment in the UK, but of a relatively better performance by Britain's other regional black spots (see Table 2).

Table 2   Unemployment in the Development Areas, 1956–64

	1956	1958	1959	1960	1961	1962	1963	1964
Scottish	2·2	3·7	4·1	3·4	2·9	3·5	4·6	3·5
Welsh	2·2	4·1	3·8	2·5	2·4	3·0	3·4	2·4
Northern	1·4	2·2	3·0	2·5	2·0	3·2	4·3	2·9
Merseyside	2·0	3·6	4·2	3·1	2·7	3·9	4·9	3·4
South-west	1·8	2·8	2·5	2·8	1·8	2·2	3·1	2·4
Northern Ireland	6·8*	9·3	NA	6·7	NA	7·5	7·9	6·6

* Figure for 1955.
NA Not available
Source. McCrone, Regional Policy, p. 154.

Before considering the effects of these results, it is necessary to bring up to date the history of the government's post-war industrial policy.

The state and the economy to 1954

In 1944 the Cabinet had decided that existing legislation aimed at diversifying the economy from its staple base was inadequate. Under the New Industries (Development) Acts of 1937 and 1942, which had offered grants towards the cost of rent and income tax, plus loans, thirty-five firms employing a total of 2,500 had been attracted.[28] It was feared that the end of the war would precipitate unemployment in the staple industries, and it was decided to introduce an Industries Development Act aimed at attracting larger enterprises by providing factory premises and equipment, with the necessary infrastructure.[29] The Act gave the government power to lease, purchase or erect premises and to let or sell them to incoming industrial undertakings. It allowed the Ministers of Finance and Commerce discretion in the type of assistance granted. Under the Act grants of up to one third of capital costs were normal, and could be exceeded in 'desirable' projects.[30] Most of the expenditure went on building factories. The rents charged were below the cost required to service the capital outlay.[31] In terms of inducements, the measures appear to have given Northern Ireland an advantage over the British regions. Because Stormont was empowered to enact this type of legislation the main foundation of British regional policy—the Distribution of Industry Act, 1945—did not apply to the province. In some ways its provisions were more stringent. A Treasury committee had to be satisfied both that each project was commercially sound and that finance could not be raised from another source. Regional policy was in any case being given a low priority in Britain at the time. The building of advance factories on the mainland was stopped altogether in 1947 and did not recommence until 1959.[32]

Northern Ireland's traditional bourgeoisie was not particularly sympathetic to a vigorous policy of industrial attraction. In January 1946 Nugent had announced that, under the new legislation, ten new plants had been established and were expected to create 4,710 jobs. They included Courtald's and Metal Box.[33] But he had already reported bourgeois disquiet over these developments to the Cabinet: 'there seemed to be a feeling that the government, in their efforts to attract new industries, were overlooking the necessity for encouraging and helping existing manufactures'.[34]

During the conflict over the Statistics of Trade Bill the representatives of traditional capital in Parliament attacked this aspect of government policy. In a debate on the Ministry of Commerce estimates in 1947 both Milne Barbour and Andrews criticised the effects of the Industries Act, which, they claimed, led to labour being drawn away from the linen industry to new firms. Andrews defended the traditional industries—'they have stood the test of time, and no matter how many of these new industries are established, it will be on the old ones that we will have to depend chiefly in the days that lie ahead'.[35]

In defending the policy Nugent and his successor, Brian Maginess, made it clear that they were relying upon the traditional industries to provide the mainstay of the north's economy for the forseeable future. In 1949 Maginess announced that, since 1945, 136 firms with an expected employment capacity of 23,000 had set up in the north. He added, however, that it was the traditional industries which 'in the testing time ahead would allow Northern Ireland to avoid large-scale unemployment by their ability to adapt and sell in competitive world markets'.[36]

Such reassurances to the bourgeoisie were given concrete form in November 1950, when a Re-equipment of Industry Bill was introduced at Stormont. It provided 'for the payment of grants towards expenditure incurred in the re-equipment or modernisation of industrial undertakings'.[37] The rationale for the Bill was set out in a speech by the Minister of Finance:

> While I am sure the [Ways and Means] committee are in full sympathy with the government's policy of attracting new industries, thereby diversifying our industrial set-up and mitigating, as far as possible, the effects of any setback in world trading conditions upon our principal export trade. There is undoubtedly a feeling that these new industries may have had an adverse effect on existing industries, notably in the attraction of labour to modern, well laid-out factories erected in many cases with generous governmental financial assistance.[38]

It was pointed out that the aim of the IDA was to expand manufacturing capacity, and that existing firms could obtain grants only if they could show that there would be a consequent increase in their work-force. Yet what existing industries needed were grants for re-equipment which would probably tend to restrict employment opportunities by increasing the productivity of the present labour force.[39] Under the new Act, therefore, grants of 33 per cent of capital cost were to be made available.

The legislation was introduced at a time when the linen industry was still experiencing boom conditions due to the effect of the 1949 devaluation on exports to North America.[40] By mid-1951 the industry was being hit by an international slump in textiles which, coinciding with a shortage of steel, led to a serious recession in local industry. Unemployment rose to 10 per cent by January 1952.[41] As the economic outlook deteriorated, the government was criticised again for 'submissiveness' to London. The issue this time was the allegedly 'crippling' levels of death duties, estate duties and excess profits tax, which were 'threatening the annihilation of the family firm'.[42] It was a popular one, since the province had a much higher proportion of family firms than the UK as a whole. The budget of 1951 conceded exemption for gifts *inter vivos* made three, rather than five, years before death.[43] But this was of little economic significance, and a section of the bourgeoisie once again revived the cry for Dominion status to ensure lower taxes and the payment of the Imperial Contribution.[44]

The political context in which these questions were debated

appear to be transformed by the return of the Conservati[v]
general election of 1951. The nine Ulster Unionist
Westminster constituted half the government majority. *The Round
Table's* commentator gave what was probably an orthodox
Unionist opinion on the new situation: 'On no previous occasion
have [the Unionists' seats] been such a material factor at a general
election. Never before has the association between the
Conservatives and Unionists proved so timely and advantageous.'[45]
Any hopes of advantage were to be confounded. To cope with the
inflationary pressure of rearmament in the national economy, the
new administration, introduced measures to restrict credit and
control public expenditure. The effect was to push local
unemployment higher. In response, some Unionist MPs began to
claim that the Cabinet was failing to assert Ulster's interests
militantly enough. At first Brooke argued that Ulster had no choice
but to suffer for the sins of national financial profligacy: 'as a nation
we have for a considerable time been living beyond our means . . .
we are now faced with the stern necessity of making our books
balance'.[46] This remark was made in December 1951, when
unemployment was 7·5 per cent. By February 1952 it had reached 11
per cent. Bourgeois disquiet about government 'inactivity'
increased, still coupled with a conviction that the solution to the
problem lay in measures to subsidise local industry and to increase
its non-taxable surplus. Faulkner continued to bemoan the
'confiscatory' level of taxation.[47] Further reductions in death duties
would be made, but their economic effect was limited.

If the Faulkner line was to be put into effect a substantial revision
of Belfast–London relations would have been involved. The
consequent threat to welfarism acted as a basic limit of the policy
options debated within Unionist politics. Throughout the decade
there was to be a largely rhetorical note in demands for a revision of
the Government of Ireland Act, which tended to collapse
pathetically into demands that the government 'at least extract
more' from the Treasury.

In 1952, however, Brooke was forced to forego his earlier fatalism
and there took place what *The Round Table's* correspondent
hailed as 'a ministerial conference without precedent in relations
between these two parts of the United Kingdom'.[48] Brooke and
four of his Ministers[49] met Churchill and other British Ministers
in London to discuss the north's economy.[50] In his report to

Stormont Brooke told MPs he had emphasised the critically high level of unemployment. It had been agreed that the British would try to increase the allocation of steel and other raw materials 'consistent with the rearmament and export programmes'.[51] Apart from this nebulous commitment, it had been agreed that the Admiralty would order three ships from Harland & Wolff, that Short's would produce the Comet airliner under sub-contract, and that 'it was hoped' ' the placing of textile orders for the defence programme would be accelerated. *The Round Table* nevertheless considered that the most important outcome was an agreement that the Chancellor and the Minister of Finance would collaborate in an investigation of those factors (including transport costs) which militated against full employment locally.[52]

In April 1952 Duncan Sandys, Minister of Supply, visited Ulster for further discussion with Cabinet Ministers and industrialists. In his subsequent comments, while agreeing that his government would do what it could to help, he concluded, 'in the long run this is an Ulster problem which only Ulster can solve'.[53]

Undoubtedly this statement ignored the effects of national economic policies on Northern Ireland. It was characteristic of what one authority has called the 'freewheeling' policy of the Conservatives towards the regions in the '50s.[54] The post-war boom in most traditional industries continued until 1955, and unemployment in many of the regions remained low. As McCrone comments,

> Governments may, perhaps, be excused for supposing during this period that the regional problem was virtually solved. In fact, however, though policy measures immediately after the war had achieved considerable success, the economies of the Scottish, Welsh and Northern regions were still heavily dependent on their traditional industries. Immense tasks remained if their infrastructure and environments were to be recreated to stimulate new economic growth. The continued boom in the traditional industries had . . . only masked [the problem].[55]

The harmful effects of shelving regional problems were compounded by those of national policies to deal with the inflationary pressures and the threat to the balance of payments that developed during the investment boom of 1954–55. As a result the regions bore the brunt of the credit squeeze and autumn budget of 1955, the post-Suez measures and Thorneycroft's increase in Bank rate in 1957.[56] Northern Ireland was particularly hard hit. The close political links between the government and the Conservatives were now to contribute to major political divisions in the Unionist ranks.

Before considering this development it is necessary to examine a further turn in Stormont's industrial policies. In March 1954 Lord Glentoran, Minister of Commerce, announced the government's decision to replace the Re-equipment of Industry Act with a Capital Grants to Industry Act.[57] Under the former grants of £3.25 million had been allocated to 150 schemes. Glentoran considered this stimulus insufficient, arguing that it had not prevented an overall decline in investment in buildings and machinery. Incentives on a much broader front were now to be offered. No longer would re-equipment schemes have to be substantial to qualify. It was proposed to give grants of up to a quarter of the cost for any investment in plant, machinery or buildings, whether it involved re-equipment or expansion in the labour force. £5 million was made available for this purpose over the next three years.

Glentoran had concluded his announcement with a plea to local industrialists to come forward with schemes. But the linen industry, despite the fact that conditions had improved, was still complaining of over-taxation. In response the Minister of Finance announced a further reduction in estate duties.[58] Again it was not enough for Faulkner, who predicted that the concession would not reverse the 'deplorable' tendency for investment to decrease.[59] A reaction to these views was also evident, however. The Round Table's correspondent reported criticism of government policy on the grounds of its over-dependence on the traditional bourgeoisie. 'Economists doubt whether this preservation of privately owned businesses can deal with the basic problems.'[60] The budget and the new Industry Bill were a challenge to the traditional bourgeoisie: if they could not make the economy viable the government would face a severe crisis. This opinion seems to have been based upon a highly critical survey of Ulster's economic structure and of government industrial policy which had been commissioned by Brooke's Cabinet, but which it was now reluctant to publish. It is with this report that an account of the political significance of economic questions must begin.

The politics of unemployment

The report, an 'Economic Survey of Northern Ireland', by two economists at Queen's University (K. S. Isles and N. Cuthbert), had been commissioned by Nugent in 1947. Its authors presented it to Glentoran in June 1955 at the latest, but it was not until over two years later that it was made public. The reasons are clear when the report's substance is considered. Although Glentoran was to claim that it broadly supported government economic policy since 1945, it in fact supported the NILP's critique of this policy.[61] It pointed out that under the IDA and the CGIA, schemes with a total employment potential of 26,000 had been introduced. This represented a yearly average of 2,500, which compared unfavourably with 'shake-out' by the staple industries. 'The degree of resilience and expansionism in the economy has not been great.'[62]

Although reference was made to the province's 'natural disadvantages' (remoteness, etc.) the authors' analysis centred on a critical view of the traditional bourgeoisie, and the government's pliability to its needs and desires. Their views amplified those of earlier critics, mentioned in chapter 4. The linen complex was dominated by small-scale family-owned units, fiercely traditional and unamenable to planned rationalisation. The preponderance of private companies (60 per cent in Ulster, compared with 35 per cent in the UK) prevented the investment of domestic savings in local industry.[63] It was the dominance of these enterprises which, they argued, was responsible for the failure of Ulster's industries—particularly textiles—to adjust to changed conditions in the world market. Principal shareholders were reluctant to seek an increase of capital for fear of losing control over decision-making. The majority of private firms had forsaken any ideas of expansion and preferred to invest their undistributed profits in government securities, or to divest them by paying high dividends and directors' salaries.[64] Lacking any breadth of experience in production, management or marketing, they were as a rule ill equiped to modernise or diversify. Indeed, Isles and Cuthbert were so critical that they probably exaggerated the inertia of local industry and its inability to rationalise.

The report also highlighted an important restrictionist and monopolist tendency which had built up in the inter-war period, when trade associations had been formed to maintain prices. There was a widespread habit of concentrating on profit margins rather than volume of sales, accentuated by a general ignorance of 'modern business methods'.[65] These tendencies had particularly bad effects in cross-channel shipping, where transport prices were needlessly high, and in the coal trade, where restrictive practices were entrenched.[66] The report recommended the creation of a nationalised cross-channel shipping service and the referral of the existing situation to the Monopolies Commission.

The most important political implication of the report was that it rebutted the state's articulation of the ideology of the traditional bourgeoisie. Lack of investment was due not to 'confiscatory' levels of taxation but to an archaic industrial structure and the myopic self-interest of local capitalists. The government, particularly the Ministry of Commerce, had failed to take a broader view in its industrial policy. In suggesting the formation of a Development Corporation to encourage the establishment of new industries, if necessary by public enterprise,[67] the report took the Ministry of Commerce to task for its failure to attract new industry, its lack of enterprise and flexibility and its wasteful concentration of resources on existing firms. The authors' criticisms were made more explicit still in their contribution to a contemporary reader on Northern Ireland—'in such a small business community as that of Northern Ireland there is inevitably a good deal of scope for the exercise of special privilege, and under self-government therefore it is difficult for the administration to always be thoroughly impartial'.[68]

In its efforts to force concessions on the Statistics of Trade Bill and death duties the local bourgeoisie had been relatively successful. In Lord Glentoran it had a rigid defender of its record against the critics. Traditional capital was also well represented in the Unionist parliamentary party. Of the fourteen Belfast MPs at this time, twelve had direct links with traditional capital as either proprietors or managing directors.[69] The two Ministers of Commerce in the '50s exemplified the close links. H. V. McCleery, who held the post from 1949–53, was a managing director of a flax spinning firm; Lord Glentoran was a member of the Dixon family, who as well as being closely involved in Conservative politics from the 1890s were ship owners and timber merchants.

The argument is not that such close personal interlocking of bourgeoisie and state apparatus determined the latter's character. A state is capitalist not because it is under the direct control of one or other bourgeois fraction, but because in a capitalist society it has the role of political organiser and unifier of the bourgeoisie, and disorganiser and disunifier of the proletariat. The significance of the heavy representation of the bourgeoisie within the state was mediated by the essential relation—that of the state towards the Protestant masses, and in particular the proletariat. If in contrast to the immediate post-war period the dominant policies appear to have reflected the wishes of traditional capital, it was because of a drop in the level of actual and potential class conflict since the earlier period. The shipyard and engineering workers who had been the prime recruiting ground for the NILP during the war years were relatively quiescent from 1950 to 1957 as the yard and the major plants maintained production. If class relations within the bloc were tranquil this allowed a certain attenuation of the state's relative autonomy to develop, and the tendency appears to have been most marked in the Ministry of Commerce.

When Isles and Cuthbert's survey was published the principal reaction in the Unionist parliamentary party was to ignore it. When its criticisms were raised by Unionists they were confined to the question of the coal trade.[70] Two of the three MPs concerned (Henry Holmes of Belfast Shankill[71] and William Fitzsimmons of Belfast Duncairn) were local bourgeoises. Not only were their criticisms of the coal importers not taken up by other representatives of their class, but when the third MP involved (Edmund Warnock of Belfast St Anne's) became persistent the possibility was raised of expelling him from the party.[72] Although productive capital had no interest in the preservation of restrictive practices, the survey induced a collective desire to close ranks and to ensure that as little open discussion as possible took place.

This recourse was hampered by a further significant rise in unemployment at the end of 1957, following a rise in Bank rate. A minority of critics now linked the question of the effects of national deflationary policy with the accusation that the government was resisting parliamentary discussion of the survey.[73] Eventually, in November, a debate took place. Glentoran attacked many aspects of the report; in particular its suggestion for a Development Corporation 'showed a sorry lack of faith in the vitality of Ulster industry'. He also rejected the authors' contentions about monopolistic practices in shipping.[74] The best the representatives of the local bourgeoisie could do was rally to the somewhat weary cry that whatever the defects of Ulster industry they were the result of the 'unfairness' of existing fiscal arrangements. According to Herbert Kirk (Belfast Windsor), British levels of taxation were inappropriate locally. Together with the consequences of unsuitable national economic policies, they justified a demand for a subsidy from the British Exchequer to offset present 'discriminatory' arrangements.

1958 saw unemployment rise to 10 per cent in the province. In Belfast it rose by almost half. The city's textile industry, which had a heavy concentration of the most viable plants, now felt the force of the depression that had eliminated firms elsewhere in the province earlier in the decade.[75] Prior to the February Stormont general election Brooke went to London for discussions on unemployment. On his return he gave a press conference at which the major announcement was a bland endorsement of UK monetary policy. 'If the value of the pound fell, nothing else mattered.'[76] The election results indicated a weakening of working-class support for Unionism in Belfast, where four seats were lost to the NILP. Three of them were marginal, and there was no question of large-scale defections, but clearly the inability of the government to reduce unemployment was diminishing its authority.

A major crisis for Belfast's economy set in at the close of 1960, when the building programme at Harland & Wolff came to an end at a time of world-wide recession in the industry. Early in 1961 the yard announced that 8,000 of its 21,000 workers would have to be made redundant by the summer. The future of 8,000 workers at Short's was also in doubt, as orders for its main aircraft were insufficient.[77] In response, the Confederation of Shipbuilding and Engineering Unions organised a mass walk-out and a demonstration of over 20,000 workers to demand government action.[78] Further marches were held during the spring as the situation deteriorated. In April the largest spinning firm in the city, which employed 1,700 and had received a substantial amount of government aid, announced it was going into voluntary liquidation.[79] In July the 8,000 shipyard workers were indeed made redundant,[80] and the regional unemployment rate stood at 7 per cent compared with 1·2 per cent nationally. Over the next twelve months 2,000 more were laid off at Harland & Wolff's,[81] and Short's management announced that unless orders were received soon the plant would close. In 1961 there were 20 per cent fewer aircraft workers than three years earlier. In the UK the contraction had been only 5 per cent.[82] By the end of the year a 'Northern Ireland Joint Unemployment Committee' was formed by local trade union branches and the NILP, with the aim of modifying government policy.[83] A 'Save Short's' campaign of demonstrations and meetings was launched. The 1962 May Day march was reckoned to have been one of the largest since the strike of 1919. While the NILP did not gain any extra seats in the Stormont election of 1962, its average share of the vote increased by 15 per cent.[84]

Between 1958 and 1962 discontent with government economic policies grew within the Unionist party. Two factors were at work. One was acute fear, especially among the Belfast MPs, that unless the government took a new initiative the drift to the NILP would intensify. At the UUC annual conference in 1961 there were complaints about government 'lack of energy' on unemployment, and the leader of the UULA delegation suggested the nationalisation of Harland & Wolff.[85] In Stormont Desmond Boal, the new Shankill MP, and Edmund Warnock led the critics. In March Boal supported a critical motion by David Bleakley of the NILP. He blamed the situation on the structure of financial relations with Westminster and the failure of the government to put enough pressure on the Conservatives. In a statement loudly cheered by NILP MPs he said, 'the government must make up its mind whether it owes loyalty to the Conservative party or to the working people of Belfast'.[88] He went on to argue that, as a 'progressive' government, the Unionists should provide full employment.

Yet if at the level of rhetoric Boal appropriated some elements of labourist ideology, the dominant critical response still centred on the long-standing dissatisfaction with existing financial relations. It was most clearly formulated by Warnock.[87] The substance of his position was that Ulster could not support the current burden of taxation. 'Why had Ulster to reply upon outsiders to provide employment? One answer was that the country had been denuded of capital to an extent which crippled development.'[88]

The second source of criticism was pressure from the traditional bourgeoisie for a 'solution' which would mean either a decrease in tax levels or a direct subsidy from Britain. Increasingly the Brooke government's problems arose not from too close a reliance on this class, as Farrell suggests, but from the critical stance it began to adopt.

The effects can clearly be seen by considering briefly the course of inter-government negotiations on the north's economy from 1958 to 1962. When in the 1958 debate on the Isles and Cuthbert survey the demand for a revision of financial relationships had been raised, the Minister of Finance, Terence O'Neill, had replied that Northern Ireland was already favourably treated by the Treasury under the terms of the various post-war agreements on 'leeway'. In particular, he added, she had been allowed a set of industrial inducements more favourable than anywhere else in the UK.[89] Under party and back-bench pressure this attitude changed drastically. In March 1961 Brooke took his principal Ministers to London for the first 'summit' (as the *Newsletter* disarmingly described it) since 1954. All he managed to extract from the Conservatives was a pledge to continue support for existing measures of industrial promotion, together with agreement to initiate a joint study of the unemployment problem and how it might be dealt with (later to emerge as the Hall report).[90]

Any positive effects he might have achieved were erased by the introduction of a UK payroll tax and a mini-budget which increased Bank rate and imposed credit restrictions. The payroll tax enraged the linen bourgeoisie, who claimed it would make their export competitiveness hopeless.[91] O'Neill managed to win the concession that the local government would have a free hand with revenue from the tax. This did not satisfy the bourgeoisie or the *Newsletter,* which became more and more critical of the government.[92] Presently Brooke had yet another meeting with London, and extracted what were announced as further concessions. There would be no slow-down in the industrial programme, local authorities would not be told to curtail any of their work programmes, and building subsidies were to be increased. In addition an Economic Advisory Office was to be created within the Cabinet secretariat under Sir Douglas Harkness (then Permanent Secretary at the Ministry of Finance).[93]

The critics were not placated. In a debate at Stormont in 1961 Warnock reiterated the traditional criticism.[94] O'Neill responded with the equally familiar reply: that solution endangered 'leeway'.[95] The government continued with its twin tactics of creating more jobs (8,000 during 1961) and making concessions to its critics (the rate of grant to firms applying under the CGIA had been increased from 25 to 33·3 per cent in 1959).[96]

The increase in the NILP vote in 1962 and continued economic difficulties further demonstrated the inadequacy of this strategy. In any case, the introduction in Britain of the Local Employment Act, 1960, had decreased the attractiveness of the inducements the Six Counties could offer.[97] The government redoubled its efforts on the joint working party to negotiate an employment subsidy from the Treasury.[98] The proposal was for a grant of 10s a week for all employees in firms qualifying for CGIA aid. It was estimated that an increase of 50 per cent in aid to industry would be involved. Ulster, the argument ran, needed to lower her costs to become competitive: labour was a prime cost, but as wage rates were tending towards parity with the UK a subsidy was the only solution. The second line of argument was that in the future a large proportion of employment would be provided by the staple industries and that it was therefore as essential to maintain employment in them as to promote new ones.

The publication of the Hall report, which was to reject this position, was crucial in the fall of Brooke. Throughout the summer the unions and the NILP had campaigned on the 'Save Short's' issue and for the recall of Stormont.[99] Brooke in response stressed that Hall would resolve all difficulties. 'We are very proud of our contribution to it. We think that the proposals it contains should go a long way to solving some of the problems.'[100] The fact that even at the time there was no definite date for publication indicated to critics (including the *Newsletter*) that the British government was unsympathetic to Brooke's proposals.[101] Meanwhile the problem became more pressing. In August 12,000 workers marched to the City Hall for a mass meeting addressed by NILP, Independent, Nationalist and Eire Labour party MPs. A resolution was passed calling on the Conservative Premier, Harold Macmillan, to take immediate steps to provide contracts and financial assistance for Short's. It was supported by Belfast Chamber of Trade and Unionist city councillors.[102] A NILP petition to recall Stormont gathered 100,000 signatures in four weeks. October saw an announcement that 620 more shipyard workers would be made redundant by November, and that 'two to three thousand more' would be paid off before the end of the year.[103]

A foretaste of the Whitehall position was received the same month. The Home Secretary, Henry Brooke, paid a visit to Belfast. He warned the population not to get the unemployment problem out of focus—'Businessmen would not plant roots where a spirit of desperation was prevalent'.[104] Shortly after, the Northern Ireland Prime Minister again visited London, drawing Macmillan's attention to the political difficulties that would accompany a worsening of the economic situation.[105] The report was published at the end of the month.

The reaction of the *Newsletter* was strongly understated: 'disappointment will be general'.[106]. The report defined the problem as 'essentially to make [Ulster's] industry fully competitive with similar industry in Britain . . . and to do so fast enough to bring about a decrease in present levels of unemployment'. The solution was to reduce costs, principally through greater efficiency and productivity. Contemporary policies were ineffective—on the assumption that the level of economic activity in the UK rose at the same rate as in the '50s, it should be possible to promote an average of 3,500 to 4,000 new jobs a year, compared with 2,500 in the '50s. Yet this would not bring about any reduction in unemployment. Labour migration would have to be encouraged.[107] Industrial policy had been biased toward propping up local industry. The 'ideal' policy would be to ensure that in future allocations of government funds preference was given to encouraging new industries. Existing ones were relatively high-cost producers with no future. A policy which aided them hindered the long-term development of the region. The proposals for subsidising Northern Ireland would have a conservative effect on the structure of industry. The more successful they were in reducing unemployment in declining industries, the less attractive Ulster would be to new firms seeking a pool of available labour. It is of interest to note that there is no evidence in the report that the British side's stress on 'modernisation' and concentration on efficient new industry found any echo among the Ulster delegation.

Brooke's leadership was fatally damaged. In Stormont all he could do was express disappointment and hope that in the 'long term' management and labour would reduce costs by increasing efficiency. The Ministry of Commerce would be redirected to concentrate on industrial development. The *Newsletter* expressed

Unionist demoralisation. The reform 'would have been wiser still a year ago'. The report was a personal crisis for Brooke.[108] Within six months he had resigned and O'Neill was Prime Minister.

Social classes and the crisis of the Brooke administration

An analysis of the political forces at work does not support the notion of a crisis of modernisation brought about by the decline of the traditional bourgeoisie and the rise of multinationals. First, the decline of traditional industry is exaggerated. By 1963 50,000 jobs had been created in government-assisted undertakings since 1945, representing 30 per cent of total employment.[109] Of these, one quarter were in firms of local origin.[110] The traditional bourgeoisie was still the predominant force in the early '60s.[111] What then was its relation to the Brooke government? According to Farrell the state apparatus was the mouthpiece of this class and its sectarian strategy towards the Protestant masses. Yet if there was a close community of interest between the traditional bourgeoisie and the state, specifically the Ministry of Commerce and Parliament, it was concerned with economic strategy rather than ideological and political relations with the Protestant masses. Even in industrial strategy the state was far from a mouthpiece. The crucial concern for dominance over the Protestant masses dictated an industrial strategy aimed at some degree of diversification. Even after the increase of grants under the CGIA it was recognised that the existing structure of incentives favoured incoming firms.[112]* It is this which explains the fact that the overriding criticism of economic policy in the early '60s was the same quaint and archaic one which

---

*Mr Denis Norman's researches provide more evidence for the general tendencies of industrial strategy outlined above but also point to the emergence of important shifts in emphasis in the mid-'50s. From 1949 to 1956 substantial amounts of finance were diverted to subsidising local industry through the RIA and later the CGIA. As a result there was a substantial fall in the number of jobs created annually. This shift in emphasis in favour of the local bourgeoisie was itself attenuated after 1956 because of its dismal results in creating employment. Norman argues that the setting up of the Northern Ireland Development Council under Lord Chandos in 1956 and subsequent substantial increases in spending on industrial attraction represented an attempt to readjust policy which was itself seriously disrupted by the results of the 1958 election.

emerged during the controversy over Dominion status. The crisis for the administration was a product not of the decline of the bourgeoisie but of its continuing strength as a political force.

It is this strength which determined the curiously hybrid nature of local attempts at solving the unemployment problem. The NILP victories of 1958 and their consolidation in 1962, together with a massive rate of actual and threatened redundancies, seemed to presage large-scale working-class defection if drastic action was postponed. To accede to the demands of Warnock and Faulkner would have been to threaten not only welfarism but regional industrial incentives. The result would not just have been to increase the danger of working-class disaffection. It would have meant renouncing the substantial benefits of existing arrangements for an uncertain gamble on the expansionary capacity of the local bourgeoisie. The outcome was a compromise. The proposals to the Hall working party defended existing financial relations and asked for a further subsidy.

The determinant social force in the crisis was the working class, in particular that section of the Belfast Protestant working class which voted NILP. Here was the phenomenon that threw existing industrial strategy into disarray and determined that a 'solution' which involved dismantling existing financial relations would be rejected. It is in this context that Babington's statement to a UULA meeting should be considered. Farrell adduces it as evidence that 'under [Brooke] the Unionists relied on traditional methods to keep their supporters loyal'.[113] In fact Babington's speech was an attack, along populist lines, on government 'inactivity' over unemployment[114]. It was repudiated, and it is noticeable that the relationship of the state to the masses throughout the period had a predominantly secular tone. There appears to have been some recognition that the NILP attacks would have to be answered on their own terms.

'O'Neillism' emerged not as the mouthpiece of a modernising fraction of capital in opposition to Brooke's sectarianism, but rather as an effect of the *impasse* which existing economic policies had reached with the Hall report and the persistence of high unemployment. The *opposition,* not the support, for Brooke came from the traditional bourgeoisie and the champions of an old-time populism.

O'Neill and planning

It is commonly argued that one of the main differences between the Brooke and O'Neill administrations was the importance O'Neill gave to 'planning'. While it is undeniable that in his early years as Prime Minister a rhetoric of regional economic planning was adopted, the significance usually attached to it is problematical. The introduction of planning is seen as heralding the novel policy of relying on multinationals, as opposed to traditional industry. Yet as incentives already favoured incoming firms (to the chagrin of traditional capital) this did not represent any basic change of policy. Where innovations occurred, they were due to the Hall report and its veto on subsidisation of the traditional bourgeoisie. Just as his predecessor had resisted bourgeois attacks upon 'socialistic' laws after the war, so O'Neill had in the post-Hall period to retain dominance over the Protestant working class even if it meant adopting measures that caused friction with local capital.

His new policies were clearly influenced by changes in regional policy at the national level. The depression in many of the heavy industries at the end of the '50s had led to increased unemployment in the British regions and a greater priority for regional policy.[115] This new concern was associated too with the first moves towards national planning. Official ideology about planning moved from a social (unemployment) to a technocratic basis (economic growth). Attention was focused on promoting regional expansion as a contribution to securing a higher national growth rate. The new ideology took shape in steps to establish growth areas and economic planning for the regions. The latter was to be related to physical and transport planning with the aim of 'creating an environment conducive to growth'. The role which new towns and infrastructural investment could play in the creation of a suitable environment was emphasised.

In his first speech as Premier to the annual meeting of the UUC O'Neill outlined a strategy that clearly mirrored the new national ideology. He referred to the Matthew report on physical planning in the province:

> Our task will be transform the face of Ulster. To achieve it will demand bold and imaginative measures. The Matthew Plan suggests a way in which Northern Ireland could capture the imagination of the world.[116]

In October 1963 he informed Stormont that he had set up an inter-departmental inquiry into the potential scope of economic planning in Ulster, with a view to the production of a 'comprehensive' plan. In fact both Matthew and the consequent 'Wilson plan' were a sham. References to 'natural properties' in Matthew's report suggest its inspiration to have been classical rather than technocratic.[117] When Professor Thomas Wilson's report was published in the winter of 1964–65 it too appeared curiously devoid of serious economic calculations. It accepted the Matthew 'growth centre' strategy as given (even though it had little academic support[118]), and argued that the main obstacles to growth were physical rather than financial. Its main proposals were improvements in infrastructure and industrial training[119]. As Steed and Thomas put it,

> Analyses in depth of the expected social and economic transformations were conspicuous by their absence—no studies providing an economic basis for the choice of regional centres, no attempt to analyse the growth potential of various industries located in these towns.[120]

Above all, the blatantly cosmetic character of O'Neillist planning was shown in the fact that no economists were taken on by the government to implement the consultants' recommendations.[121] Planning merely represented, in a phrase which evidently pleased O'Neill, 'stealing Labour's thunder'.[122]

Behind the ideology of 'transforming the face of Ulster', planning represented an intensification of post-war dependence on subsidisation by London. It meant working hard on the leeway argument to extract subsidies for a large-scale public works programme of housing, motorways, a new airport and improved port facilities. If subsidies were to be refused for traditional industry, then the new ideology could at least be used to extract resources providing employment in construction and services.

While this strategy offered the possibility of recuperating Unionist losses amongst the Protestant working class, it was to create new conflicts within the party. The most serious of these before 1965 arose from the effects of the Matthew recommendations on the relationship between central and local government.

One of the main recommendations—a new Ministry of Planning and Development—was originally turned down by the Cabinet. In explaining its decision, W. J. Morgan, Minister of Health and Local Government, observed that the suggestion was the most difficult in the report, and that action on it depended on the outcome of negotiations with the local authorities.[123] The implications of planning for local government were to prove a thorn in O'Neill's flesh.[124]

Subsequent legislation (the New Towns Act (Northern Ireland)) transferred the planning powers of local authorities in development areas to central government. The Ministry responsible—Development—had been created only as a result of O'Neill's adoption of what his critics inside the party referred to a dictatorial style of politics. In the summer of 1964 he attempted to overcome resistance of his proposals by a Ministerial reshuffle, setting up the new department while most of his colleagues were on holiday.[125]

The *Newsletter* observed at the time that the July reshuffle was surprisingly limited in terms of changes in personnel. In fact the paper criticised him for his continuing reliance on Ministers from the Brooke administration.[126] The most significant change was a realignment of Cabinet responsibility which concentrated powers over planning, transport, roads, local government and housing in the Ministry of Health and Local Government, restyled the Ministry of Development in January 1965. The new Ministry, with its task[127] of developing a 'master plan' for Ulster, was the centrepiece of O'Neill's strategy for dealing with the NILP. Right from the beginning, however, it was clear that resistance from local Unionist power centres would have significant effects on the implementation of the strategy. Thus the existing Minister of Health and Local Government, who was believed to have antagonised the Unionist-controlled Belfast Corporation, was replaced by William Craig in a cosmetic attempt at appeasement.

More significantly, actual and potential resistance appears to have had a measurable influence on both the decision to create the 'new city' at Lurgan–Portadown and the Lockwood report's recommendation that a new university be sited at Coleraine. Both projects were vital symbols of 'modernisation' and both were the product of a specific kind of political calculation. It had obviously been decided to treat the inevitably hostile reaction of local Unionists in the west of Ulster as a necessary price for the political benefits to be gained from concentrating resources in the

Protestant 'heartland' of the east. The existence within the Derry Unionist leadership of a significant group that saw 'modernisation as disruptive of the local power structure may have encouraged the O'Neill entourage to hope that resistance to Lockwood would be seriously weakened.[128]

'Modernisation' under O'Neill combined an overriding concern with symbols of a new direction with a series of piecemeal attempts to placate and divide the Unionist opposition at the local level. The controversy over Craigavon and Lockwood was in fact relatively easily contained. It did become linked up with a province-wide resistance to the government's New Towns Bill and its encroachments on the powers of local councils.[129] However, O'Neill was able to placate some of the opposition by emphasising his basic commitment to some of the most traditional aspects of Unionist rule. In a revealing interview with a *Newsletter* reporter he replied to a question about the youth of Ulster getting tired of hearing about 'Derry, Aughrim and the Boyne', 'I do not think we could or should turn our backs on a very honourable tradition which still means a great deal to the majority of Ulster people. What we have to do is to build modern policies upon the foundations which these traditions have given us.'[130] The ideology of modernisation could function quite simply to defend sectarian activity by defining Nationalist and NILP concern as 'reactionary' or 'living in the past'.

The degree to which modernisation was aimed not at dismantling sectarian structures but at denying the legitimacy of a reformist strategy in this area was soon apparent to some of O'Neill's erstwhile liberal supporters. In March 1964 *The Round Table* discussed this question:

> It is indicative of government reluctance to admit that grievances exist and to forestall political attack that the National Assistance Board, the Housing Trust and the newly appointed Lockwood committee on university expansion are without Catholic members'.

It speculated that O'Neill's failure to act would consolidate the growth in the Catholic community of the Campaign for Social Justice and eventually make liberalisation 'from above' impossible. It continued:

> Captain O'Neill's series of speeches on the 'New Ulster', stimulating as these have been in terms of a more modern outlook

1 and country planning ... have not further defined the
; of what he earlier called a 'unity of purpose'. 'A change of
> quote another phrase, has not been applied beyond civic
pride and a quickening of the economy. The impression is that he has
decided that material well-being is enough, without running the risk
of dissension in his party through a direct attempt to ease the
problem of segregation.

O'Neill's economic policies bore no relation to intercommunal
relations. Their *raison d'être* lay only in political conflicts within the
Protestant bloc. In June 1964 his disinclination even to begin the
process of breaking down discrimination was confirmed for *The
Round Table*. Two prominent Catholic professional men had
written a series of letters to him enquiring why he continued to
follow the traditional policy of not appointing Catholics to public
boards. The letters were published because he did not reply. On
the day of publication he attacked the Catholic hierarchy for
maintaining social divisions by insisting on segregated education.[131]
The feebleness of his conciliationism (not to mention its illogicality)
was demonstrated when, within a few days, he made his famous
visit to a Catholic school.

The political concerns of 'O'Neillism' had been determined by
the loss of dominance over a section of the Protestant working
class. The new departure required the centralisation of initiative at
Stormont within a relatively small group of Ministers and civil
servants. This led to charges of Ministerial and bureaucratic
dictatorship from local Unionists. Opposition was manifested
within the parliamentary party itself, especially over the New City
and Lockwood decisions. Nevertheless it is noticeable that up to
the end of 1965 the critics within the party at all levels could still be
treated as a small if vigorous minority. Desmond Boal and Edmond
Warnock attempted to associate O'Neill's meeting with Sean
Lemass, the southern Prime Minister, with the general question of a
secretive and anti-democratic style of operating which supposedly
threatened Ulster's security.[132] But whilst there was undoubted
dissatisfaction in the parliamentary party over particular decisions it
did not reach the level of a significant political division about the
overall direction of government policy. The latter appeared to be
successful in its object of reconstituting Unionist hegemony over
the Protestant working class. The O'Neillite manifesto for the 1965
election crystalised the ideology of modernisation—'Forward

Ulster to Target 1970'. The vote showed an average swing to the Unionist party of 7 per cent and a reversal of the Labour inroads of 1962, with the NILP losing two of its Belfast seats.[133]

The political success of O'Neill's strategy made it difficult for his critics to consolidate what could be represented as merely selfish local concerns. More significant, however, were the clear signs he had given of having no positive strategy for reform in the areas of civil rights and discrimination. The main question for the future development of his administration was whether the disorganised and passive state of Catholic politics would continue to allow him the political space for intra-Unionist dispute to be localised and defused.

Notes to chapter 5

[1] Farrell, *Orange State*, p. 227.

[2] *Belfast Newsletter*, 8 March 1961. But see below, p. 151.

[3] Quoted in Poulantzas, *Political Power*, p. 49.

[4] Farrell, *Orange State*, p. 328.

[5] *Ibid.*, p. 329.

[6] *Ibid.*, p. 329.

[7] L. Althusser, *Lenin and Philosophy and Other Essays* (London, 1971), p. 160.

[8] *Ibid.*, p. 156.

[9] Cf. A. Boserup, *Who is the Principal Enemy?* (Square One pamphlet No. 5, London, 1973).

[10] Cf. Patterson, *Protestant Working Class*.

[11] Gibbon, *Origins*, pp. 112–42.

[12] Farrell, *Orange State*, p. 228.

[13] K. S. Isles and N. Cuthbert, 'Ulster's economic structure', in T. Wilson (ed.), *Ulster under Home Rule* (Oxford, 1955), p. 101.

[14] *Ibid.*, p. 97.

[15] M. D. Thomas, 'Manufacturing industry in Belfast', *Annals of the American Association of Geographers*, 46 (1956), p. 189.

[16] *Ibid.*

[17] K. S. Isles and N. Cuthbert, *An Economic Survey of Northern Ireland* (Belfast, 1957), p. 382.

[18] G. P. Steed, 'Internal organisation, firm integration and locational change: the Northern Ireland linen complex, 1954–64', *Economic Geography*, 47 (1971).

[19] *Ibid.*

[20] One example was the important Herdman company. In this period it acquired two mills, one of which had been recently re-equipped. The mills were dismantled and sold off, whilst the best equipment was transferred to the main Herdman plants in Belfast and Sion Mills (*ibid.*).

[21] Government of Northern Ireland, *Report of the Joint Working Party on the Economy of Northern Ireland*, Cmd 446 (Belfast, 1962) (hereafter 'Hall'), para. 19.

[22] G. P. Steed, 'The changing milieu of a firm: a case study of a shipbuilding concern', *Annals of the Association of American Geographers*, 58 (1968).

[23] G. McCrone, *Regional Policy in Britain* (London, 1969), p. 117.

[24] Steed, 'Changing milieu'.

[25] This process began during the war: in 1939 there were 350 tractors in Ulster, by 1960 30,000 (Hall, para. 23).

[26] *Ibid*.

[27] Hall, paras. 25 and 26; Government of Northern Ireland, *Economic Development in Northern Ireland*, Cmd 479 (hereafter 'Wilson') (Belfast, 1965).

[28] PRONI Cab. 4/604/8.

[29] *Ibid*.

[30] Hall, para. 48.

[31] *Ibid*.

[32] McCrone, *Regional Policy*, p. 115.

[33] *Belfast Newsletter*, 7 January 1946.

[34] PRONI Cab. 4/619/12.

[35] *NIHC*, Vol. XXXI, c. 916.

[36] *Ibid*., Vol. XXXII, c. 579.

[37] *Ibid*., Vol. XXXIV, c. 1928.

[38] *Ibid*., c. 1000.

[39] *Ibid*., c. 1982.

[40] *The Round Table*, XL (1950).

[41] *Ibid*., XLII (1952).

[42] Brian Faulkner was one of the chief proponents of this quaint analysis; cf. *NIHC*, Vol. XXXV, c. 1105.

[43] *The Round Table*, XLI (1951).

[44] See Sinclair's attack on them, *NIHC*, Vol. XXXV, c. 1023.

[45] *The Round Table*, XLII (1952).

[46] *NIHC*, Vol. XXXV, c. 2572.

[47] *Belfast Newsletter*, 20 February 1952.

[48] *The Round Table*, XLII (1952).

[49] Those of Finance, Commerce, Labour and Agriculture.

[50] *Belfast Newsletter*, 19 March 1952.

[51] *Ibid*.

[52] *The Round Table*, XLII (1952).

[53] *Belfast Newsletter*, 3 April 1952.

[54] McCrone, *Regional Policy*, p. 116.

[55] *Ibid*., p. 117.

[56] *Ibid*., p. 117.

[57] *NIHC*, Vol. XXXVIII, c. 1499.

[58] *Ibid*., c. 1830.

[59] *Ibid*.

[60] *The Round Table*, XLIV (1954).

[61] *Belfast Newsletter*, 14 September 1957.

[62] Isles and Cuthbert, *Economic Survey*, p. 382. (It is significant that the survey, unlike the later one by Wilson, was not published as a Command Paper.)

[63] *Ibid*., p. 183.

[64] *Ibid.*, p. 187.

[65] *Ibid.*, p. 189.

[66] *Ibid.*, p. 350.

[67] *Ibid.*, p. 197.

[68] Isles and Cuthbert, 'Ulster's economic structure', p. 101.

[69] From the extremely useful appendix of biographical notes on Unionist MPs in Harbinson, *Ulster Unionist Party*, pp. 188–203.

[70] *Belfast Newsletter*, 23 October 1957.

[71] An ex-chairman of the NILP.

[72] *Belfast Newsletter*, 4 November 1957.

[73] *Ibid.*, 11 October 1957.

[74] *Ibid.*, 14 November 1957.

[75] *The Round Table*, XLIX (1959).

[76] *Belfast Newsletter*, 28 February 1958.

[77] *The Round Table*, LI (1961).

[78] *Belfast Newsletter*, 3 March 1961.

[79] *Ibid.*, 25 April 1961.

[80] *Ibid.*, 21 July 1961.

[81] *Ibid.*, 16 June 1962.

[82] *Ibid.*, 19 and 20 June 1962.

[83] *Ibid.*, 20 October 1961.

[84] *Ibid.*, 1 June 1962.

[85] *Ibid.*, 12 April 1961.

[86] *Ibid.*, 12 April 1961.

[87] In an open letter to Brooke, *ibid.*, 28 April 1961.

[88] *Ibid.*, 24 May, 22 June 1961.

[89] *Ibid.*, 15 November 1957.

[90] *Ibid.*, 12 April 1961.

[91] *Ibid.*, 18 April 1961.

[92] *The Round Table*, LI (1961).

[93] *Ibid.*

[94] *Belfast Newsletter*, 26 October 1961.

[95] *Ibid.*

[96] *Belfast Newsletter*, 23 June 1962.

[97] Hall, p. 11.

[98] *Ibid.*

[99] *Belfast Newsletter*, 23, 26, 27 June 1962.

[100] *Ibid.*, 19 July 1962.

[101] *Ibid.*, 23 July 1962.

[102] *Ibid.*, 18 August 1962.

[103] *Ibid.*, 13 October 1962.

[104] *Ibid.*, 3 October 1962.

[105] *Ibid.*, 16 October 1962.

[106] *Ibid.*, 24 October 1962.

[107] Hall, p. 11.

[108] *Belfast Newsletter*, 31 October 1962.

[109] Wilson.

[110] Hall, p. 75.

[111] It should be noted in passing that the traditional bourgeoisie should not be thought of as a wholly local one. Isles and Cuthbert estimated that

about a third of total paid-up capital in all public and private companies registered in Northern Ireland was owned outside the province (*Economic Survey*, p. 161). In a sample of public companies it was as high as 76 per cent. The investment of mainly British external capital in both shipbuilding and engineering sectors became significant in the inter-war period (although John Brown's had bought a controlling interest in Harland & Wolff as early as 1906). This non-local section of traditional capital does not appear to have been interested in asserting an independent line in local politics or employment practices.

[112] Hall, p. 50.

[113] Farrell, *Orange State*, p. 227.

[114] *Belfast Newsletter*, 8 March 1961.

[115] McCrone, *Regional Policy*, p. 120.

[116] *Belfast Newsletter*, 6 April 1963.

[117] The three major reasons Matthew gave for siting the new city (Craigavon) in north Armagh were: '(1) [the] location . . . beyond the head of the Lagan valley is in the *natural direction of development* . . . (2) [Lurgan/Portadown] have good rail connections . . . and can easily be linked to the proposed motorway . . . *their proximity to Lough Neagh could take advantage of water transport should it develop* . . . (3) *The configuration of the land is well suited to building* . . .' (emphasis added). Government of Northern Ireland, *Belfast Regional Plan*, Cmnd 451 (Belfast, 1963), p. 37.

[118] M. D. Thomas, 'The Northern Ireland case', in United Nations Research Institute for Social Development, *The Role of Growth Poles and Growth Centres in Regional Development* (Geneva, 1968).

[119] Wilson, pp. 188–90. It should be said in mitigation that some of Wilson's recommendations were not included in the accompanying White Paper, in particular that the government enter into negotiations with the Industrial and Commercial Finance Corporation about the possibility of establishing a new finance agency, and that it set up a full-scale enquiry into cross-channel shipping charges (*Belfast Newsletter*, 3 February 1965).

[120] G. P. Steed and M. D. Thomas, 'Regional industrial change in northern Ireland', *Annals of the Association of American Geographers*, 61 (1971).

[121] The number of economists (other than agricultural economists) employed by the Northern Ireland government in 1963 was two. In 1968 it was still two. (*NIHC*, Vol. LXIX, c. 1404–5.)

[122] T. O'Neill, *Autobiography*, p. 47.

[123] *Belfast Newsletter*, 9 May 1963.

[124] It prompted a sharp reaction from local authorities (*ibid.*, 4 July 1964).

[125] *The Round Table*, 216 (1964).

[126] *Belfast Newsletter*, 23 and 24 July 1964.

[127] *Belfast Newsletter*, 30 December 1964.

[128] The role of Derry Unionists in resisting the idea of expanding the local Magee College as an alternative to Coleraine was first underlined in an article by Ralph Bossence in *The Newsletter*, 19 February 1965.

[129] In 1965 the Ulster Unionist Conference passed a resolution condemning 'the dictatorial outlook of recent government planning proposals' (*Belfast Newsletter*, 1 May 1965).

[130] *The Round Table*, 214 (1964).

[131] *The Round Table*, 215 (1964).
[132] *Belfast Newsletter*, 4 January 1965.
[133] J. A. V. Graham, '*The consensus-forming strategy of the NILP*', unpublished M.Sc. thesis, Queen's University, Belfast (1972), p. 183.

6

COLLAPSE, 1965–72

In 1972, after little more than fifty years of devolved power, the British government terminated the existence of an autonomous administration in Northern Ireland. Parliament at Stormont was prorogued, and the civil service absorbed in to a new Northern Ireland Office under a Secretary of State who was to take responsibility for most Stormont Ministers' former functions. This process coincided with the administrative centralisation of almost all the hotly disputed functions of local government in Northern Ireland. Jointly these events signified the end of the state in Northern Ireland.

Formally speaking, the death of the state was occasioned by the refusal of its last Prime Minister, Brian Faulkner, to cede responsibility for security matters to Westminster. In fact, as one historian has already pointed out, 'the move was evidently well prepared. It seems clear that the threat to take over Stormont's security powers was only a way to precipitate a crisis . . .'.[1] The British actually dismantled Stormont because it had ceased to deliver ruling class dominance and the subordination of the masses. The real collapse took place not on 24 March 1972 but during the preceding four years, as a result of an unprecedented combination of developments. This conjuncture, and its relation to some of the tendencies already described, are the subject of this chapter. For the collapse of the state was just as dependent on the regime's historically specific qualities as its survival had been.

There is an enormous range of interpretations of the failure of the state in Northern Ireland and little consensus even about its principal empirical dimensions. Nevertheless most commentators have generally agreed in emphasising three issues. First, the changes in Catholic politics associated with the rise of the civil rights movement. These have generally been treated as the political expression of a novel social and economic force in the province, a Catholic middle class. Second, the policies of the British government. There is no agreement on what these policies were, though, let alone their precise effects. Third, there is the issue of divisions within Unionism, the main subject of this study. Broadly speaking, Unionist differences in the period have been attributed to the same process which purportedly led to the rise of O'Neillist 'reformism' in the early '60s—a polarisation between declining, reactionary traditional capital and progressive, modernising monopoly capital. This polarisation is said to have intensified as a result of an increasing 'dissolution effect' of the latter upon the former. While their interpretation will be disputed, these three dimensions of the state's collapse may be taken as a starting point.

Changes in Catholic politics

In 1968–72 the politics of the Catholic population underwent a fundamental restructuring. The process was characterised by two main trends. Firstly, almost the entire Catholic population became a united militant political force, at least for a short time in 1968–69. This unity was to swallow most nationalist-oriented organisations and assumed institutional form with the creation of the Social Democratic and Labour Party in August 1970. Secondly, and somewhat paradoxically, there was the reappearance after 1969 of a strong republican undertow—especially in the most deprived Catholic urban areas—which was to find expression in the Provisional IRA.

The first of these trends was unprecedented in Northern Ireland, at least since the formation of the state. Directly and indirectly its effects were dramatic. Terence O'Neill was prevented from consolidating a moderate political centre and the stage was set for the events that were to lead to direct rule. The second, parallel impulse, which began to make itself felt more strongly after August 1969, amplified the overall effect of Catholic political mobilisation while simultaneously reducing the ability of its formal leadership to 'deliver' support for any particular compromise it was offered.

For a prolonged period this twin tendency, towards formal unity on the one hand and the recreation of a familiar kind of disunity on the other, was to be buried beneath a general celebration of Catholic political mobilisation as such. So novel was the scale of this development that it intoxicated the Catholic masses and their political representatives alike. Bernadette Devlin observed that the atmosphere in Derry in January 1969, at the conclusion of the march from Belfast organised by People's Democracy, was 'like that of V Day: the war was over and we had won'.[2] The sentiment was to surface frequently in the next three years. Shortly before Bloody Sunday, Austin Currie addressed an anti-internment rally in Falls Park in equally triumphalist terms:

> When Brian Faulkner turns on his TV set and sees the crowd here, by God, it will be the longest day of his life. Reginald Maudling came on TV and said we should be prepared to talk. I say to him, why the hell should we be prepared to talk to him ? Because we are winning and he is not . . . Even if Maudling got down on his bended knees and kissed all our backsides we would not be prepared to talk . . .[3]

Mobilisation itself was being accounted victory.

The novelty both of Catholic mass activity and the relative unity which became associated with it is best appreciated by a glance at post-war Ulster Catholic politics.[4] The major political division in the Catholic population between 1945 and 1965 was that between town and country. Rural areas were dominated by the Nationalist party, a segmentary political organisation embracing all constitutionally minded Catholic activists. Supporters not only of the old Redmondite party, but of Cumann na nGaedheal/Fine Gael and Fianna Fail had fallen in behind the Nationalists long before the war. Until the 1960s, however, the Nationalists had no party apparatus to speak of. Most parliamentary candidates were still selected by conventions dominated by the clergy and middle class of the small towns. Their only form of organisation was often the registration committee which doubled for the Republican candidates who by mutual agreement stood in place of Nationalists at Westminster elections. In 1965, as a result both of Sean Lemass suggesting they become an official parliamentary opposition[5] and of increasing competition from Belfast MPs, the Nationalists endeavoured to create a proper political machine.

Catholic politics in Belfast and one or two larger towns (e.g. Dungannon) were somewhat different. Until the 1940s most of the Catholic vote in these areas was accounted for by the NILP (which until late in the decade took no explicit line on partition). In some constituencies (e.g. Oldpark) this continued to be the case during the '60s. In constituencies where Catholics formed a reasonable majority, however, the NILP never recovered from its 'constitutional' stand. In its place appeared various versions of Catholic labourism. According to Rumpf and Hepburn,

The confusing multiplicity of party labels in the Central, Dock, Pottinger and Falls constituencies between 1945 and 1969 was the result of an inability on the part of local politicians to agree on what sort of anti-partitionist party should fill the vacuum created by the expulsion of both the Nationalists and the NILP from Belfast Catholic politics. The main difficulty was simply that there were fewer seats than there were aspirants, while there were no compensating pressures to encourage political unity . . .[6]

Catholic politics in post-war Belfast were characterised by competition between hustling politicians with a labourist rhetoric and personal followings established by brokerage. By 1966 the one with the largest following was Gerry Fitt, whose election to Westminster that year as a 'Republican Labour' candidate was to prove significant.

The Catholic masses meanwhile showed considerable apathy towards these forces. Actual numbers involved in any organisation, whether Nationalist, Catholic labourist or Republican, were minimal. The bread and butter of Catholic politicians remained patronage and brokerage. Fitt, for example, despite forays into 'Connolly socialism', was as suspicious of the professionalism and secularism of the Northern Ireland Housing Trust as back-bench Unionists and Nationalists:

> Mr Fitt. . . . One of the points of criticism in which members of both sides have joined over a period of time is that as elected representatives we should have some say . . .
>
> Miss Murnaghan. They should have none at all.
>
> Mr Fitt. It is quite all right for the Hon. and learned member for Queen's University to say that we should have no say at all, but she has got no constituency interest in this . . .[7]

The vehicle for the unparalleled Catholic popular mobilisation which this stiuation gave way to was of course not the Nationalist party, nor the political retinues of figures like Fitt, but the civil rights movement, an entirely new force.

The first and subsequently most influential interpretation of the movement's wide appeal was that its growth was due to the emergence in the 1960s of a 'much larger Catholic middle class . . . which is less ready to acquiesce in the situation of assumed (or established) inferiority and discrimination than was the case in the past'.[8] This stratum was created by the extension of secondary and higher education to Catholics after the war, an innovation which had a dual effect. Integration into the British educational system, particularly in higher education, supposedly diminished the appeal of Republicanism to the post-war generation, leading it to demand a role within the state. The civil rights movement was an expression of that demand.

While aesthetically pleasing, the 'Cameron interpretation' is deficient in a number of ways. Firstly, its protagonists offer little or no empirical evidence for the 'expansion' of the Catholic middle class nor even any precise definition of who comprised this class.[9] Secondly, as will be seen, Catholic middle-class political activity in the immediately preceding period evinced little evidence of any general trend towards secularisation and moderation as a consequence of educational changes. Thirdly, and most strikingly of all, this interpretation fails to show why such a narrow impulse should have generated such broad appeal and impact. Even if the 'expansion of the Catholic middle class' thesis is accurate in identifying the source of civil rights agitation, it hardly shows why the movement was to acquire an irreversible momentum among the Catholic population at large.

The problems underlying these difficulties may perhaps best be solved by an empirical investigation of the Cameron hypothesis. In 1975 E. A. Aunger published a review of the results of the 1961 and 1971 Northern Ireland censuses of religion and occupational class.[10] His figures indicate that in the intercensal period there was virtually no change in the social structure of the male Catholic population.[11] The finding that the male Catholic middle class was immobile rather than expanding might itself be thought sufficient ground for rejecting the Cameron argument, but it should rightly be placed in the context of a longer-term view of changes in social structure.[12] The censuses of 1926, 1937 and 1951 lacked the necessary tabulation of occupation by religious affiliation, but that of 1911 did not. Its results are retabulated here as far as possible according to procedures identical to those employed by Aunger.[13] (The figures include all economically active males and females; because these figures were not available for 1961, comparison is made only with Aunger's figures for 1971.)[14]

The last sixty years have, of course, been characterised by substantial general changes in social structure, even in modern industrial societies. The most notable have been a decline in the numbers employed in agriculture, a dilution of the craft skills of the

Table 3   *Religion and occupational class, Northern Ireland, 1911 and 1971(%)*

Occupational class	Catholic		Protestant		Total	
	1911	1971	1911	1971	1911	1971
Professional, managerial	5	12	8	15	7	14
Lower-grade non-manual	23	19	18	26	20	24
Skilled manual	24	17	34	19	31	18
Semi-skilled manual	28	27	22	25	24	26
Unskilled	20	25	18	15	18	18

N (1911) = 423,448; (1971) = 564,682
Source. See text and appendix.

manual working class and an expansion of intermediate and higher-grade non-manual strata.[15] The trends were reflected in Ulster as in the rest of the kingdom. Notable in Northern Ireland, however, is the way in which the last two of these trends have worked out differently for Catholics and Protestants. Starting from a position in 1911 in which they were disproportionately over-represented in semi-skilled manual and non-manual occupations, and under-represented in skilled manual and non-manual ones, Catholics have moved towards a position where they are today over-represented in unskilled manual occupations and under-represented in semi-skilled non-manual ones. In other words, Catholic 'wastage' from semi-skilled non-manual and skilled manual occupations has been polarised into skilled non-manual and unskilled manual ones. This trend is in marked contrast to changes in the Protestant social structure, where skilled manual labour has been displaced fairly evenly into all other strata except the unskilled. The proportion of unskilled Protestant workers has indeed actually fallen.

While the figures therefore to some extent confirm the Cameron hypothesis they show that it describes only part of the overall picture. The proportion of Catholics in professional and managerial occupations has risen sharply—more sharply in fact than for the population of the province as a whole. But two other conclusions are equally significant. First, expansion at the top end of the Catholic social scale has been balanced by an expansion at the other end. Second, most of the changes seem to have taken before 1961 and not to have been directly related to ved educational provisions after 1944.[16] (The provisions were in any case delayed in their local implementations.)

These qualifications illuminate the question of the origins and effects of the civil rights movement more than the original hypothesis. The movement's timing in relation to structural change suggests a specific political trigger to Catholic middle-class impulses for reform in the mid and late '60s rather than a purely economic one. On the other hand, the expansion at the base of the Catholic social structure throws light on why the movement should have had popular impact among the working class, whose enthusiasm was to prove more enduring than that of its leadership.

A possible trigger to Catholic middle-class political activity in the '60s that has often been mentioned is a growing awareness of Protestant monopolisation of recent expansion in the state sector of the economy and infrastructure.[17] *The Plain Truth*,[18] *Fermanagh Facts*[19] and other civil rights publications concentrated much of their attention upon the non-absorption of the Catholic professional classes into public service. Indeed, as has been noted, O'Neill was criticised by liberal Unionists as early as 1964 for failing to encourage appointments of this kind. No doubt there were real grievances amongst the middle class, but grievances alone do not generate political involvement. Two factors which had a bearing upon mobilisation as such appear to have been the return of a Labour government to Westminster in 1964, and the response of the Nationalist party to O'Neillism.

There can be little doubt that the Labour victory of 1964 raised Catholic political expectations. Obviously it made the position of Unionism somewhat delicate. Moreover it invoked other echoes. The period of the last Labour government in Britain (1945–51) had seen a large-scale mobilisation of Irish Catholics in the anti-partition campaign of 1949. Though in most respects a dismal failure, the campaign had succeeded in establishing a core of committed anti-Unionists within the parliamentary Labour party. Thirty Labour MPs became associated with Geoffrey Bing's 'Friends of Ireland' group, and many more—including Harold Wilson—could be regarded as sympathetic. Some of this group were to provide the nuculeus of Paul Rose's 'Campaign for Democracy in Ulster', founded in June 1965 at a meeting attended by sixty Labour MPs.[20] The CDU gained impetus with the return of

Gerry Fitt to Westminster in 1966, and its membership soon rose to ninety.[21] Evident numerical support and general sympathy in Parliament for the Campaign created a favourable atmosphere within Northern Ireland for a 'responsible' reform movement. Equally significantly, it was to have an important effect upon the forms of public protest the movement was to adopt. Another influential factor was developments within the Nationalist party, and local Catholic politics generally, in the period 1965–66. The O'Neill–Lemass meeting of 1965 had been the occasion of the Nationalist party's official reversion to constitutional opposition, but it had been edging in that direction for some time before. While retaining an essentially conservative outlook on social and economic questions, the party moved rapidly towards a conciliatory stance on community relations immediately after O'Neill's accession. It not only responded to O'Neill's gestures with what Farrell has called 'pathetic gratitude',[22] but reciprocated them disproportionately. In particular, traditional hostility to the security forces was abated noticeably. In 1963 one of the party's senators described the RUC as 'a fine body of men who are doing a good job'.[23] By February, 1968, when it was proposed at Stormont to grant a supplementary estimate of £29,000 for the B Specials, the party leader, Eddie McAteer, agreed to the proposal without qualification.[24] Reception of the administration's other policies was equally gentle, not to say deferential. When in April 1968 the government announced the appointment of Professors Wilson, Matthew and Parkinson as consultants for the 1970 economic plan, McAteer fatuously remarked, 'That would be a hell of a half-back line—those three.'[25] Indeed, as McAteer was himself to reveal inadvertently during the February 1968 debate on Brookeborough's retirement from Stormont, the party's assumption of official opposition had had the practical effect of opposition being renounced completely:

In some way or another I am reminded of a very recent experience which I had discussing with a veteran Nationalist some of the difficulties surrounding the new soft-line approach. I talked for some time and I recall that he looked at me sorrowfully and said, 'Ah, sure, Eddie, there is hardly any such thing as politics now at all . . .'[26]

The Nationalist party had vacated its traditional role, possibly as much in response to the prevailing religious ecumenism as to local political realities, without finding a new one. This was most apparent on civil rights questions. Individual Nationalists continued to raise cases of discrimination against their constituents, but the party had a less coherent approach to the issue than either the Liberals or the NILP.[27] When a Unionist White Paper on local government was discussed early in 1968 McAteer was obliged to confess, 'I want to say frankly that our party's view has not yet fully crystallised on this subject.'[28]

Probable external receptiveness to a local 'civil rights' campaign, together with the Nationalist party's loss of direction, ushered in a general period of fluidity and competition in Catholic politics, which created opportunities for marginal groups of Marxist revolutionaries to capture the stage briefly. The tendency was strongest in Derry, where after the riots of 5 October 1968 it impelled the local middle classes to head off what was perceived as growing popular support for Eamonn McCann:

> ... word got round during the afternoon that 'all interested parties' were meeting to 'consider the situation' ... In the room upstairs there were about a hundred and twenty people. The Catholic business community, the professions, trade union officialdom and the Nationalist party were well represented ... Various speakers congratulated us on the marvellous work we had done over the past few months. A few expressed their regrets, apologies, etc, that they had not 'been so active in the past as I would have liked'. All urged we now all worked together . . .[29]

The truth is not, as Cameron suggests, that a newly radicalised Catholic middle class dropped from the sky (or at least from post-Butler secondary and higher education). While growing in numbers, the middle class actually remained remarkable more for its conservative than for its radical qualities.[30] The situation was rather one in which the social basis, the political space and impetus and the opportunity of apparent success for a middle-class reform movement all coincided.

The movement's instantaneous popularity is another matter. Two factors, already mentioned in passing, may be considered here. Firstly it is evident from the statistical account of changes in social structure that the relative position of the Catholic lower strata deteriorated during the existence of the Northern Ireland state. Most significantly, while everywhere else (including the Protestant community) the unskilled section of the working class was diminishing as a proportion of the work-force, in the Catholic community it was actually increasing. No less than a quarter of the non-agricultural work-force was consigned to the residuum of unskilled labour, excluded not only from political life but also from social rewards. This sector constituted an immense reservoir of opposition to Unionism and indifference to moderation.

The stimulus for the involvement of this and other strata of the Catholic population in the civil rights movement was partly provided by the new-found activism of influential and respected, not to say patrimonial, community figures, as McCann has pointed out.[31] Perhaps more importantly, it was provided by the forms of public protest which this stratum had specifically devised as a means of capturing the outside world's attention and sympathy. While these forms of protest—the street march, the sit-down, etc.—had their immediate pedigree in the moderate American civil rights movement and were intended to evoke its image, in practice their impact in Northern Ireland was at variance with this secular inspiration.

In Ulster demonstrations had distinctly non-secular implications. Marches in particular meant, and still mean, the assertion of territorial sectarian claims. To march in or through an area is to lay claim to it. When so many districts are invested with confessional significance by one bloc or another, undertaking a 'secular' march creates the conditions for territorial transgressions and counter-transgressions. Most incidents of this nature occurred, as a matter of probability, in the inner urban areas inhabited by the unskilled as efforts at secular demonstrations spilled from town centres to adjacent zones. Quite apart from any independent sectarian attraction such demonstrations may have had for a portion of the population, they inevitably had a further tendency to involve involuntarily the unskilled working class, possibly in submission to arbitrary violence. This tendency gave rise to feelings of local solidarity and thus to the creation of 'militant areas' on behalf of civil rights.

Catholic unity reached its high point under the leadership of the Catholic middle class late in 1968 and early in 1969. Its volatile and somewhat contradictory character was exemplified in the remarkable selection (and subsequent election) of a Trotskyist woman, Bernadette Devlin, as pan-Catholic candidate for Mid-Ulster in the spring of 1969. Thereafter, and without ever having been complete,[32] unity declined. The circumstances in which it did so were to reflect the disparity within the movement's social basis and to be critical for future developments.

As sections of both the Catholic and Protestant communities became more belligerent in the early summer of 1969, leading figures of the previous year lost influence to a greater or lesser degree, particularly in working class districts. As early as May 1969 members of People's Democracy were ejected from Ardoyne.[33] As popular participation in public demonstrations increased, so did the unsought involvement of entire areas in violence, which became commonplace, even casual.[34] These events escalated into the quasi-civil war of August 1969, when the prevalence of intimidation and flight mobilised entire districts. The 'breakdown of public order' in July and August 1969 led to the evacuation of 1505 of Belfast's 28,616 Catholic households.[35] Such ills inevitably inspired local remedies—barricades, vigilantes, citizens' defence committees, etc. Where these prevailed, the leadership of the professional middle classes was broken.

Yet while conditions at one level were working towards a breakdown in the effective social unity of the Catholic community, other factors were promoting the formal institutionalisation of its political unity. Principal among these was British military intervention in August 1969 and the support it implied from British public opinion for amelioration of the Catholic position. As the formal civil rights organisations were now either in abeyance or had lost their authority, pressures which had begun after the collapse of the Nationalist party in 1969 to favour a reorganised 'United Opposition' intensified. These were perhaps increased by the common desire of most Catholic politicians to isolate Bernadette Devlin, who they perceived as bringing their cause into disrepute.[36] Even so, competing personal ambitions seem to have delayed the setting up of the SDLP for a further year. Once formed, however, it rapidly came to monpolise Catholic political representation.[37]

Although Catholics now had a more effective political voice, the SDLP found that in some districts it had at least to coexist with a new, localistically oriented current of Republicanism which had evolved from the 'local solutions' of August 1969. While Unionist policies became more extreme in 1971 and 1972 this undertow, crystallising in the Provisional IRA, temporarily dictated the pace and content of the SDLP's moves. Unionism faced a more determined opposition than ever before. Yet despite its relative homogeneity, the authority and internal control of its constitutional leaders were weak. This discrepancy was to redouble the obstacles to Unionist dominance.

There remains the question of how this restructuring of Catholic politics, which proved so full of difficulties for Unionism, was influenced by the tendencies embodied in the apparatuses of the state prior to 1968. They appear to have affected it in two clear ways.

The more extensive effects were those due to the exclusivism institutionalised by successive Unionist regimes. The most obvious consequences were the well known grievances over status among the Catholic middle class and the steady augmentation of a reservoir of potential support for extreme politics among unskilled Catholic workers. A corollary of these largely administrative and economic aspects was a political exclusivism towards the Catholic political parties which, with some Nationalist collusion, deprived Catholics of effective political representation. When a slightly more accommodating stance was eventually taken by Terence O'Neill, Unionist exclusivism ironically took a still heavier toll. Continued Unionist preoccupation with the border as the only permissible area of political controversy had enabled the Nationalist party to survive as a credible political force despite its almost total lack of formal organisation and hence of close communication with its constituency. The party's lack of contact with informed middle-class Catholic opinion was to rebound on it when in response to O'Neill's gestures it chose to adopt 'pathetic gratitude' as a political line.

A second aspect of the Unionist state apparatus directly affecting the restructuring of Catholic politics was the mutual insulation between it and the British state, tacitly and directly encouraged by both regimes. As will be seen, the consequences were most severe for British and above all Unionist politics. Its effects on Catholic politics were nonetheless real. The fact that civil rights leaders recognised its existence dictated the spectacular forms of public protest which they devised, and which had local repercussions well beyond their original intentions. Perhaps, however, this insulation had a further consequence with as much impact as any of those mentioned. It led to a common lack of cynicism about British politicians' intentions among both Catholics and Protestants. There seems little reason to doubt that both communities believed their grievances would ultimately be remedied, one way or another. For the leadership of the Catholic community this seems to have acted as a restraining influence. Perhaps above all it prevented major political defections from that most conservative of communities. Had Catholic politicians taken a more militant stand in 1971–72, for example, they would surely have been overplaying their hand. As recent research has shown, even at the height of the rent and rate strike of that year less than a quarter of the province's Catholic households were taking part.[38] Traditional conservative nationalism never really showed its face between 1968 and 1972, but it is far from clear that it disappeared. By holding the movement back in the way it did, the SDLP was to keep this force submerged and so maintain a high degree of pressure on Unionism.[39]

The policy of the British state

There is some dispute whether the British state had an Irish policy at all in the period 1965–72 (not to say since 1972). Cecil King and Joe Haines have categorically stated that it did not.[40] Most of the left-wing literature, on the other hand, inspired possibly by the Trotskyist dictum 'the bourgeosie thinks in decades and centuries', have concluded that a coherent British ruling-class strategy did exist but that its implementation was obstructed and modified by events.

Evidence can be produced to support both views. The apparently frank memoirs of both Haines and Richard Crossman show that discussion of the Irish question in the Cabinet was perfunctory, inconclusive and ill informed (at one stage in his diary Crossman refers to 12 July as St Patrick's Day). On the other hand, leading British politicians with special Irish interests were in the habit of regularly making public statements embodying reformist zeal and seeming to disclose an intention of initiating long-term structural reforms.

To determine the real nature of British strategy it is necessary to examine the determinants of ruling-class opinion on this question, and the general political objectives of the Wilson and Heath governments.

First, the development of ruling-class interest as regards Ireland, north and south, after 1925. Between the wars two economic trends in Anglo-Irish relations stand out. One is the completion of large-scale British landed disinvestment in southern Ireland. The landed British had been withdrawing since the Land War but even in 1921 retained substantial interests. Against general imperial trends[41] these were now almost wholly terminated. While commercial and financial investment was maintained, the value of property sold off before 1939 well exceeded new investment.[42] The other is the increasing marginality of Northern Ireland's bourgeoisie. At one stage of the nineteenth century it could almost have been regarded as an integral part of the metropolitan bourgeoisie, not simply sharing the latter's sources of finance but engaged in substantially the dominant industrial pursuits—shipbuilding and textiles. After 1925 an increasing disparity became evident. Ulster saw very little of the 'rationalisation' applied to these industries in Britain and none of the growth of monopolistically shaped consumer industries which in the Midlands and south-east came to dominate the industrial sector of the metropolitan bourgeoisie.

In the post-war period the currency of this trend not only in Northern Ireland but in Wales, Scotland and parts of England too became recognised as the 'regional problem'. Regional bourgeoisies were considered backward, inflexible and incapable of delivering full employment. While not seeking to disengage themselves from them entirely, the metropolitan bourgeoisie's relation to its regional counterparts was no longer one of simple solidarity. As marginalisation continued, some enterprises were forced to site plants in the regions to avoid so-called 'overheating' in the metropolitan areas, while others went there voluntarily to take advantage of investment incentives and relatively cheap labour. To this extent the economic interests of the metropolitan ruling class were physically extended. Yet the overall amount of investment was relatively small and in general the regions were an economic embarrassment. By the 1970s the *annual* subvention to Northern Ireland easily exceeded the total amount of modern industrial capital there.[43]

Politically speaking, too, Ireland became marginal after 1925. By 1940 Ulster demonstrably had no part in the long-term political and strategic calculations of the British ruling class. That summer Churchill effectively offered the province to de Valera on condition that he joined Britain in the war against Germany.[44] The Empire was no longer considered an inviolable entity, and a strong current of opinion favoured intelligent adjustments to local opinion wherever it became organised, or even sacrificing large slices of territory where expedient. In the post-war period both the Empire and Ireland became even less important political considerations. At any rate, no coherent force within the British ruling class lobbied for the question to be reopened.

One political consideration not touched upon should be mentioned. This was Anglo-American relations. Because an Irish cultural identity persisted among a substantial sector of the American people the US government felt periodically obliged to take up the mantle of guarantor of Irish national aspirations. After the second world war, with the emergence of the 'special relationship' (heavy British economic, political and military dependence on the USA), the potential significance of American government opinion increased.

A second general determinant of policy towards Northern Ireland was the institutional form of state-to-state relations between Britain and the province. These relations were largely conducted through Parliament, the Treasury and the Home Office. Constitutionally, Britain began insulating herself from the affairs of the Northern Ireland state even before partition took place. The process was completed by 1923 when the first definitive ruling was given that matters of administration for a Minister in Northern Ireland could not be discussed.[45] In so far as this convention was modified it was on the terms of the Unionists.

A process of insulation is also evident in the practices of the Treasury and the Home Office. The Treasury's control of financial matters has been discussed at length, and only two remarks will be made here. First, financial relations between the two areas, which had always been to Northern Ireland's benefit, became more and more so. Second, the Treasury's autonomy in handling these relations appears to have been very extensive indeed. It is doubtful whether Ministerial decisions were involved in all the post-war period. Certainly Crossman did not recall them coming up before the Cabinet:

> Neither Jack Diamond nor the Chancellor knew the formula by which Northern Ireland gets its money. In all these years it has never been revealed to the politicians and I am longing to see whether now we shall get to the bottom of this very large and expensive secret . . .[46]

Predictably, they did not.[47] The major *quid pro quo* of all this, from the Treasury's point of view, seems simply to have been that the Northern Ireland Ministry of Finance satisfy Whitehall that they were applying Treasury-style monetary management policy and techniques.

The Home Office was theoretically the main channel of inter-state relations, and Northern Ireland affairs were strictly speaking the responsibility of the Home Secretary. Yet just as in practice the various state departments in Britain serve as 'sponsors' of particular economic and political forces, rather than as executors of an independently conceived government policy, so the Home Office over the years acquired the role of sponsoring the Unionist interest in British ruling-class circles. This was made stunningly clear by Sir Frank Newsam, Permanent Under-Secretary of State at the Home Office in 1954. Newsam listed the Northern Ireland functions of the Home Secretary as follows:

> 1. To act as the official channel of communication between the Governments of the United Kingdom and Northern Ireland.
> 2. To ensure that Northern Ireland's constitutional rights are not infringed and to watch Northern Ireland's interests generally.
> 3. To safeguard her interests with regard to schemes under the Agricultural Marketing Acts...
> 4. To ensure that the views of the Government of Northern Ireland on matters affecting them are made known to the Government of the United Kingdom.
> Questions of law and order are entirely for the Government of Northern Ireland...[48]

He added:

> Personal contacts that have been established between Home Office officials and their Northern Ireland colleagues have led to mutual understanding and goodwill in the handling of thorny problems, despite occasional differences of opinion. The Northern Ireland Government has attached to the Home Office a responsible member of their Civil Service so that close liason may be maintained both with the Home Office and with other departments of the United Kingdom Government. The Home Office has found this arrangement most helpful.[49]

Charles Brett, a Northern Ireland Labour Party leader who in the mid-'60s made considerable efforts to persuade the Labour government to adopt a more active reformist position on Ulster, recorded: 'The Home Office officials were not only unhelpful, they were downright obstructive, and we had grounds for believing they were secretly furnishing Stormont with reports to Labour Ministers.[50]

This situation seems to have prevailed as late as 1971. According to Joe Haines, a senior civil servant assisting Wilson and himself on a trip to Ireland had never been to the south. Such visits were 'not encouraged'[51] by the Home Office.

Not only was Northern Ireland economically and politically marginal for the British bourgeoisie, but the latter had done much to keep it so. The forces for retaining such a relationship were powerful, outside and inside the state apparatuses. It would have required a major strategic departure to implement or even formulate a reformist strategy for Ireland.[52]

A third general determinant of British strategy was the political objectives of contemporary British governments.

Initially the Labour government of 1964 declaimed reformist intentions of a general sort. Labour rhetoric envisaged considerable structural change, particularly in the economy, where its programme was one of energetic modernisation. This was supposed to involve 'putting teeth' into planning (with a National Plan), blunting what was perceived as the excessive influence of the Treasury and the City (through the DEA), regional development, industrial reorganisation and insistence that growth in incomes should be tied to advances in productivity. The objectives of modernisation and a higher growth rate naturally required a favourable economic climate, however. As the government saw it, the most obvious route to this climate was devaluation. But devaluation was held to involve unacceptable political costs. Opposition to it came from the City, which believed the consequent reduction in sterling balances would damage its international position, and from the United States, which believed it would lead to a run on the dollar. Both advanced the rather curious argument that calls for devaluation were inspired by de Gaulle, who saw it as a means of weakening Anglo-American influence.[53] Structural reform was sacrificed to this opposition.[54] By 1966 the rhetoric of reform was abandoned. The Labour government became obsessively cautious in all its actions. Its response to crises was managerial and institutional—problems were invariably met by setting up new bodies, usually involving the same individuals and invariably lacking the impulse or power to implement departures in policy.

The Heath government, elected in 1970, had by the spring of 1972 reached the same position, though from a different route—that of the so-called 'Selsden' policies, which were as rhetorically radical as Wilson's, but in a neo-liberal sense. They involved a commitment to substantially reducing the role of government, cutting the level of public expenditure, having wider recourse to the market and attacking the 'privileged' position of the trade unions. In so far as these policies were implemented they gave rise to a quite remarkable degree of political conflict, much of it involving the masses. After the fiasco of a defeat by the miners in February 1972, Heath's government was obliged to return to the same managerialist path trodden by Labour for most of 1966–70.

The general managerialist strategy of the Labour government disposed it towards a 'minimal' Irish position. So did that of the Conservatives, from spring 1972 at any rate. Before then they inclined to neo-liberal solutions, which would have had much the same effect.

Yet if the determinants of government strategy all point to non-intervention, events like the dispatching of troops, the Downing Street declarations, the Hunt committee and direct rule seem inexplicably reformist as they were sold to the British public. Either they *were* reformist, and the general determinants of government strategy were suspended, or they were not reformist at all and had other objectives.

Enough is known today about at least some of the interventions to make the second answer the more plausible. Its coherence depends upon the validity of a preliminary distinction, however—one which the Unionists *en bloc* failed to make: between the subjective views of Harold Wilson and actual government policy.

As anyone who reads Wilson's memoirs will perceive, he was much concerned with historical immortality. As his policies were thoroughly nondescript he became susceptible to a certain adventurism, which he liked to confuse with statesmanship. It should not be thought that this reflected any particularly interesting psychological trait—on the contrary, it expressed and sometimes even fulfilled a need of the Labour party for some identifiable public achievement. For years Rhodesia seemed capable of presenting such an opportunity. Wilson seriously underestimated the durability of Ian Smith, though, and after the debacle of the *Tiger* talks he concentrated his attention elsewhere. Securing a negotiated peace in Vietnam was, of course, the jewel in the diplomatic crown of the '60s, but despite frantic efforts the 'special relationship' alone made it unlikely that any of the parties to the conflict would take him seriously as a potential mediator. Ireland was a different matter entirely. Here were two dependent states still within the receding British sphere of influence ripe for persuasion, if not bullying—that is, for statesmanship. Even before becoming Prime Minister, he had shown himself disposed to make diplomatic gestures on Ireland. From a Unionist viewpoint the most alarming ones occurred between 1964 and 1966; they will be discussed in the next section. Others followed regularly, and their flavour may be appreciated from an incident in 1966. Shortly before the Westminster election that year he made a speech to the NILP which was reported to be about 'abhorring sectarianism'. A few days later, however, a rumour circulated that Wilson had privately suggested transferring the functions of the twelve Unionist MPs at Westminster to a joint Eire–Ulster committee with a British chairman.[55] Publicly and semi-publicly he urged a united Ireland, preceded by interim tripartite arrangements. He continued to push this line, to the horror of other members of the Cabinet, even after the crisis had begun to take shape in 1968. Crossman reported being told by Denis Healey in May 1969,

> You have no idea what it was like before you came on the [Northern Ireland] Committee [of the Cabinet]. The P.M. was always demanding active intervention early on, with this crazy desire to go over there and take things over, that we side with the R.C.s and the Civil Rights movement against the government, though we know nothing at all about it . . .[56]

Wilson must have been overruled, since the 'crazy desire' was not fulfilled in the course of the Labour government. Nor indeed did anything come of his other suggestions. Two months after the 1966 speech he was faced with a demand by Fitt for a commission to investigate the discrimination he had condemned. Wilson rejected the idea, commenting blandly, 'there are allegations and counter-allegations on both sides'.[57] This was no *volte-face*, but simply the voice of the Cabinet, the state apparatuses and the British ruling class.

Brett has recalled what he regards as the majority viewpoint: 'This is the twentieth century, not the seventeenth, and it is just not possible to believe that the religious divisions of Ireland could lead to violence ever again.'[58] He had added: 'A dozen times since then I have been reproached by friends in the British Labour Party: "Why ever didn't you warn us of what was coming?" I have never yet succeeded in finding words adequate to reply to that question.'[59] Brett is particularly eloquent in his condemnation of the inactivity of the Home Secretaries, Sir Frank Soskice and Roy Jenkins.

The *Sunday Times* 'Insight' team's work,[60] Crossman's diaries, Chichester-Clark's review of Wilson's memoirs[61] and other recent work[62] all suggest that British intervention in August 1969 was planned and executed as *the minimum possible form of intervention* by the British state. The Downing Street declarations and to some extent the Hunt committee embodied the same principle, modified by a dash of institutionitis and, as will be seen, a severe miscalculation on the part of the Unionist Cabinet.

Every effort seems to have been made to forstall military intervention, and then to minimise and terminate it. The main tactic had been to threaten the Northern Ireland government that to call upon troops would bring about direct rule.[63] The Unionists were encouraged instead to use first CS gas and then the B Specials against rioting Catholics.[64] By mid-August 1969, when it became obvious that the Northern Ireland government would have to call in troops whatever the consequences, the British Cabinet made it known that no strings would be attached to their use after all, provided Chichester-Clark could dispense with them quickly.[65] To facilitate this, they were initially sent only to Derry. Callaghan sat in the Home Office listening to reports of the killings in Belfast and waited for a further specific request before he ordered them there the next day.[66] In any case, so few troops were made available that they had little immediate impact. All this took place in the Cabinet's full knowledge that it could not escape a legal obligation to provide troops in the long run. The point had been established in April 1969 at the latest, and was made somewhat revealingly by Crossman:

> I went through all the papers. I found the committee had already come to the conclusion that it was *impossible to evade* British responsibility if there was a civil war or widespread rioting. Strictly speaking the police in Northern Ireland or the Government can ask

for British troops to come in.[67]

The troops having been dispatched, and it being established by 19 August that they could not be immediately withdrawn, discussion took place on what policy to present to Chichester-Clark. The main concern seems to have been to discover a means by which orderly military disengagement might take place. Differences arose over the conditions under which this could be achieved. Some, including Callaghan, felt that institutional changes (stopping short of giving Catholics a share of power) were necessary. Others, notably Healey, felt that 'they must push Chichester-Clark only as far as he wanted to go'.[68] The latter view seems to have been accepted, and all that was anticipated from Chichester-Clark's visit was a new Head of the RUC and a promise of a reivew of the position of the B Specials and the local authorities.[69]

Chichester-Clark's perception of the needs of the situation—specifically the need to pacify Wilson—led him to propose a more radical course of action: a complete British take-over of security and a full-scale inquiry into the police and B Specials.[70] The Cabinet could hardly reject it, and pondered the implications. The most obvious was that the B Specials, who were responsible only to themselves, would have to go. Wilson, who had wanted this all along, promptly announced their impending dissolution—without informing Chichester-Clark, who was under the impression that they would come under military control.[71]

Within five weeks, the Cabinet had decided these measures were insufficient. On 11 September:

> [Callaghan] said life was very bleak . . . there was no prospect of a solution. He had anticipated the honeymoon wouldn't last very long and it hadn't. The British troops were tired and were no longer popular and the terrible thing was that the only solutions would take ten years, if they would ever work at all . . .[72]

The Cabinet agreed on the necessity of administering another bout of institutionitis. This was the background of the Hunt and post-Hunt reforms. It was considered, however, that further serious change would repel Protestant support and hence postpone military disengagement. The reforms of 1969 were to be the last. By mid-1970 a consensus had emerged between Labour and Conservative leaderships that the road to a solution lay elsewhere.[73]

The necessity of avoiding a confrontation with the Protestants, with its implication of greater military involvement, appears to have become by 1970 the major influence upon government policy. After the election of that year the Conservatives were also anxious to re-insulate the whole question from British political life. The army was given tactical control over the situation and a convention was evolved to keep the army satisfied: it would have the power of veto over suggestions by the Stormont-dominated Joint Security Committee.

Despite a number of diplomatic blunders the army settled relatively well into its authoritarian position. It was unable to prevent the growth of the IRA, though, and its 'long haul' aim of 'reducing the IRA's capacity to conduct terrorist warfare'[74] fell considerably short of Unionist expectations. Once Brian Faulkner became Prime Minister and a bolder Unionist policy was adopted towards London, Unionist rhetoric began to have an effect on the British Cabinet. In the general context of a substantial increase in IRA activity, not to say a continued wariness about introducing direct rule, the notion of engineering a swift conclusion to the troubles began to appear attractive. It could be achieved, according to Faulkner, by a strategic shift to a short-run policy of aggression.

From August 1971 to February 1972 Faulkner was given his head, and army, not to say Ministry of Defence, opinion was systematically overruled. This was certainly the case with respect to internment[75] and the toleration of the UDA[76], and it seems likely also to have been behind the loosening of UDR recruiting standards and the reorganisation of the force on local lines.[77] It should not be thought that the new policy reflected merely the personal weakness of Reginald Maudling, as Callaghan suggests in his book. On the contrary, some powerful figures supported it, among them Cecil King[78] and the former champion of reform, Sir John Hunt.[79] At the time it was widely said to be supported by Callaghan, though later, when it had demonstrably failed, he was to argue that his backing had been conditional upon its accompaniment by a 'political initiative'. [80] Strictly speaking, of course, it was.[81]

As his gamble collapsed Faulkner became reduced to increasingly desperate measures. The decision that live rather than rubber bullets should be available during the Bloody Sunday operation was his direct responsibility—one that was to cost him dearly. The events of that day inspired the Catholic masses to go further over to the offensive. By February 1972 it was clear that far from creating the conditions for British disengagement, Faulkner was creating a minor Vietnam.

Direct rule was received as an abandonment of 'temporary' considerations of minimisation. Some even believed it to be the prelude to integration. But if the idea of integration was ever entertained it was only in the context of a review of various long-term strategies. In February 1972 a Northern Ireland Cabinet Minister voiced a more realistic appraisal: 'Look, let's face it. Ted Heath regards us as his doorstep Cyprus. Don't be surprised by anything that happens—I won't.'[82]

The same month marked the onset of Heath's phase of 'U turns', most notably on incomes policy. The impetus within the state apparatus for these changes came from the Central Policy Review Staff, adapted by Heath to act as a Prime Ministerial department. The CPRS enabled him to climb down on a number of issues. Northern Ireland was among those it considered, and direct rule was its suggestion.[83]

It is clear from the literature on the subject that the Think Tank's suggestions were intended as interim rather than final solutions for urgent problems.[84] In view of this it seems likely that direct rule was recommended on account of its potential for opening up new possibilities rather than as an end in itself.

Ruling-class political thinking about 'ends in themselves' concerning Ireland had not come far since 1964. The major development was that more British politicians were coming round to Wilson's views on unity. Figures as mainstream as Roy Jenkins, Peter Carrington and William Whitelaw were now said to be espousing this line. Certainly the Labour party had been discussing it seriously (under the melodramatic code name 'Algeria'[85]). The reasoning seems to have been that the IRA was strong enough to make any other solution unworkable. This was confirmed in Wilson's mind (and possibly Heath's, since he was kept informed) by a secret meeting he held on 13 March 1972 with leaders of the Provisionals. Wilson came away impressed both by David O'Connell and by the Provisionals' claim to be in a position to step up their campaign.[86]

Clearly the British ruling class was not about to capitulate to the

IRA, but it now had every reason to develop a policy that would make withdrawal and a united Ireland possible.[87] Despite London politicians' contempt for those in Dublin, it was widely accepted that if such a solution were adopted the southern government could deliver the Provisionals[88]. The army and the Ministry of Defence themselves favoured a policy of this kind, since in their view southern collaboration had to be secured if they were to handle the IRA in the north.[89]

Support for a policy that would make withdrawal feasible also came from the United States, which at this time began to exert strong pressure upon Heath. 'London has not had an easy time with overseas governments, including some of Britain's principal partners in the world, since the engagement of British military forces in Northern Ireland,' observed *The Times*[90]. Demands for drastic action apparently quickened after the burning of the British embassy in Dublin. M. J. Killeen, managing director of the Irish Industrial Development Association and a frequent spokesman for American interests, was reported to have said, 'The burning of the British embassy had particular significance. The Americans regard embassies as symbols of stability. They could not believe it when an embassy was burned in a peaceful country like Ireland . . .'.[91]

The day direct rule was introduced Whitelaw told Cecil King, 'in the end the answer must be a united Ireland'.[92] At the time it looked as if direct rule was actually the interim solution that Wilson had been talking of for so long. Whilst the Protestant reaction was feared, withdrawal meant that ultimately it would be somebody else's problem. In the meantime the reaction could be contained by Ian Paisley, whom Whitelaw was said now to be calling 'the future leader of Northern Ireland'.[93]

In the event few real steps towards a united Ireland were actually taken and Whitelaw pursued instead the Sunningdale strategy, which was itself fated to collapse within a year. Sunningdale was remarkable in *being* a strategy, however: it was the first identifiable set of constructive British goals to emerge since 1922. This is not to agree with King and Haines that there was no consistent policy on Ireland throughout the period. There was one—one, indeed, which was bipartisan. Though it was the organising principle for British action, its nature meant that it was disclosed only in times of crisis like 1969. The policy, which was manifest in every twist and vacillation described above, was to *minimise British involvement,* politically and militarily. Action was taken only where the alternative appeared ultimately to entail a greater degree of involvement. It was always designed as a short-term stop-gap unavoidable if the *status quo ante* in British–Ulster relations was to be restored. In reality there were no long-term commitments to integration or to unity, since either implied the probability of a temporary or permanent *increase* in engagement. The underlying continuity of British strategy was an absence of active desire to do anything at all, except to avoid getting further ensnared. Even the sort of disengagement that was favoured was limited, since a more comprehensive variety had unpredictable elements.

While the durability of this policy obviously had much to do with Ireland's declining importance for British economic interests, it was clearly also to some extent self-perpetuating. The deliberately insulatory measures undertaken by both the Unionists and the British in the 1920s generated a mutually welcomed mutual ignorance of each other's political arena. Absorbed by the Home Office, probably one of the least energetic departments of state, consideration of Northern Ireland was insulated even from the development of the limited forms of diplomatic knowledge and strategic thinking operative in the Foreign Office.[94] Under these conditions it was impossible for any informed Irish policy to emerge at all. Specific crises—especially where they could be assimilated to 'messy' history (Crossman)—served only to reinforce the tendency towards minimising involvement, since, as Healey remarked, 'we know nothing at all about it'. Short of total Unionist loss of control or the intervention of 'powerful allies' there was no way in which this circuit could be broken, and no guarantee that even if it was anything novel would happen.

Minimal involvement had, of course, an ambiguous effect on Northern Ireland. For fifty years it preserved the state from certain pressures for change, and allowed the Unionists to maintain a specific kind of exceptional state. In the long run, however, it meant that the government had little or no recourse to British support. Obligations were admitted (as in 1949 by Attlee) only when they seemed to forestall events which would have disrupted the condition of mutual insulation. When times changed, obligations were modified and redefined. The lability of 'Loyalism' once more found itself mirrored in the lability of British solidarity.

Unionist divisions

At the risk of tedium, allow a final rehearsal of the orthodox liberal and socialist view of the nature of Unionist divisions. On the one hand, backwardness and sectarianism, the expression of 'declining' traditional capital. On the other, progressive non-sectarianism, representing internationalised monopoly capital and its rise. The theoretical basis of this reduction has already been evaluated. So too has the 'decline' of traditional capital. It is nevertheless profitable to take the remaining part of the equation as a starting point in examining the dissolution of Unionist dominance. The character of 'internationalised monopoly capital' in Northern Ireland illuminates much that is of interest. Consider, for example, four of its characteristics.

First, internationalised monopoly capitalism in Northern Ireland could not be said to be in any way a homogeneous entity. Certainly many multinational companies set up or acquired branches in the Six Counties during the '50s and '60s. Dupont, Enkalon, Michelin, Courtauld's, ICI, Goodyear, Hoechst, ITT, Molins, Baird, and Monsanto all did so. There no doubt either that some of these enterprises made very substantial investments. With its roughly pound-for-pound investment grant policy, Stormont paid out over £200 million between 1945 and 1972 for 'new projects'. Total investment in them therefore amounted to £400–£450 million.[95] American holdings made up £125 million of this; Dupont's contribution alone came to about £25 million[96] Other major multinational investments included Courtauld's £13 million plant at Carrickfergus[97] and Hoechst's £10 million plant at Limavady.[98] But such large-scale projects were exceptional. Many of the multinational operations were small and corporately marginal enough to be painlessly terminated during the recession of the early '70s.[99] Different levels of commitment to Northern Ireland, economic and political, must have existed.

Second, internationalised monopoly capital was only a *part* of the 'new capital' invested. The average contribution of enterprises themselves to new projects was well under £1 million (£200 million + spread over about 250 projects[100] About one in ten of the new projects was attracted by some existing link with an enterprise already based in Northern Ireland[101] In this sense 'new' capital was no more unambiguously external than pre-1945 capital (linen

excepted) was unambiguously local. Some of the largest
investments involved competitive capital. For example, from 1955
Cyril Lord, a Lancashire carpet firm which was put in the hands of
the receiver in 1968, obtained £900,000 in grants, a free purpose-
built factory at Carnmoney and further grants and loans of £2·8
million towards plants at Donaghadee and Rathgael.[102]

Third, internationalised monopoly capitalism's 'dissolution
effect' upon traditional capital apparently continued to be limited.
Objections to new industry by local capitalists recurred,
particularly from linen manufacturers in small towns, whose profit
margins were tied tightly to low wages.[103] As a rule, though, they
remained rare. While evidence suggests a progressive relative
disinvestment by the local bourgeoisie in traditional industry[104], the
economic statistics indicate that on the whole local capital was
reproduced at least at its former rate during the '60s and early '70s.
A general decline in its fortunes appears to have occured in the
1964–69 period, but a recovery had at least compensated for this by
direct rule.

The blunting of the 'dissolution effect' was due to a number of

Table 4 Quinquennial averages (1950–74) of Northern Ireland
joint-stock company registrations, formations, liquidations and
paid-up capitals

	1950–54	1955–59	1960–64	1965–69	1970–74
Total registered companies	3,327	3,771	4,809	5,851	6,775 [a]
Average paid-up capital	£20,218	£22,618	£28,799	£27,338	£29,444 [b]
Average new registrations p.a.					
• Public	0·8	0·6	1·0	1·2	1·0
Guarantee	2·2	3·8	7·8	10·4	5·2
Private	135·8	196·6	343·6	300·6	534·6
Average No. of liquidations p.a.	22·6	30·0	46·6	63·6	53·2

a 1970–73.
b 1970–71.
Source. Government of Northern Ireland, Digest of Statistics
(Belfast, annual, 1954–   )

factors. The Ministry of Commerce 'consciously avoided aiming primarily at attracting labour-intensive concerns'.[105] The maintenance of high direct and indirect subsidies to old capital was important (the shipyard, upon which much of the engineering industry of east Belfast relied, received a staggering total of £70 million from the state up to 1973[106]). Some new projects had their own multiplier effects. Dupont, for example, were said in 1963 to purchase goods and services from 130 Ulster firms.[107] In any event, old capital's dissolution—though continuing—was slowed. In 1970 60 per cent of the manufacturing and 86 per cent of the total work-force were still employed outside the new projects[108]. Although no direct comparision is possible, the figures suggest a slower rate of dissolution than in other development areas, such as Scotland[109]

Fourth, there is little evidence that representatives of new capital sought any political system other than the established Stormont one. Some dissatisfaction was expressed with local government on the score of physical planning[110]. Also, according to Callaghan, 'major industrialists' approved his 1969 reforms when directly asked[111]. Hitherto no pressure for reforms was ever evident from this source. A good many new businesses conformed without protest to the practices of old capital. In 1965, when new industry provided about 60,000 of 190,000 manufacturing jobs, the first Development Plan complained that only 10 per cent of new vacancies were being filled through labour exchanges[112] Evidently Orangeism was becoming absorbed into the new workplaces.

New capital actually had as much interest as old capital in an undisturbed continuation of Stormont. The advantage for both was described as early as 1953 by a senior civil servant, L. G. P. Freer:

> Senior officials of the various departments are known personally to those with whom they have dealings to an extent which would be impracticable in a larger area of administration . . . Administrators in Northern Ireland find it easier to assess what the results of any particular line of action are likely to be, and when action has been taken, to correct more quickly any untoward consequences which may appear likely to arise . . .[113]

Consciously or unconsciously, this point is the essence of Lawrence's defence of Northern Ireland.[114] It was most succinctly recapitulated by Terence O'Neill, who himself supported Stormont's existence to the end:

small area with a regional or provincial government can take
strative decisions and can take them quickly within the limits
of its powers . . . *incoming industrialists are delighted to be able to
deal with a small, local and intimate government . . .*[115]

Industrialists of all species benefited from the sympathetic
attention of the Ministry of Commerce, whose generosity was
unchecked by Whitehall, or, probably increasingly, by the Ministry
of Finance either. Among the consequences was that in Northern
Ireland each job cost roughly twice as much to create as in Wales or
Scotland[116]. With eggs like this, few recipients were interested in
the colour of the goose.

This is not to imply ruling-class political unanimity. Divisions
existed—but not on one fundamental. Recognising this is of vital
importance to understanding the nature of the divisions that did
occur. *All the bourgeoisie, all its fractions, wanted to maintain
Stormont.* Stormont's development funds seemed inexhaustible,
and whatever its other deficiencies it represented the best possible
political arrangement. Divisions revolved around the question of
how to maintain it.

The main political problems of the bourgeoisie were to this
extent common problems. At the beginning of the '60s they had
concerned the defection of Protestant working-class support in
Belfast to the NILP. By 1964, though, O'Neill was on the road to
resolving this difficulty. In the mid-'60s a far more serious one
arose. In various forms it was to divide and redivide Unionists and
finally to ensure the collapse of the state. It was the problem of
developing a policy to meet what was perceived as a
transformation, or potential transformation, of traditional
London–Belfast relations.

Substantially increased dependence on British subsidies, and
centralised control in Belfast over their distribution, was one aspect
of this transformation which was to give rise to tensions. More
fundamental was the change of British government that brought
Harold Wilson and the Labour party to power in 1964. The effects
on Catholic politics have been described. Among Unionists it
generated considerable apprehension. This was not simply
because Labour governments, unlike Conservative ones, had
actively to 'demonstrate [they were] as staunch friends of Ulster as
were the Labour leaders of twenty years ago'.[117] There was also the
question of Harold Wilson's surrogate Irish nationalism.

Concern about Wilson's politics was created not only by various off-the-cuff pronouncements in favour of a united Ireland, or gestures like his return of the remains of Sir Roger Casement to the southern government[118], but by a specific commitment he appeared to have entered into shortly before the 1964 general election. On 5 October the *Newsletter* published a letter from him to Patricia McCluskey, who was shortly to found the CSJNI. It promised, should Wilson be elected, to implement large-scale changes in Northern Ireland.[119] While this incident had only a tenuous connection with Britain's actual Irish policy, it seemed to make development of a 'Wilson strategy' imperative to Unionism.

Although O'Neill had encountered resistance in the execution of his strategy against the NILP, it did not last long. The reduction in local government powers and certain infrastructural decisions caused brief furores,[120] but opposition to them failed to coalesce. As has been demonstrated, those on the right of the party specifically failed in their endeavours to assist the process.

This relative success inspired O'Neill to undertake what must have seemed at the time a relatively daring 'Wilson' strategy. He embarked on a series of progressive-looking public gestures towards the south and towards public opinion in Britain. Such gestures—the invitation to Lemass, for example—would convince Wilson of Unionism's reforming intentions and thus induce him to keep at bay what were thought of as the Labour party's wilder counsels. The timing of the meeting with Lemass might even have been regarded as somewhat cautious: the *Newsletter* had chided O'Neill in November 1964 for refusing to meet the southern Premier when he came to Belfast to speak at Queen's University[121].

O'Neill was careful to indicate the bounds of this strategy, however, and in particular to distinguish it from a secularisation of the state machinery. He went out of his way to point out that no changes were contemplated in the field of discrimination. In February 1964 he strongly rebutted accusations of 'apartheid' in Northern Ireland. In March 1966 he described such accusations as 'facile'. In January 1967 he advised his supporters to 'forget jargon words ... like community relations', while in April 1967 he described the views of the CDU as 'baseless and scurrilous'[122].

The opposition to O'Neill found a voice in Brian Faulkner. Faulkner advanced the view that the only way of handling Wilson was to recreate 'lost' Unionist unity around the party's traditional positions. This would call Wilson's bluff and force him to abandon his reformist pretensions. Gestures such as the invitation to Lemass simply whetted his nationalist appetite. Support for Faulkner's view came when, three months after Lemass's visit, Wilson called for tripartite talks on the future of Ireland[123]

Even after this O'Neill's position remained relatively firm, however. At least, it was firm enough to enable him to seek, in his future efforts at conciliating Wilson, to damage the right-wing critics endeavouring to unify opposition to him. His first and most serious attack upon the right was on the extra-parliamentary wing of the party, Paisleyism. Ian Paisley and his supporters, who were the most vocal supporters of the notion that there was a general undesirable anti-Unionist streak in all O'Neill's policies, laid themselves open to attack by embarking upon a 'strategy of tension' during the spring and summer of 1966. According to the Belfast correspondent of *The Economist,* O'Neill welcomed the opportunity to 'lance this boil of simmering nastiness'[124]. After incidents outside the Presbyterian General Assembly in June he called the Paisleyites 'Nazis', practitioners of 'obscenity and sedition' using 'the sordid techniques of gangsters'[125]. After the Malvern Street murders he banned the UVF, which he said was associated with Paisley, commenting, 'this [is] an evil thing in our midst . . . a very dangerous conspiracy [which] . . . we cannot and will not tolerate . . . one cannot touch pitch without being defiled'[126]. When Paisley was imprisoned for his part in the trouble outside the Assembly his supporters demonstrated in Crumlin Road. The RUC dispersed them using baton charges, armoured personnel carriers and—for the first time—water cannon.[127]

O'Neill's opponents now tried to link this policy to his general gestures of reform and his alleged anti-Unionism. Faulkner claimed the Assembly had been used to disseminate an inaccurate report on discrimination, and that the Paisleyites had been provoked.[128] Moreover 'Mr Paisley in prison is more an embarrassment to the government than an asset'[129] Brookeborough agreed: 'Many of us do not like the way things have been going of late . . . may I offer a grave warning at this time—never at any time can we Unionists afford to forget that in unity and unity alone rests all our strength.'[130]

Despite such powerful opposition, O'Neill was still strong enough to add to his gestural attacks on the right by dismissing

Harry West in April 1967. Faulkner continued to articulate opposition: 'the Unionist party inside and outside of parliament is tired of crises which serve only to disrupt and divide'[131]. A few days later he was once more condemning as 'nonsense' O'Neill's view that fascist extremism was a force in Ulster politics.[132]

O'Neill's position was not, of course, wholly determined by the Wilson problem. The strategy of reformist gestures accorded with his earlier outflanking of the NILP, and was accompanied by an ideology of modernisation. In most instances his policies were successful, too. This served to diminish opposition and to forestall its unification.

But his situation was a precarious one. An independent political factor was working for the unification of opposition to him. Most of his policies had as a necessary consequence the reduction of different aspects of the state's relative autonomy. The threat from the NILP, the importance of reducing unemployment, the desire for indicative planning, the need to control Paisleyism, all involved centralisation under tighter bourgeois control. This trend should not be exaggerated, since the populist discriminatory core of state autonomy remained intact. The consolidation of O'Neill's position turned on whether the distinction could be maintained. Until the emergence of the civil rights movement in 1968 the problem did not arise.

The crisis provoked by the arrival on the scene of the civil rights movement was therefore not restricted even to the great fundamental issue of discrimination. Involved with this basic problem were all the tensions raised by earlier crises of the '60s.

For O'Neill the dilemma was excruciating. On the one hand, placating the civil rights movement was likely to mean consolidation of the opposition to him. On the other, failing to do so would probably lead—in his eyes at least—to British intervention and a complete dissolution of local autonomy. O'Neill chose the road of minimal appeasement (the five-point programme of November 1968[133]), emphasising that Wilson had made it 'absolutely clear that if we did not face up to our problems, the Westminster Parliament might well decide to act over our heads . . . .'.[134]

From that moment he was probably doomed. Even a purely placatory line towards Catholics proved difficult to implement with the machinery at his disposal, while dissatisfaction with the way it was put into effect further cemented opposition to him. This was most sharply illustrated in the question of the civil rights movement's 'freedom to march'. From the beginning the right to hold marches was not recognised by a substantial number of Unionists, for whom it connoted a decisive modification in the nature of the state. The feeling was shared by at least a segment of the repressive apparatuses, whose reluctance to grant it coincided with popular Protestant views. These were in any case well represented in the bodies concerned: for example, over a quarter of the RUC were former B Specials,[135] a further 300 Specials were fully mobilised into the force in 1968–69,[136] and eighty of these were to be found in the Reserve Force (riot squad).[137] Sections of the judiciary were seen in a similar light. Judge Topping, a former Minister of Home Affairs who in 1947 had declared, 'the enemy today is no different from what it had been 257 years ago',[138] and who was said in Parliament to have appointed himself Recorder of Belfast in 1959 (an event exceptional even by Unionist standards) was a particular target of criticism.

As the civil rights movement continued its progress, both the heightening of tensions in the organs of state which it provoked, and the increasing efforts to centralise control over them which this inspired, served to coalesce previously disparate forms of opposition to O'Neill and to isolate him within both the state apparatus and the party leadership. As a result O'Neill began to appear weak and impotent. It seems likely that it was grounds such as these, rather than a 'revulsion against violence' or the development of class opposition to his 'aristocratic' qualities, that were the basis of the collapse of O'Neillism as a popular position.

Its collapse was fairly dramatic, as during 1968 at least O'Neill seems to have been far from isolated within the Protestant community as a whole. After his 'Ulster at the crossroads' speech of 9 December over 150,000 letters or telegrams of support were received, while another 120,000 newspaper coupons supporting the speech were returned. By the 1969 Stormont election this support appears to have diminished, although it was still substantial.

Boal and Buchanan have shown that definite voting trends were discernible among the Protestant community at this election (although they probably misinterpret them).[139] Pro-O'Neill votes tended to be highest in surburban Greater Belfast, anti-O'Neill votes most substantial along the border and in working-class Belfast constituencies. It has been argued in explanation that since these regions contained a concentration of deprived Protestants, and since the opposition to O'Neill was frequently classist in its rhetoric, class antagonism underlay popular preference for O'Neill's opponents[140]

While a rhetoric of class did consistently surface in the contest[141] a simpler explanation is available. As Boal and Buchanan themselves point out, both on the border and in working-class areas of Belfast Protestant communities were in close proximity to zones of high Catholic concentration. In both, the Unionist bourgeoisie had historically been obliged to especially extend the relative autonomy of the state from central bourgeois control in order to maintain its dominance. Likewise, these were areas of high workplace exclusivism. Although it was articulated along anti-'big house' lines, opposition to O'Neill seems to have been most obviously founded upon the question of the state's relation to the Protestant masses. Anti-O'Neill areas were those which had been bastions of populism, and which were therefore most sensitive to its erosion—a phenomenon popularly designated as 'Lundyism'.

On the other hand, support for O'Neill was clearly not based simply on those with an interest or even a belief in greater centralisation of bourgeois control. While the best successes of the O'Neillists were in the kinds of area where suburban middle-class subscription to an ideology of modernisation might have subsumed this view, O'Neill's colleagues also did surprisingly well in working-class and rural constituencies (except Bannside), where they were opposed by Paisleyites[142]. A striking feature of the election was indeed the remarkably good performance of official Unionist candidates whether pro- or anti-O'Neill. In twenty-two contests where they faced unofficial Unionist opposition (of whatever variety) only two resulted in official Unionist defeat (Bangor and Willowfield, where pro-O'Neillists were returned). In eight constituencies where moderate official Unionists were opposed by unofficial Unionists or Paisleyites, moderates won on each occasion. In the fourteen constituencies where official anti-O'Neill Unionists stood against unofficial pro-O'Neill opponents, all but the two mentioned won. Official Unionism, whatever its colour, bestowed a high probability of success on its bearer. A large part of both the pro- and anti-O'Neill camps appear to have been traditional—might one say deferential—in their attitudes.

In this sense 'pure' O'Neillism represented only a part of an artificially inflated 'popular' O'Neillism. As alternative centres of official Unionism emerged these trends became distinct. In April 1969, four days after a series of explosions which seemed further evidence of O'Neill's weakness, he resigned. His successor, Chichester-Clark, was to face identical difficulties.

If anything, the situation confronting Chichester-Clark and his successor, Brian Faulkner, was even more acute than that which had defeated O'Neill. Both necessarily had to resolve the question of the nature of the state in Northern Ireland, and both faced the question—in a much sharper form than O'Neill had—of handling the British. In August 1969, with the greatest reluctance, Chichester-Clark called in British troops. Subsequent events were overshadowed by the apparent imminence of direct rule.

Chichester-Clark and his supporters evidently took the position, like O'Neill, that the threat of direct rule was the major imperative governing policy, and that questions about the shape of the local state must temporarily be dictated by it. For Chichester-Clark, as for O'Neill, Stormont's autonomy was the major issue. In order to preserve it the various reforms Britain was expected to demand should be pre-empted. Later the traditional form of the state could be retrieved by stealth[143]. Chichester-Clark volunteered to transfer security decisions to the army and to set up a commission of inquiry into the RUC;[144] he accepted, without argument, proposals for investigations into housing, local government and community relations. As for public order, he institutionalised distinct RUC and army jurisdiction.

Not only was gestural appeasement reproduced in identical form, but so was its opposition, which continued—as under O'Neill—to argue for party unity and the calling of Britain's bluff, coupled now with the demand for restoration of control over security.

So too, in an intensified form, were its effects. The 'gestural' changes of 1969 and after were to prove far from minimal. As Poulantzas has pointed out, one of the most significant characteristics of exceptional states is their rigidity and brittleness.[145] The cumulatively destabilising effect of reforms, especially when they reached the repressive apparatuses, increased in geometric progression. Efforts to improve and centralise control, prior to 1972 at least, were to prove unsuccessful and disruptive. The RUC in particular suffered from an almost total loss of efficacy between 1969 and direct rule. Other parts of the state apparatus seem to have assumed an informal or unofficial guise: the B Specials in paramilitary organisations, local government in the Vanguard movement, etc. As a result, Chichester-Clark's and later Faulkner's isolation was to be far more complete than even O'Neill's. Both became extremely susceptible to increases in Catholic militancy. Chichester-Clark's fall was directly precipitated by the first dramatic signals of the Provisional IRA's offensive. In consequence both, but especially Faulkner, were to be driven to desperate attempts to preserve their credibility in the face of accusations of weakness. Chichester-Clark pressed the Falls curfew on the army and then proposed that a 'third force' of civilian volunteers should be re-formed[146]. Faulkner's initiatives were more dramatic—an ill prepared internment operation and Bloody Sunday. The point had been reached at which the repercussions began to impinge directly on British politics, provoking direct rule.

To interpret the significance of these events in relation to the history of the state as a whole we must consider for a moment one of this final period's most extraordinary features. In view of the nature of much of its original support, its isolation from the state apparatus, etc., it is not surprising that the party's 'centre' collapsed and failed (reappearing later in the Alliance Party). Much more remarkable was the failure of the right to take advantage of the centre's unpopularity. It was surprisingly timid throughout the period, for reasons which at the time were not altogether clear. It was even more timid when direct rule was actually introduced—the threatened holocaust dissolved into a series of peaceful rallies. In fact the right (and even then this did not include much of the parliamentary right) was not to launch a real offensive until the UWC strike of 1974.

A clue to this curious conduct, which in a sense provides a key to the period, was provided by William Craig in an interview in 1976. Questioned about the significance of Chichester-Clark's resort to British troops, he explained, 'at that point in time I was convinced that it was only a matter of time until the parliament of Northern Ireland was abolished . . . once the army came in and the way they came in . . . there could be only one end to it . . .'.[147] The statement has both immediate and longer-range implications.

Immediate implications: Craig provides a reason for the right's quiescence. It was due not to an ideological crisis about 'ultimate loyalties' but to a calculation that the British ruling class had the will to take the loyalists on. Militarily this would almost certainly have meant that the loyalists would be crushed. Paisley continually echoed this argument in the winter of 1971–72 in his declarations that another 1912 was not on. His own opportunistic solution was full integration—another form of words for the anticipated direct rule (though when it came he opposed it). Paisley's vacillations, and Craig's essentially reflected not only their need to take account of the hostility of the Protestant masses to Chichester-Clark and Faulkner, but their conviction that they would soon be required to treat with whatever instrument of direct rule Westminster selected. Hence the constant jockeying for position within rightist politics, which made a mockery of all calls for unity. Hence too the somewhat eccentric dove-like positions[148] adopted (presumably for British consumption) by Paisley's Democratic Unionist Party shortly after its formation.

Broader implications: if this view held by the right, which was presumably shared by the centre too, is related to the motives behind O'Neill's movement towards general placation in 1964, a compelling continuity appears. There was a common conviction throughout Unionist politics and throughout the eight years preceding direct rule that a substantial British intervention in Northern Ireland was a significant probability.[149]

Any such intervention would obviously present a grave threat to the two key aspects of the Unionist position. On the one hand, it appeared to put in question the status of Northern Ireland with respect to the Republic (this was particularly evident in Wilson's earlier years). On the other, and probably more directly, it threatened Northern Ireland's independence from the rest of the United Kingdom.

Insistence on autonomy had at first been based on Britain's unreliability as an ally, evident between 1918 and 1922. Its consequences were the incorporation of private violence into the state apparatus, the creation of a predominantly populist political regime and the extension to an exceptional degree of the state's relative freedom from central bourgeois control. Henceforth the Unionist regime was to absorb these characteristics indelibly and to acquire a high degree of rigidity where they were concerned.

One aspect of this rigidity was a certain inflexibility over reform, whose effects have already been described. More perceptive unionist leaders than Chichester-Clark recognised that an end to Unionism's autonomy within the United Kingdom was undesirable not only for material reasons but because it would very likely make reformist demands upon a state apparatus too inflexible to cope with them. Hence the preference for the disastrous course of gestural, then actual, reform.

The question remains of what gave birth to a widespread belief in the likelihood, of British intervention, which was contrary both to historical indications and the reality of British strategy. The fact is that this universal misperception arose from precisely the situation which Unionists sought to preserve—the autonomy of the local state. This autonomy, welcomed as it was on both sides of the water, was associated—as has been noted—with a progressively distancing of the political life of Britain and Northern Ireland. From time to time the insulation was weakened, by the war or the rise of the 'regional problem'. These difficulties failed to touch at the heart of the state though. Unionism managed to contain them, and to reaffirm a general insulation. Partly it consisted in a mutual ignorance of the strategic realities of British and Irish political life. While Crossman could confuse St. Patrick's Day with 12 July, O'Neill, Craig and Paisley could confuse the rhetoric of British politicians with their actual intentions.

This structural misperception, arising out of a specific form of inter-state relations, was the source of Ulster politics' fatal irony. In order to safeguard Northern Ireland's autonomy from what was regarded as the near inevitability of British intervention, a section of the Unionist party actually began to dismantle the populist structures whose preservation was a large part of the regime's raison d'être. Directly and indirectly the move led to conditions under which the populist class alliance at last began to founder and break up. The state's autonomy was designed to preclude a united Ireland and reduce dependence on an unreliable ally. Success depended on creating a class alliance which would perpetuate that autonomy. Yet autonomy failed to endow Unionists with a realistic perception of the prospects of securing external assurance that it would continue. In consequence they embarked on a strategy which not only removed its motive force but in so doing destroyed the state's autonomy itself.[150] It remains to be seen what, if any, final intentions will emerge from the unreliable ally, and what, if any, implications, they have for a united Ireland.

Notes to chapter 6

[1] Farrell, *Orange State*, p. 291.
[2] *The Price of My Soul* (London, 1969), p. 143.
[3] *Belfast Newsletter*, 3 January 1972.
[4] The following two paragraphs rely on the final chapter of Rumpf and Hepburn, *Nationalism and Socialism*.
[5] *Irish Times*, 3 February 1965.
[6] Rumpf and Hepburn, *Nationalism and Socialism*, p. 191.
[7] *NIHC*, Vol. LXX, c. 507–8.
[8] Government of Northern Ireland, *Disturbances in Northern Ireland*, Cmd 532 (Belfast, 1969) (hereafter 'Cameron'), p. 15.
[9] The nearest approximation to such support is McCann's figures on enrolment at the major Catholic boys' grammar school in Derry, which increased from 725 in 1959 to 1,125 in 1967 (*War and an Irish Town*, London, 1974, p. 212).
[10] E. A. Aunger, 'Religion and occupational class in Northern Ireland', *Economic and Social Review*, 7 (1975).
[11] No comparison is possible for the Catholic middle class as a whole.
[12] The authors are obliged to J. H. Whyte for this point.
[13] See appendix.
[14] Aunger convincingly argues that there was probably little overall change between 1961 and 1971 for this population.
[15] Cf., e.g., G. Routh, *Occupation and Pay in Great Britain* (Cambridge, 1965), table 1.
[16] Routh's figures show that in Britain expansion in the upper white-collar sector was most rapid in the period 1931–51 (*ibid.*).
[17] Cf. the argument of Lyons, in *Ireland since the Famine*.
[18] Campaign for Social Justice in Northern Ireland (Dungannon, 1969).
[19] Fermanagh Civil Rights Association (Enniskillen, 1969).
[20] *Irish Times*, 3 June 1965.
[21] *Ibid.*, 26 May 1966.
[22] Farrell, *Orange State*, p. 240.
[23] McCann, *War*, p. 213 (speech by Patrick O'Hare).
[24] *NIHC*, Vol. LXVIII, c. 1270. Later, apparently after press comment, the matter was taken up by O'Reilly, Diamond and Fitt (*ibid.*, c. 1344–7).
[25] *NIHC*, Vol. LXIX, c. 782.
[26] *NIHC*, Vol. LXVIII, c. 1140.
[27] The position of the NILP was far from a militant one, however. Agitation was directed only at securing reforms 'from above', and in any case diminished in conviction after an embarrassingly unsuccessful visit by Paul Rose in 1967 (Graham, 'The strategy of the NILP', p. 187).
[28] *NIHC*, Vol. LXVII, c. 1445.
[29] McCann, *War*, p. 44.
[30] Just a few weeks before the civil rights explosion the northern

correspondent of *Hibernia* described the lack of discussion among northern Catholics of a recent Papal encyclical on contraception. He commented, 'it must be accepted that there has not yet evolved in the north the type of middle-class liberal intellectual society which might be expected to participate [in this] controversy' (*Hibernia*, September 1968).

[31] McCann, *War*, p. 47.

[32] It is evident that many Catholics, even in this period, resisted mobilisation. Some of these probably retained the support for O'Neillist Unionism apparent in the surveys of R. Rose (*Governing without Consensus*, London, 1970) and I. Budge and C. O'Leary (*Belfast: Approach to Crisis*, London, 1973).

[33] Government of Northern Ireland, *Violence and Civil Disturbances in Northern Ireland in 1969*, Cmd 566 (Belfast, 1972) (hereafter 'Scarman'), p. 27.

[34] In Derry in July 1969, according to D. I. McAtamrey (RUC), 'stopping somebody in the street and asking him what religion he was' became common. 'If he gave the wrong answer, he would be assaulted' (*ibid.*, p. 31).

[35] 315 of 88,379 Protestant households were also evacuated (*ibid.*,p. 248).

[36] Cf. Devlin, *Price*, p. 193.

[37] For the authorititive description of the SDLP's formation see I. McAllister, *The Northern Ireland Social Democratic and Labour Party* (London, 1977), pp. 29–34.

[38] McAllister, *SDLP*, p. 101.

[39] As McAllister has shown, this achievement was practically realised in a purely negative way, through the SDLP's inability to generate any concrete policies prior to direct rule (*ibid.*).

[40] C. King, *Diary, 1970–74*, p. 80; J. Haines, *The Politics of Power* (London, 1977), p. 112.

[41] M. Barratt-Brown, *After Imperialism* (London, 1963).

[42] 'According to McGilligan's statement at the Imperial Conference in 1930, Irish capital in British industry was estimated at £90 million, and British capital in Irish industry at only half that amount' (E. Burns, *British Imperialism in Ireland*, Dublin, 1931, pp. 63–4).

[43] *Financial Times*, 22 November 1976.

[44] The offer was made in the course of a letter to Roosevelt, who was evidently in touch with de Valera. The letter is reprinted in W. S. Churchill, *The Second World War*, Vol. II, *Their Finest Hour* (London, 1949), pp. 498–9.

[45] H. Calvert, *Constitutional Law in Northern Ireland* (London, 1968), pp. 95–6.

[46] R. H. S. Crossman, *The Diaries of a Cabinet Minister*, Vol. III, *1968–70* (London, 1977), p. 187.

[47] They should have read O'Nuallain, *Finances*.

[48] F. Newsam, *The Home Office* (London, 1954), pp. 168–9.

[49] *Ibid.*, p. 170. Confirmation of this position is provided by Brian Faulkner: 'The relationship between Stormont and Westminster [in 1960] makes an interesting contrast with the one which developed later. As Minister of Home Affairs I was in charge of the counter-terrorist measures. Westminster was helpful and co-operative at all times, providing troops

when they were needed for a particular operation and making various representations to Dublin . . . its rôle was very much a supportive one, standing aside from day-to-day decisions . . .'. (B. Faulkner, *Memoirs of a Statesman*, London, 1978, p. 24.)

⁵⁰ C. E. B. Brett, *Long Shadows Cast Before* (Edinburgh and London, 1978), p. 135.

⁵¹ Haines, *Politics*, pp. 121–2.

⁵² Southern Ireland shared both in this insulation and in an anomalous and obscure set of inter-state relations with Britain (see below also). (J. Peck, *Dublin from Downing Street*, Dublin, 1978, pp. 16, 26, 44–5, 116.)

⁵³ Callaghan, then Chancellor, voiced this argument with characteristic banality: 'the whole thing was a wicked French plot to bring down the dollar by bringing down the pound first and making Paris the financial capital of the world' (King, *Diary, 1965–70*, London, 1972, p. 83).

⁵⁴ According to John Steven, Treasury representative in Washington, 'Johnson made it quite clear to Wilson that the pound was not to be devalued' (*ibid.*, p. 78). In fairness it should be pointed out that there is considerable doubt whether the National Plan and Wilson's structural reforms had sufficient credibility to be worth gambling on anyway. Cf. A. Budd, *The Politics of Economic Planning* (Manchester, 1978, pp. 115–18).

⁵⁵ *Irish Times*, 25 and 29 March 1966.

⁵⁶ Crossman, *Diaries*, Vol. III, p. 478.

⁵⁷ *Irish Times*, 27 May 1966.

⁵⁸ Brett, *Shadows*.

⁵⁹ *Ibid.*, p. 139.

⁶⁰ *Sunday Times* Insight Team, *Ulster* (London, 1972).

⁶¹ *Belfast Newsletter*, 27 July 1971.

⁶² E.g. R. Maudling, *Memoirs* (London, 1978) and Faulkner, *Memoirs*.

⁶³ 'Insight', *Ulster*, pp. 84–5, 110.

⁶⁴ *Ibid.*, pp. 109, 111–12; Crossman, *Diaries*, p. 601.

⁶⁵ 'Insight', *Ulster*, p. 121.

⁶⁶ *Ibid.*, p. 137.

⁶⁷ Crossman, *Diaries*, pp. 463–4; emphasis added.

⁶⁸ *Ibid.*, pp. 621–3.

⁶⁹ *Ibid.*; 'Insight', *Ulster*, p. 144.

⁷⁰ Crossman, *Diaries*; *Belfast Newsletter*, 27 July 1971.

⁷¹ 'Insight', *Ulster*, p. 146; *Belfast Newsletter*, 27 July 1971.

⁷² Crossman, *Diaries*, p. 636.

⁷³ Nor was encouraging a shift to a two-party British-style political system the answer, although it was at one time favoured both by Callaghan (*A House Divided*, London, 1973, pp. 151–2) and Quintin Hogg.

⁷⁴ *The Times*, 17 March 1972.

⁷⁵ 'Insight', *Ulster*, p. 265.

⁷⁶ The unqualified opposition of Carrington and Tuzo was reported in the *Belfast Newsletter*, 2 October 1971.

⁷⁷ *NIHC*, Vol. LXXXII, c. 877–8, 1258, 1283.

⁷⁸ King, *1970–74*, pp. 99–100.

⁷⁹ *Belfast Newsletter*, 15 March and 9 July 1971. (Baron Sir John Hunt should not be confused with Sir John Hunt, shortly to become Cabinet secretary.)

[80] Callaghan, *A House*, pp. 168, 174.

[81] The obvious corollary of British support for this policy was British pressure on the southern government to cut the supply lines of the IRA and—when necessary—to introduce internment themselves. However, this policy was pursued ineptly and half-heartedly. Lynch was asked if he would introduce internment in the south, but not until twelve hours after it was actually implemented in the north (Peck, *Dublin*, p. 127).

[82] *Belfast Newsletter*, 4 February 1972.

[83] J. Leruez, *Economic Planning and Politics in Britain* (London, 1975), p. 238. However, in his memoirs Maudling himself claims responsibility for this recommendation (together with power-sharing and appointing Whitelaw as Secretary of State) (p. 185). This seems somewhat unlikely, since according to Faulkner Heath had a low evaluation of Maudling's contribution to Irish strategy (*Memoirs*, p. 129).

[84] H. Heclo and A. Wildavsky, *The Private Government of Public Money* (London, 1974), p. 320.

[85] Haines, *Politics*, p. 114.

[86] *Ibid.*, pp. 125–9.

[87] On 8 February 1972 Cecil King met Whitelaw at the House of Commons. 'Whitelaw was ... very frank. Things cannot possibly be allowed to go on as they are; Stormont will have to be closed down; confidence in Faulkner has gone. They have looked at the possibility of incorporating Northern Ireland in the UK [*sic*] ... They have also considered moving the border. To both policies there are insuperable objections ... the plain impression left was that they had decided on a united Ireland...' (King, *1970–74*, p. 178).

[88] *The Times*, 28 March 1972.

[89] *Ibid.*, 17 March 1972.

[90] *Ibid.*, 28 March 1972.

[91] *Irish Times*, 8 March 1972. Pressure from France seems to have been strong too (Faulkner, *Memoirs*, p. 140). There is evidence also that the Foreign Office by this time were beginning to argue that further 'drift' might irreparably destabilise southern politics (cf. Peck, *Dublin*, pp. 4, 12).

[92] King, *1970–74*, p. 181.

[93] *Ibid.*, p. 188. King and Hugh Fraser, MP, had for some time led a campaign for the rehabilitation of Paisley in ruling-class circles. King himself found Paisley 'nearly as tall as I am ... an honest man and a nice man. It is not clear to me why Tory Ministers regard him as a sort of pariah' (p. 138). It should be pointed out that King, an easily puzzled man, was equally baffled by the unpopularity of Mosley.

[94] To make matters worse, the Foreign Office only took charge of relations with southern Ireland in October 1968 as a consequence of the merger of the Foreign and Commonwealth Offices. Until Peck's arrival as ambassador in Dublin in 1970 it concerned itself only with the 'butter wrangle' and provided no intelligence for London on southern politics. Peck appears to have remedied this situation, but in 1971 responsibility for Irish affairs was shifted within the Foreign Office to a desk whose concern was defence and liaison between the FO and the Ministry of Defence. This meant that intelligence from Dublin was subsequently evaluated only militarily. (Peck, *Dublin*, pp. 45–6, 116.)

95 M. Blades and D. Scott, *What Price Northern Ireland?* (Young Fabian Pamphlet No. 22, London, 1970).

96 *Fortnight*, 17 September 1971.

97 *The Economist*, 6 May 1972.

98 *Ibid.*, 2 March 1968.

99 *Ibid.*, 23 February 1974.

100 Government of Northern Ireland, *Industrial Development in Northern Ireland* (Belfast, 1973), p. 8.

101 P. D. McGovern, 'Problems of industrial dispersal in Northern Ireland' (unpublished Ph.D. thesis, London University (1963), p. 38.

102 *NIHC*, Vol. LXX, c. 2136. Lord's repaid a total of £768,000 before they went bankrupt. In this and other cases it was claimed that incoming firms and their directors had received additional undisclosed perquisites.

103 Government of Northern Ireland, *Development Programme, 1970-75* (Belfast, 1970), p. 15.

104 Estate duty: analysis of property (proprietary shares or debentures in joint-stock companies (£000), selected years ending 31 March):

Companies	1952	1957	1962	1967	1972	1974
NI private	1,007	754	549	879	781	985
NI public	536	324	792	941	355	282
GB private	1	4	4	4,404	6,568	7,446
GB public	2,350	2,556	4,493	4,404	6,568	7,446
Foreign	329	383	475	530	689	621

Source: Government of Northern Ireland, *Digest of Statistics* (Belfast, annual, 1954–   ).

105 Steed and Thomas, 'Regional industrial change'.

106 *The Economist*, 27 July 1974.

107 McGovern, *Problems*, p. 41.

108 J. V. Simpson, 'Population, employment and urbanisation trends in Northern Ireland', *Journal of the Statistical and Social Inquiry Society of Ireland*, 33 (1976).

109 Cf. J. Foster, 'Capitalism and the Scottish nation', in G. Brown (ed.), *The Red Paper on Scotland* (Edinburgh, 1975).

110 *Development Programme, 1970-75*, p. 24.

111 Callaghan, *A House*, p. 88.

112 Wilson, p. 80.

113 L. G. P. Freer, 'Recent tendencies in Northern Ireland administration', in D. G. Neill (ed.), *Devolution of Government: the Experience of Northern Ireland* (London, 1953).

114 R. G. Lawrence, *The Government of Northern Ireland* (Oxford, 1965).

115 T. O'Neill, *Autobiography* (London, 1973), pp. xi-xii. An almost identical formulation may be found in Faulkner's *Memoirs*, p. 31.

116 Blades and Scott, 'What price?' Whereas public anxiety was rife in the '20s about the closeness of government and people in Northern Ireland, it re-emerged in the '60s about the proximity of government and incoming industry. An admission by Faulkner does nothing to dispel this anxiety: 'Goodyear was another "blue chip" American firm which came to Ulster in 1966 after long negotiation . . . I was led to understand at the conclusion of

these ... that if I ever decided to get out of politics the Chairman of Goodyear would have a job waiting for me' (*Memoirs*, p. 31). As it turned out, he did.

[117] *Belfast Newsletter*, 30 March 1965.

[118] H. Wilson, *The Labour Government, 1964–70: a Personal Record* (London, 1971), p. 75.

[119] *Belfast Newsletter*, 5 October 1964.

[120] The most notable of these concerned the siting of the New University of Ulster and Craigavon New Town. In the case of the university Warnock observed, 'a very reluctant Unionist party was compelled to vote against its intentions' (*Irish Times*, 13 May 1965). Craigavon's siting was opposed by north Armagh farmers (*ibid.*, 17 December 1965). In order to deflect opposition to the University proposal, O'Neill moved his Minister of Development (William Craig) to Home Affairs (*ibid.*, 1 May 1965).

[121] In a leader the *Newsletter* argued that such a meeting in no way threatened the constitutional position (20 November 1964).

[122] The first three speeches referred to are to be found in T. O'Neill, *Ulster at the Crossroads* (London, 1969). The last was reported in the *Irish Times*, 20 April 1967. A similar sentiment was expressed in an interview with Mervyn Pauley in the *Newsletter*, 12 January 1965.

[123] *Irish Times*, 18 March 1965.

[124] *The Economist*, 2 June 1966.

[125] *Irish Times*, 16 June 1966.

[126] *Ibid.*, 29 June 1966.

[127] *Ibid.*, 23 July 1966. The vehicles carrying water cannon had been adapted to this function only shortly before; cf. Scarman, p. 7.

[128] *Ibid.*, 20 June 1966.

[129] *Ibid.*, 29 August 1966.

[130] *Ibid.*, 24 September 1966.

[131] *Ibid.*, 1 May 1967.

[132] *Ibid.*, 8 May 1967.

[133] *Belfast Newsletter*, 23 November 1968.

[134] *Ibid.*, 10 December 1968.

[135] *NIHC*, Vol. LXXIII, c. 1454.

[136] Scarman, p. 7.

[137] *Ibid.*, p. 19.

[138] Quoted in *NIHC*, Vol. LXXXIV, c. 48.

[139] F. W. Boal, and R. H. Buchanan, 'The 1969 Northern Ireland general election', *Irish Geography*, Vi (1969).

[140] One of the present authors argued similarly some years ago, cf. P. Gibbon, 'Ulster: the dialectic of religion and class', *New Left Review*, 55 (1969). Boal and Buchanan's interpretation is close to this: 'These are slender indications of change within the Unionist Party yet . . . they reveal basic differences relating to class and region . . . which could be exploited by a party concerned more specifically with policies of economic and social development' ('The 1969 election').

[141] 'It is a long time since the word "class" has been bandied about so freely [here]'—R. Porter (O'Neillist), *The Times*, 18 February 1969.

[142] E.g. Victoria: Unionist 9,249, NILP 2,972, PU 2,489; North Antrim: Unionist 9,142, PU 3,241.

[143] This was the interpretation of Callaghan, *A House*, p. 96.

[144] *Ibid.*, p. 51; *Belfast Newsletter*, 27 July 1971.

[145] N. Poulantzas, *Crisis of the Dictatorships* (London, 1976).

[146] *NIHC*, Vol. LXXVI, c. 1988–2000.

[147] R. Deutsch, Interview with William Craig, *Etudes Irlandaises*, 1 (1976), p. 163.

[148] E.g. its calls for dissociation of the Orange Order and Unionist party, or, more remarkably, Paisley's interview on RTE in November 1971 (*Irish Times*, 29 November 1971).

[149] Cf. Faulkner on Callaghan: 'it was soon clear that Callaghan was determined to use any military involvement to allow him to intervene decisively in the political situation . . .' (*Memoirs*, p. 62). The unreality of this judgement is itself acknowledged in the next sentence '. . . though he did not put to us anything he thought we ought to be doing but were failing to do.' (*ibid.*).

[150] Faulkner effectively acknowledges this argument in his autobiography: '. . . we were too absorbed in our own affairs. The only real contacts with Westminster were Ministerial. There was precious little other contact because Westminster was not interested in Northern Ireland and similarly Northern Ireland was not interested in Westminster. The important place politically was Stormont. And I think that was a mistake, a weakness. It led politicians in Northern Ireland into illusions of self-sufficiency, of taking part in a sovereign parliament. It created separatist tendencies. It also meant that the crisis of 1969 hit an unprepared Westminster between the eyes. Both sides must accept responsibility for that situation.' (*Memoirs*, p. 26.)

7

CONCLUSIONS

In conclusion, two sets of issues will be returned to. First, the results established by the research described here will be employed to propose definitive answers to the principal questions raised over and over again by Northern Ireland's historians and commentators. Second, some basic questions concerning the significance of the Marxist concept of the state will be briefly explored.

Traditional controversies

In the literature on the Northern Ireland state certain controversies recur. There is the problem of British endorsement of the regime. There is the question of the role and extent of anti-Catholic discrimination. Associated with them are questions concerning the participation of Catholics in the state, and the effects in the north of events in southern Ireland. In the light of the research presented in this book it is possible to offer a resolution of these controversies.

The nature of British endorsement of the Northern Irish state has provoked several bitter disputes and it lies at the heart of one recent exchange. Michael Farrell has argued that British military and financial support has always been the state's 'ultimate line of defence'.[1] Against this, it has been stressed that those who argue that Unionism made a show of militancy only when British backing was ensured are simply empirically wrong. 'Think of 1886, 1912 and 1921, when the British ruling class were by no means unequivocal in their support. Think also of 1935 and 1969, when unofficial Protestant violence was unleashed largely without even the local state apparatus's support.'[2]

The second argument makes the point that popular Unionism is a relatively autonomous force and not a paper tiger. However, the British state has undeniably played a critical role with respect to

Unionism, a role which cannot be understood without reference to its overall objectives in Ireland. In the period 1918–72, British policy can be divided into a number of distinct phases.

First, the period of state formation. Here it was increasingly unpredictable. It was complicated both by sudden changes in the situation and by internal divisions. There was, however, generally acceptance that the British government could not physically coerce the Ulster Unionists. At the same time the British had the primary objective of reaching a settlement that would install in Dublin the 'moderate' wing of Irish nationalism, the Free State party. There can be no doubt that the period of maximum British pressure on the Unionists (May–June 1922)[3] coincided with the maximum vulnerability of the Free Staters to Republican charges of having 'deserted our co-religionists in the north', etc. With the onset of civil war and the victory of the Free Staters the British saw no further *need* to interfere in Northern Ireland.

Conflicts with the Ulster regime increasingly lost their political dimension and became, from the British government and Treasury viewpoint, largely financial—the struggle to restrain 'extravagance'. Although these conflicts had political implications within the Six Counties, for the British state machine it is clear that financial considerations alone were significant. Embarrassing incidents in Ulster such as the outdoor relief riots (1932) or the sectarian riots of 1935 were simply hushed up. It was not until the Anglo-Eire negotiations of 1938 and the onset of the Second World War that the Ulster issue again became politicised. In this period it is clear that the desirability of pressurising Ulster to subordinate itself to British strategic interests was accepted in certain ruling-class circles.[4] When it became clear that this would not deflect de Valera from his chosen course, pressure was rapidly abandoned. Indeed, Eire's eventual neutrality in the war strengthened the Northern Irish position within the UK. Nevertheless it still remained a peripheral region quite deliberately insulated from the mainland.

When the crisis broke in October 1968 Ulster was economically and politically marginal for the British bourgeoisie. It is this fact which partially explains the difficulties experienced by the British government in formulating and implementing its strategy.

The role of discriminatory practices in the history of the state is again the subject of debate. Certain recent commentators have tended to minimise its significance or to refer to minor injustices.[5] In this view, Catholic opposition to the state on religious and nationalist grounds is the crux of the matter. No doubt the Unionist leadership occasionally overstepped the boundaries of what might be considered just, but this was an 'understandable reaction' to the enemies in their midst.

Against this position it must be said that discrimination against Catholics in the NICS, for example, cannot be explained by reference to the Nationalist party's negative attitude towards the state. In fact, the party sought to involve itself in civil service selection procedures, but was rebuffed.

On the other hand, accounts which stress the central role of discrimination are often heavily moralistic and lack any attempt to locate its precise political significance. It has been argued in this study that, until 1945 at least, Unionist dominance was articulated through the integration of discrepant and to some extent contradictory practices—the dominant populist and the subordinate anti-populist ones. In populist practice, sectarian forms of Protestant exclusivism played a major role in ensuring the unity of the Unionist class alliance. Although the populist–anti-populist division was displaced after the war in the context of welfarism, there was no change in the role of sectarianism. The dominant policy of the state towards Catholics was still exclusivist, and this remained the case until 1972. If any evidence other than the Cameron report is required, Cecil King's diaries should be considered. On 28 March 1972 William Whitelaw, the new British Secretary of State for Northern Ireland, lunched with King and told him:

> There were three grades of civil servant [at Stormont]: the best were delighted with the take-over; the second best were pleased; the duds were shocked—they gave Willie the impression they were political appointees...[6]

On 14 April King and Whitelaw lunched together again.

> Whitelaw said the Augean stables were nothing to the mess he had found at Stormont. Disproportionate ... salaries ... jobs for the Protestant boys; every power of the government used to depress the Catholics. Whitelaw obviously thought that the Catholics had far more to put up with than he realised...[7]

Events in southern Ireland have often been held to explain much about Ulster Unionism. John Whyte has cogently argued, 'dispassionate studies are now available of the role of the Catholic Church, and the position of the Protestant minority in the south since independence. While [they] disprove the more extreme criticisms, they do show that northern Protestants were not without grounds for concern.'[8] It is, however, also true that the Unionist leadership has persistently played up the alleged nationalist irredentism of Dublin governments. The Provisional government in 1922 bitterly resented Craig's refusal to acknowledge publicly their *de facto* recognition and practical assistance of the northern state.[9]* The ploy of exploiting alleged southern intransigence—explicable in the de Valera period—was continued by no less a figure than O'Neill well into the Lemass era. Interestingly, it was the authentic Unionist organ the *Belfast Newsletter* which played a significant role in forcing O'Neill to drop this rhetoric and meet Lemass.[10]

More recently new themes have been developed in the literature. In particular there has been a growing emphasis upon the financial constraints which reduced the Ulster regime's capacity for generous policy-making. For example, indignation at the brutal way in which the state dealt with unemployment and distress riots in 1932, Patrick Buckland has suggested, should be tempered by knowledge that 'the government of Northern Ireland's room for manoeuvre in the face of acute distress was severely limited'.[11]

There is a danger here that the debate on the significance of an important incident may be reduced to a dispute about one question only—whether the regime's financial resources were

---

* The problem of Collins in 1922 is clarified by a letter to L. G. Walsh of 7 February that year (National Library MS 3486). He believed that he was capable of reducing 'the North East area to such limits that it can not exist without us'. However, he ruled this out because he feared that such a course 'will leave . . . minorities which it would be impossible to govern'. De Valera clearly had a more militant, rhetorical stance. Even so, his letter to Cahir Healy of 20 July 1935 should be noted. At a high point of sectarian tension in Ulster he claimed, 'This situation is causing me great anxiety,' but, he added, 'I do not want to add fuel to the north' (N.L.I. MS 2796). In 1937, however, his new constitution claimed for the Dublin government the whole island of Ireland.

sufficient. In fact it is possible to say a great deal more about the outdoor relief affair. Indeed, it is only when more has been said that the true nature of the crisis becomes clear.

Briefly, the outdoor relief crisis reveals the play of populist–anti-populist divisions. The populists, true to their traditions, favoured the expenditure of cash on relief works to head off any possibility that distress would create unity amongst Protestant and Catholic workers.[12] The anti-populists—equally true to form—pointed out that at that very moment the British Treasury had explicitly stepped up its opposition to such expenditure. While sympathetic to the plight of those on relief, they pointed out that the responsibility for the low rates of relief in Belfast lay not with the government but with the Poor Law Guardians, the Belfast Corporation and the ratepayers. The populist response was to avoid major conflict with the Guardians, the Corporation and the ratepayers and to authorise government expenditure of £300,000 on relief works, riding roughshod over Ministry of Finance and Treasury objections.[13]

In the light of this, the emphasis upon financial constraints is somewhat sterile. Money *was* found to deal with the problem. It is the way money was found that is interesting, revealing again the significance of the populist–anti-populist division, discussion of which is the core of the earlier sections of this book.

It may be argued further that the regime's capacity for manoeuvre was nonetheless still limited—that it was caught between a strong sovereign Parliament at Westminster and strong local government bodies in Ulster itself. However, it is difficult to see the relevance of this point. If through an analysis of the populist–anti-populist division we have successfully reconstructed the dynamic of the regime before the war, then it is likely that the strength of Unionist local authorities (revealed by the constant concessions to them) was a product not of any intrinsic quality but of a *general political strategy*. Certainly this was how the anti-populists viewed the question. As for Westminster allowing Stormont more freedom for fiscal manoeuvre, this refusal was no more than a reflection of the increasing dependence of the populists upon the Treasury in order to finance their strategy.

Much of this polemic in the traditional literature is in reality linked to a more complex set of problems. Repeatedly the traditional debate relies upon the notion that a particular group of religious subjects (Protestants as such, Catholics as such) *ought* to have behaved better, been more generous, etc. For example, Protestants *ought* not to have discriminated against Catholics, or Catholics *ought* to have recognised the state. In certain variants it is asserted that Protestant behaviour cannot be judged by abstract canons of generosity, given the existence of a 'continuous Catholic threat' to the state.

It requires a considerable effort to make the point against this prevailing orthodoxy that the problem cannot be understood at the level of 'the Protestant community' on the one hand and 'the Catholic community' on the other. It must be insisted that the problem of the 'two communities' is the problem of the reproduction of two class alliances. If this declaration does not immediately illuminate, it still has a consequence which demands careful consideration. The activity of the state in Northern Ireland cannot be reduced to the questions described above. The state had certain peculiarities—as do all states—but it was undeniably a capitalist state. As such, its basic function was to hinder the unity of the dominated classes. Conceiving the Northern Ireland state in this way, based on a particular kind of power bloc linked to the maintenance of a particular mass line, dissolves the primacy of the problem of Protestants and Catholics as generic subjects, however often or importantly these ideological forms have been reproduced in political struggle.

This argument raises the general issue of the applicability of Marxism to the Northern Ireland situation.

The state, Marxism and Northern Ireland

It was argued in chapter 1 that the Marxist concept most pertinent to an analysis of politics in Northern Ireland was that of the state. The possibilities of such an approach were emphasised by comparison with the failure of an interpretation based on Marxist concepts of the Ulster question, the national question, imperialism and the social structure of Irish nationalism. This of course is only part of the story. The concept of the state is important not merely because the alternatives fail to produce a coherent analysis but because it can illuminate problems inadequately handled or unrecognised from other positions.

First, however, one general issue must be mentioned. The

development of political forces in Ulster before and since the creation of the state has seemed to many commentators a test case for Marxist theory, and one which has thrown doubt on its basic explanatory value.[14] What is the merit of 'class analysis' when the obvious forms of cleavage cut across class lines?

Traditionally such reservations have been voiced by conservative anti-Marxists, but recently they have been put forward by more 'enlightened' writers. The modern British textbook of revisionism, *Marx's Capital and Capitalism Today*,[15] contains arguments which would lead to the conclusion that the defects of Marxist analyses of Ulster are a result of the 'inherent' reductionism of Marxism itself. The implications for the present work are serious. In their critique of classical Marxism's handling of the relation between classes and politics the authors write:

> Classes do not immediately and directly represent themselves. When we examine political and ideological struggles we find state apparatuses, political parties and organisations, demonstrations and riotous mobs ... but we cannot find *classes* lined up against each other. Nor do we find that the issues in political struggles take the form of direct conflict between classes for political hegemony or over the specific character of the relations of production . . .[16]

They argue that this limitation is so pressing that it was in fact habitually registered by the most intelligent Marxists of the past. While 'in theory' Marxism insists that political and ideological struggles should be conceptualised in class terms, 'in practice the classics of Marxist politics have come to terms with the specificity of political forces and issues'.[17] Hence, for example, one finds a tension even in Marx's own writings between a dogmatic approach to political analysis (political tendencies = class interests) and a more 'sensitive' recognition of the autonomy of the political.[18]

The tension between the realities of politics and efforts to conceptualise politics in class terms is allegedly reflected in the emphasis Marxists place upon the concept 'relative autonomy of the political'. This concept serves to shore up the possibility of maintaining that 'obviously' non-class phenomena have a class significance. The weight of their attack is directed against this supposedly 'half-baked'[19] notion.

A number of arguments are adduced. The notion is first said to lead to inconsistency in political explanation. Second, it is said to be founded upon a contradictory interpretation of a concept (that of representation). Thirdly it is said that the concept falls since it requires, but fails, to stipulate a general principle governing representation.

Present purposes are served simply by reviewing the second, undoubtedly the one on which Cutler *et al.* lay most stress. They claim that the notion both implies and repudiates the concept of 'representation' and is therefore incoherent. At the same time they seem to be arguing that the concept of 'representation' is itself essentially incoherent. The thesis is as follows:

1. The difference between what is represented and its representation presupposes a specific and determinative effectivity of the means of representation.

2. Since the means of representation are specific, determinative and therefore independent, it can make no sense to conceive of them as tending or being constrained to represent anything in particular. 'If political institutions . . . are not determined . . . by a system of economic class relations then they cannot also be constrained to function as the means of representation of those relations.'[20]

Step 1 can be admitted without dispute. A sportsman represents a country by means of a national team, implying determinative practices of selection, a 'standard', a given national context of competition, a managerial apparatus, etc. The notion of representation is really shorthand for 'representation by means of . . .'.

Step 2 is more dubious. It is claimed that, in order to count as a genuine means of representation (in order for relative autonomy to be autonomous), something cannot be constrained in a determinative way (cannot be relatively determined). Specifically, if something is *not* determined completely by a given entity or range of entities it cannot be constrained to represent them. Since counter-examples spring readily to mind, it seems hard to understand how this could be argued seriously.

Consider an independent means, the camera, by which visual images can be represented in photographs. The camera exists perfectly independently of these images. They do not conjure it into existence. Its conditions of production are social, economic and technological. There can be a plurality of types of camera, each with a specific way of being effective. Yet a genuine constraint is present. To function *qua* camera, the camera is constrained to produce photographic representations of visual images. If it does not, then it ceases to be a working camera. For all its independence of origin and independent effectivity it can only represent a strictly specifiable set of entities. There is *no* necessary incompatibility between the effectiveness of a practice and constraint upon it to represent a set of entities. Nor, more generally is there a necessary incompatibility between autonomy and its limitation. Cutler *et al.* fail to demonstrate that 'representation' is an incoherent notion. It is not the concept of relative autonomy which is half-baked, but their objections to it.

It remains to be shown what further light may be thrown on other general interpretations of the Northern Ireland state by the theoretical positions adopted here. While alternative explanations have been commented on in passing, they have not been examined systematically from this viewpoint. Modern general interpretations of the Ulster state fall into two categories, Marxist and non-Marxist. In turn, the latter divides into two basic positions, best represented by J. F. Harbinson and P. J. Buckland.

Harbinson's interpretation may be designated 'sectarian voluntarism'. According to Harbinson, the secret of Unionism is that the Unionist bourgeoisie has at various stages in the past simply decided to promote sectarianism. The decision has been institutionalised in the state as an act of will. Harbinson's characterisation of Unionist politics is a good summary of this view:

> After 1920 their objective was to maintain the Union. The strategy they employed was simple, short term and effective. They maintained themselves in power by banging the big drum, waving the flag, and playing upon the emotions of the Protestant population.[21]

He argues that some Unionist leaders had more liberal inclinations but failed to convince the party of the need for change. No analysis of the basis of different positions is offered, and the general impression he gives is that the leadership adopted a primarily sectarian strategy because it made life easier.

Adopting the Marxist concept of the state enables these deficiencies to be met. The different strategic positions within the Unionist leadership were related to political forces which had divergent objective relations to determinate practices like Orange triumphalism, workplace exclusivism and unofficial violence. *Both* sets of relations to these practices had material determinants based on class divisions within the Unionist bloc. It was these divisions, not the 'wish' of a class, that gave rise to sectarianism.

The second variant of non-Marxist analysis is the apparently more realistic attempt to locate a material basis for Unionism in terms of external threats to the Protestant community. In his account of Ulster Unionism Patrick Buckland chides its critics for ignoring the real or imagined fears of the Protestant community:

> Ulster Unionists thus [a reference to IRA attacks in the 1920s] felt like an embattled community under seige from the forces of evil, a feeling renewed by occasional IRA campaigns against Northern Ireland and perpetuated by the longevity of Unionist politicians . . .[22]

The British and Irish Communist Organisation's 'two nations' view can be included in this line of argument, since it shares its basic principle of explanation—the treatment of the 'Protestant community/nation' as the crucial historical subject. In this account the state becomes a mere expression of 'real or imagined' fears, that is, it effectively ceases to exist at an objective level. In the same way, classes are themselves abolished. All that remains is a history of 'community' reaction to external threats. This interpretation takes its point of departure from the undoubted fact that Unionist ideologies were influenced by the actions of successive southern governments and northern republicans. However, treating these as unproblematical 'threats' is to ignore the fact that they had no *independent* significance.

They acquired significance as 'threats' not to the extent that they represented real opposition from the south, but according to whether an ideology of external threats was dominant or subordinate in the north. This in turn was a matter of class relations. Harbinson argues that Unionists banged the big drum because they wanted to delude the workers; Buckland that they did so because they had to. In fact they banged the big drum when the class struggle dictated greater bourgeois forbearance of independently generated popular Protestant activity.

An interesting example is provided by the Unionist leadership's reaction to the Free State army 'mutiny' of 1924. The mutiny did not in any sense signal a shift towards militant republicanism in the south. This much was clear to all observers at the time (including the British government), yet the Northern Irish government attempted to exploit the affair in order to gain more British financial support for the Specials. It can be readily seen here that relations within the Protestant bloc, and not the objective significance of the issue, determined how much weight the Unionist leadership gave it.[23]

The weaknesses of both these non-Marxist positions stem from their failure to consider the role of class relations in determining the nature of the state. Both, for this reason, reduce to a moral discourse in which the state 'creates' its evil aspects by an act of will (Harbinson) or has them thrust upon it involuntarily by external forces (Buckland). Their relation to the traditional ideologies of Nationalism and Unionism should not need underlining.

It may be expected from the discussion in chapter 1 that the concepts governing modern Marxist efforts to analyse Ireland might render their treatment of the Northern Ireland state theoretically deficient. Not only is this in fact the case, but the interpretations suffer from the same drawbacks as non-Marxist ones. Class relations are again ignored or subordinated.

The first important characteristic of most Marxist analyses is their failure to focus seriously on the nature of bourgeois political and ideological dominance. Instead, they provide a more or less elaborate account of the various sectarian and discriminatory aspects of central and local state apparatuses. These are analysed in terms of their supposed function of uniting the Protestant masses behind the bourgeoisie by the grant of material privileges. The state is treated as both an instrument for differential allocation of rewards and an institution to which social classes are completely external. Ideological and political relations are seen as simple expressions of a basic material relationship—bourgeoisie–state apparatus–labour aristocracy— in which the state is conceived in purely institutional terms. Given these terms, the logical conclusion is that until the state is destroyed the possibility of winning any section of the Protestant masses to the side of progressive forces is non-existent.

The question at issue is not the undoubtedly sectarian aspects of both central and local state apparatuses. It is the absence from an allegedly Marxist interpretation of any attempt to relate them to the basic disposition of the main social classes within the Protestant bloc. By omitting to ask which relations of social forces the main ruling-class strategies correspond to, this type of analysis fails even to register what has here been demonstrated—that the Unionist state was torn by continuous conflicts and that populism prevailed owing to the triumph of a certain set of political and ideological relations between the Unionist leadership, sections of the state apparatus and the Protestant masses.

Two aspects of this current form of Marxist analysis need to be drawn out in more detail for the practical results of these shortcomings to be appreciated: the notion of a labour aristocracy, which lies at their heart, and the political strategy proposed to counter its opposition to progress.

The notion of labour aristocracy in these analyses is tied inseparably to the notion of privileges. The labour aristocracy is created by the award of privileges, which then provide the raw material for 'false consciousness' to feed on. Protestants acquire privileges and then rationalise them vis-à-vis Catholics in Orangeism.

The assumptions about ideology in this presentation are clearly problematical—it is treated as ideas or chimeras in peoples' minds, without material expression. Yet the formulation concerning the labour aristocracy's constitution is more problematical still. It is characterised by imprecision and sociologism, slipping from reference to the skilled and unionised section of the Protestant working class to the class as a whole. In Farrell's analysis the two senses can even appear in the same sentence. In his explanation of the 'utter failure of the labour movement' he writes:

> This failure can only be understood against the background of religious discrimination in employment which divided the working class, giving the Protestants a small but marginal real advantage and creating a Protestant 'aristocracy of labour', particularly in the Belfast engineering industry . . .[24]

The conclusion appears to be that the Protestant working class, and engineering workers in particular, have been unproblematically Orange supporters of the Unionist bourgeoisie. Yet the Protestant working class has by no means supported its bourgeoisie through thick and thin. Through the medium of the NILP it frequently opposed it in secular class terms. In the early '60s opposition was very strong indeed. Moreover the backbone of the NILP was the engineering workers, that is, the body here identified as the most unrepentantly Orange.

For similar reasons, serious Marxist analysis of British history has recently questioned the use of the term 'labour aristocracy'. In a review of recent Marxist analysis of class relations in Victorian Britain, Gareth Stedman-Jones has written:

> In most Marxist writing, the use of this idea has been ambiguous and unsatisfactory. Its status is uncertain and it has been employed at will, descriptively, polemically or theoretically, without ever finding a firm anchorage . . . the term has often been used as if it provided an explanation. But it would have been more accurate to say that it pointed towards a vacant area where an explanation should be . . . there has never been any simple correlation between degree of privilege and political or industrial behaviour. What matters is not the fact of differentials but what type of differentials and, above all, in what political and social context they operate in . . .[25]

In his important analyses of class forces in nineteenth and twentieth century Britain John Foster has demonstrated the continued force of the Leninist definition and the vast distance that separates it from the usual reductionist use of the term. He follows Lenin in arguing that the labour aristocracy was 'the temporary product of a particular phase in the development of British capitalism'.[26] However, referring to the nineteenth century, he points out that a crucial element in the constitution of this stratum was a change in ruling-class strategy. 'Instead of continuing a policy of blanket opposition to virtually any independent working-class organisation, it had been decided to permit and then actually encourage simple, moderate "non-violent" trade union organisation'.[27] Foster insists on the inadequacy of reducing the term to one of descriptive sociology and emphasises that it must refer to specific ruling-class strategies towards the masses.

It is clear also that the term has no theoretical significance beyond a specification of a *national* conjuncture, that as it depends on both a periodisation of the dominant mode of production and the development of specific strategies by the ruling class, its application to a particular locality is conditional. It depends upon the degree to which the disposition of class forces there reflects the dominant national trends. At the economic level the position of the labour aristocracy in Ulster in the period after the First World War did reflect the national trends, which were severely adverse. The war had seen a massive increase in the unionisation of all grades of work, an associated shift in the labour movement's internal balance towards the un-skilled, and a decline in the relatively privileged economic position of the skilled.[28] In the inter-war period it was the traditional industrial bases of the labour aristocracy, particularly heavy engineering and shipbuilding, that suffered severe unemployment. Foster's interpretation of ruling-class strategy towards the working class between the wars takes account of this external undermining of the stratum on which pre-war strategies of incorporation had been based. The main strategy now was to 'educate labour'.

> It would now be the Labour Party itself which would have to act as the basic anchor. By adopting the Labour Party as a legitimate governing party ... these organisations might themselves be transformed into the primary institutions of control ... remoulding the ideas of the great mass of working people ...[29]

The significance of this analysis is its demonstration that the cluster of forces denoted by the term 'labour aristocracy' no longer existed, and that Marxism had to comprehend the class basis of a new strategy towards the masses.

Particular local shifts in class relations and not 'privileges' have been the critical element in the formation of Protestant working-class politics. While privilege was and is a real fact, it fails to account for differentiation and transition in Protestant politics. The use of the term 'labour aristocracy', in explaining everything, explains nothing.

Finally, the question of political strategy. Only two strategies may be derived from the 'labour aristocracy' thesis, and both lead to similar conclusions. Either the Protestant working class is written off completely as irredeemably reactionary and an attempt made to blow it to pieces, or it is argued (by Farrell and others) that, since the state is both the source and guarantee of this stratum's privileges, its destruction will equalise the status of Catholics and Protestants and accelerate the development of progressive unity. This is not the place to develop an alternative perspective. Consider merely some consequences of the strategy of destroying the state.

An 'anti-imperialist struggle' which focuses on the destruction of a set of institutions and completely ignores the political and ideological practices embodied in them can only have the most reactionary effects. Just as it was possible to destroy the Stormont apparatus of 1921–72, so it might be possible to destroy the existing apparatus of direct rule. The question is what would be the effect of a strategy designed to achieve this upon the balance of forces within the Protestant bloc.

It is a crucial question, for contrary to common assumption there is nothing inherently reactionary about the Protestant working class or, for that matter, a national frontier which puts Protestants in a numerical majority. As we have tried to show, the sectarian and supremacist ideologies of the Protestant masses have been condoned and encouraged by the ruling class throughout the history of the state. But at various times the predominant populist strategy has been incapable of producing hegemony. Important sections of the Protestant proletariat have come under the influence of relatively secular labourism. The continuing existence of populism and the associated characteristics of a Protestant state could not prevent important and progressive transformations in the political and ideological configuration of the Protestant bloc.

Even earlier 'anti-imperialist' struggles had little effect on this process. It is only with the present one that progressive tendencies in this bloc have been completely submerged.

There is lesson here. The social republican and republican Marxist characterisation of the Protestant working class is based upon a self-fulfilling prophecy. Because national liberation and socialism are indivisible, a 'progressive' position on the national question is regarded as an essential qualification for admission to the ranks of progressive forces. The progressive forces can then be 'unconditionally' or even 'critically' supported in their struggle to complete the national revolution. Since this involves destroying the northern state, it also involves stimulating a shift within the Protestant political bloc, with inevitably reactionary effects. This in turn becomes further evidence for the exclusion of the Protestant working class from the category of potential progressive forces.

Only when the terrible weakness of the forces of the left in Ireland, north and south, is realised will there be a stimulus to re-think this nexus. In the present stage, while consciousness of this is only dawning, a decisive break with Irish Marxism's subordination to bourgeois ideology is necessary. Only on this basis can a political strategy eventually be developed which can work towards the destruction of those political and ideological conditions which have underlain the Northern Ireland state and which, if British troops were withdrawn tomorrow, would create another more reactionary one.[30]

Notes to chapter 7

[1] M. Farrell, 'Northern Ireland – an anti-imperialist struggle', in R. Miliband and J. Saville, *Socialist Register, 1977*, p. 92.

[2] P. Gibbon, 'Some basic problems of the contemporary situation', in *ibid.*, p. 87.

[3] The evidence that Unionist difficulty was at its peak in late May 1922 is clear. In March 1922 members of the Lloyd George group, L. Curtis and Tom Jones, had written critically of the Unionist security build-up: 'it is impossible to assume that the formidable forces now being organised under the guise of police are being directed solely against the danger from the south. The British government has armed and is paying for forces which it is told by the one who controls them (i.e. Craig) will in certain eventualities be turned against itself' (PRO C.O. 906/30, Memorandum on the present position of the Imperial Government on Northern Ireland, 18 March 1922). Moreover, by 25 May 1922 even that ardent champion of Loyalism, Churchill, felt it necessary to rebuke Craig because of the Ulster Premier's denunciation of the Boundary Commission (D. W. Harkness, 'The ill-fated Boundary Commission and a rebuke for Craig', *Irish Times*, 21 April 1976). This, in Churchill's view, implied the very possibility that Curtis and Jones had warned against.

[4] T. R. Dwyer, *Irish Neutrality and the USA, 1939–47* (Dublin, 1977), p. 54. Before leaving for the Six Counties (in June 1940) David Gray, US Minister to Ireland, was visited by Sir John Maffey, Britain's representative there. Maffey told him that Craigavon had recently been called to London, where he had been given 'merry hell' and all but ordered to 'end partition on the best terms he could'.

[5] A. T. Q. Stewart, *The Narrow Ground* (London, 1977), pp. 173–9.

[6] King, *1970–74*, p. 188.

[7] *Ibid.*, p. 194; cf. also p. 214.

[8] J. Whyte, 'Interpretations of the Northern Ireland problem: an appraisal', *Economic and Social Review*, 9 (July 1978), p. 259.

[9] Tallents to Masterson Smith, 6 December 1922, PRO 739/1.

[10] *Belfast Newsletter*, 20 November 1964.

[11] Buckland's comments appear in a notice of Farrell's work in *History*, 63 (1978), p. 160.

[12] PRONI Cab. 4/304/21, Cabinet memorandum on distress, 8 July 1932 (Dawson Bates is the author).

[13] For anti-populist views see Spender, *Financial Diary*, 28 November 1932 and 9 January 1934. For a wider analysis cf. P. Bew and C. Norton, 'Class struggle and the Unionist state: the outdoor relief riots of 1932' *Economic and Social Review*, 10, No. 3 (April 1979).

[14] For a review of this literature see P. Bew, 'The problem of Irish Unionism', *Economy and Society*, 6 (1977).

[15] By A. J. Cutler, B. Hindess, P. Q. Hirst and A. Hussain, 2 vols (London, 1977–78).

[16] Vol. I, p. 232.

[17] *Ibid.*, p. 233.

[18] This is held to be true of the work of Lenin and Mao also. A lacuna in

the work of today's rigorous anti-reductionists is any indication of what theory does guide the 'sensitive' elements of the work of these figures. In fact the authors seem to rely on a rather primitive notion of 'genius' in this instance. Additionally, the 'tension' itself is not properly demonstrated. For example, a false opposition is established between reductionist and non-reductionist analyses supposedly existing within a few pages of each other in Marx's *Eighteenth Brumaire* (Culter et al., Vol. I, p. 183–4). Yet Marx does not analyse the 'Republican fraction', for all its undoubted autonomy, without being very careful to specify its crucial relation to the industrial bourgeoisie. Equally, the analysis of the division of Royalist fractions is critically dependent on the notion that the different Royalist lines (Bourbon, Orleanist) helped to secure the *political conditions* of the dominance of different forms of property, landed and industrial capital respectively.

[19] Cutler et al., 'Marxist theory and socialist politics', *Marxism Today*, November 1978.

[20] Cutler et al., *Marx's Capital*, Vol. I, p. 234.

[21] Harbinson, *Ulster Unionist Party*, p. 166.

[22] Buckland, *Ulster Unionism*, p. 177.

[23] See especially A. Henderson to Londonderry, 4 April 1923, PRONI Cab. 7A/4/3. Henderson wrote, 'We have very good evidence that the Republican party was not behind the mutiny, which was rather in the nature of a strike against the demobilisation scheme put forward by General Mulcahy.'

[24] Farrell, *Orange State*, p. 11.

[25] G. Stedman-Jones, 'England's first proletariat', *New Left Review*, 90 (1975).

[26] Foster, 'The state'.

[27] *Ibid*.

[28] *Ibid*.

[29] *Ibid*.

[30] These issues are explored in more detail in our 'Aspects of Irish Marxism, 1968–78', in A. Morgan and B. Purdie (ed.), *Ireland–Divided Nation, Divided Class* (London, 1979).

Appendix

NOTE ON THE CONSTRUCTION OF TABLE 3

The section of this table referring to 1971 is reproduced from Aunger's 1975 article.[1] The section referring to 1911 was constructed from the 1911 *Census of Ireland* for the counties of Armagh, Antrim, Down, Fermanagh, Londonderry and Tyrone and the cities of Belfast and Londonderry. To assist comparability the principles used in its construction followed as far as possible those used by Aunger. Economically active males and females were first divided, by occupation, into seven basic strata: (1) professionally qualified and higher administrative, (2) managerial and executive, (3) inspectorial, supervisory and other non-manual (higher grade), (4) *ibid*. (lower grade), (5a) routine non-manual, (5b) skilled manual, (6) semi-skilled manual, (7) routine manual. The criterion for this division used by both Aunger and ourselves is an adapted form of the Hall-Jones scale of occupational prestige. For details of this scale, see J. Hall and D. C. Jones, 'Social grading of occupations', *British Journal of Sociology*, Vol. 1, No. 1 (1950). A chart indicating the position of specific occupations is given in A. N. Oppenheim, *Questionnaire Design and Attitude Measurement* (London, 1966), pp. 275–84. As in Aunger's table, persons with the following occupations were excluded from the classification for 1911, as their occupational descriptions provided insufficient information for grading: farmers, farmers' relatives, 'others concerned with agriculture', 'others', members of the armed forces, and students. A number of conventional decisions on categorisation of occupations not on the Hall-Jones scale had to be made. It seems probable that Aunger had to make similar decisions. Since there is probably a degree of inconsistency between these decisions, comparison between 1911 and 1971 cannot be said to be completely valid.

The arrangements described gave the following results for 1911 (the very small number of Jews being included in the figures for Protestants). N= 423,498.

[1] 'Religion and occupational class'.

Class	Protestant	Catholic
1	6,596	1,819
2	3,754	902
3	11,774	4,122
4	1,911	2,728
5a	49,457	30,256
5b	94,596	35,382
6	62,209	40,666
7	48,798	28,537
Total	279,086	144,412

(The decline of the agrarian population is, of course, the main factor in the enormous intercensal growth of what is couted here as the economically active population.)

To produce the scale in the main text, grades 1, 2 and 3 were taken together to give 'Professional, managerial' (I); grades 4 and 5a were taken together to give 'Lower-grade non-manual' (II), and grades 5b, 6 and 7 were renumbered III, IV and V respectively.

Index